LANDMARKS IN RHETORIC AND PUBLIC ADDRESS

A COURSE OF LECTURES

ON

ORATORY AND CRITICISM

BY JOSEPH PRIESTLEY

EDITED BY *Vincent M. Bevilacqua*
AND *Richard Murphy*

FOREWORD BY *David Potter*

Southern Illinois University Press · *Carbondale*

FOREWORD

By David Potter

AUTHOR OF SOME TWO HUNDRED articles, treatises, and books which cover much of the intellectual spectrum of the eighteenth century, Joseph Priestley is recognized today primarily for his discovery of oxygen. Yet, as the editors of this edition of *A Course of Lectures on Oratory and Criticism* point out, Priestley's contemporary reputation rested upon a broader foundation—witness his election to the Royal Society for literary ability—and his present significance deserves far greater emphasis.

Throughout an eventful life, Priestley was deeply concerned with the establishment and maintenance of freedom of inquiry and the continual betterment of mankind. This concern is evinced throughout his many publications and decisions, whether scientific, religious, or educational. It is a basis for the important and virtually unobtainable *Course of Lectures*.

This volume, in keeping with the policy of the "Landmarks in Rhetoric and Public Address" series, is based upon the best available edition, that printed for J. Johnson in 1777. Because of the size of the original and the attractiveness of its type and composition, an offset process has been used with only a minor reduction in type size and a resultant variance with the original "Landmarks" format. There are three differences between this edition and the original. We have added a portrait of Priestley, a much needed index, and a lucid introductory essay which places the author in the mainstream of eighteenth-century enlightenment and traces vital influences upon his thinking in general and his rhetoric in particular.

The editors of this "Landmarks" edition are thoroughly conversant with the *Lectures*, their author, and the century in which they were produced. Professor Bevilacqua, a member of the speech faculty of the University of Virginia, has specialized in the critical writings of Lord Kames as well as the rhetorics of Priestley and Adam Smith. Professor Murphy, of the speech faculty of the University of Illinois, is one of the most widely recognized members of the speech profession, a bibliophile, author, editor, and director of many theses and dissertations in British Public Address.

This definitive edition makes an important volume readily available to scholars, should extend the reputation of the author and his editors, and affords further proof of the generosity of college librarians—we are indebted to the University of Chicago Library for the loan of a rare copy of the Johnson imprint.

CONTENTS

Joseph Priestley, LL.D., F. R. S.

by Rembrandt Peale

By Vincent M. Bevilacqua
and Richard Murphy

JOSEPH PRIESTLEY, scientist, educator, theologian, Unitarian preacher, libertarian, polemicist, inventor of soda water, and discoverer of oxygen, was a prodigious writer on a phenomenally wide range of subjects. His nonscientific writings extend to twenty-six volumes. His first work on language, *The Rudiments of English Grammar*, written when he was twenty-seven, went through nine editions from 1761 to 1833. In his last hour, in his seventy-first year, although aware that he was sinking into death, he dictated corrections for writings to be published posthumously.

Priestley was born near Leeds, Yorkshire, March 13, 1733. He died at Northumberland, Pennsylvania, February 6, 1804. His father was a woolen-cloth dresser of moderate means. His mother died when he was five, and he later lived with his father's sister. He attended grammar school at Batley, and various independent schools conducted by dissenting ministers. At twelve he was studying Latin and Greek, and learning Hebrew during holidays. At sixteen he stopped attending school because of what he describes as "a weakly consumptive habit," and learned French, Italian, and High Dutch without a master. He also studied Chaldee, Syriac, and Arabic.[1] In 1752 he attended a nonconformist academy at Daventry, and, because he was older and more advanced than most of the students, completed the work in three years. There was a spirit of liberal inquiry at the school. Priestley enjoyed the disputations. "In this situation," he wrote, "I saw reason to embrace what is generally called the heterodox side of every question,"[2] a practice he maintained through life. In 1755, he took appointment as assistant to a Presbyterian minister at Needham Market, in Suffolk. Indifferently received, however, he removed to a congregation at Nantwich, Cheshire, in 1758. Here he opened a school with thirty boys in one room and a half-dozen girls in another. It was for this school he wrote *The Rudiments*.

Finding teaching pleasant, and not being very successful as a minister, in 1761 he accepted appointment as tutor in languages and belles lettres at Warrington Academy, north of Nantwich, and midway between Liverpool and Manchester. Despite his slight formal academic background, he applied himself to his duties, as he said, with great assiduity. He taught history, grammar, oratory, and elocution, and investigated botany, astronomy, and electricity. He composed, in addition to the work on oratory here reprinted, lectures on the theory of language, history and general policy, and the laws and constitution of England. Of his brashness in this period Lord Brougham huffed:

> How well he was qualified to write on oratory and on English law, we may easily conjecture, from the circumstance that he could never have heard any speaking save in the pulpits of meeting-houses, and in all probability had never seen a cause tried; . . . it is difficult to imagine anything more adventurous than the tutor of an academy, afflicted with an incurable stutter, and who devoted his time to teaching and to theology, promulgating rules of eloquence and of jurisprudence to the senators and lawyers of his country.[3]

He was ordained a dissenting minister May 18, 1762, and was married to Mary Wilkinson the following month, June 23. The marriage was a happy one; Mrs. Priestley managed home and family in orderly fashion. The Christmas holiday of 1765–66 he spent in London. His visit there "was unquestionably the turning point in Priestley's great career," writes W. Cameron Walker. He met John Canton, Richard Price, Benjamin Franklin, and developed the desire to become a member of the Royal Society. His visit "marked the change from School Master to Scientist and from preacher to political and religious reformer."[4]

In 1767, pressed by the urge to preach and by some instability at the school, Priestley took a charge at Mill Hill Chapel, Leeds. His house was next to a brewery, where he was able to observe and collect gases. In 1772, he became librarian and literary companion to Lord Shelburne (William Petty Fitzmaurice, first Marquis of Lansdowne, prime minister 1782–83). He was given a house at Calne, near Shelburne's seat at Bowood Park, a hundred miles west of London, and quarters in Lansdowne House in London. His patron supplied a laboratory and an assistant; it was at Bowood Priestley discovered oxygen. Through Shelburne, patron of the arts, collector, ardent Whig and friend of the American colonies, Priestley met many celebrities of the day, especially Whigs, such as Sheridan and Burke. He regularly saw Benjamin Franklin. In 1780 there was some estrangement between Priestley and his patron—the reasons are not clear. Shelburne had remarried after the death of his wife, he was much saddened by the death of his youngest son, he had been wounded in a duel, and he did not appreciate Priestley's instructions on his complex political life. The separation was amicable; Priestley received a pension of £150 for life, and years later Shelburne asked him to return to service, but the invitation was declined.

Upon leaving Calne, Priestley took appointment in Birmingham as a minister in the New Meeting Society. His duties were light, and he was able to carry on his studies and writing. His support of French Republicanism and dissenting religious views aroused resentment. On July 14, 1791, a dinner celebration of the fall of the Bastille was held. Priestley's name was published as one of the sponsors, although he did not attend. A mob formed in protest of the event, descended upon Priestley's meeting house and burned it, and then sacked and burned his house and laboratory. Priestley retreated to London, and was appointed to teach at Gravel-Pit Meeting, Hackney, on the death of Richard Price, the celebrated mathematician, libertarian, and friend of Priestley. He also lectured in chemistry at the New College in Hackney. In 1792, he accepted French citizenship, but declined the French government's offer of sanctuary and patronage. Life in London became more difficult. Because of his political views, he was snubbed by his old friends in the Royal Society. When some of his associates received sentences for seditious libel under "Pitt's reign of terror," he decided to emigrate to America in 1794. His three sons had gone there the year before. He settled with them in Northumberland, at the junction of the north and west branches of the Susquehanna, in north-central Pennsylvania. There were hopes for a colony of liberty-loving English, but this did not develop. His home is now maintained as a museum by The Pennsylvania Historical and Museum Commission.

Here he lived quietly, supported by grants from friends in England and an annuity from his brother-in-law, John Wilkinson, a wealthy iron manufacturer. He gathered a library and set up a laboratory. He was offered the chair of chemistry at the University of Pennsylvania Medical School, and gave the offer some consideration because he thought he might be able to establish a

Unitarian church in Philadelphia. Although today Priestley is regarded as one of the fathers of modern chemistry, the discoverer of nine gases, he recognized his lack of formal training. Lecturing every day for four months did not appeal to him. He wrote to a friend: "For, though I have made discoveries in some branches of chemistry, I never gave much attention to the common routine of it, and know little of the common processes."[5]

Not only his views and accomplishments were distinctive, but also his personality and mannerisms. In physical appearance, Priestley was described by a contemporary[6] as about middle stature, five feet eight in height, slender and well proportioned. His complexion was fair, his eyes gray. He often smiled but seldom laughed. He was very active, and was "a most excellent pedestrian," walking with a long cane in his right hand. He wore a cocked hat, a black tailed coat, waistcoat with wide cravat, breeches and stockings, with buckles on his shoes. On going to America, he gave up his wig, not being able to find a suitable wig-dresser in the remote recesses of Northumberland County.

In the last lecture in this book, Priestley speaks of "people who are inclined to stammer," and adds in parenthesis, "as I know by experience." He speaks of his difficulty in his *Memoirs*. The stammer was "inherited from my family," he wrote.[7] Although a "thorn in the flesh," it "has not been without its use." Without it he felt he might have become "disputatious in company," or "might have been seduced by the love of popular applause as a preacher." While serving at Needham, he had been so tortured by his stammer that he went to London and paid "one Mr. Angier" twenty guineas for a cure. He received "some temporary benefit, but soon relapsed again, and spoke worse than ever."[8] To cure himself he read very loud and slowly every day, speaking a word at every step as he paced, and was able to keep the impediment in control.[9] In the pulpit he spoke conversationally, with little gesture, and a marked Yorkshire accent.

Priestley's ambition to be a practicing rhetorician in the pulpit was never completely fulfilled, but he maintained the desire to the last. He was hurt that he was invited only once to preach at the local Presbyterian church in Northumberland. He held regular Sunday services at his home, however, for his family, servants, and friends. He gave two series of sermons in Philadelphia and published them. Not as a platform man, but as a pamphleteer and tractarian was his desire to preach most gratified. Aroused by Edmund Burke's opposition to the French revolution as expressed in his *Reflections*, Priestley published his answer in *Letters to the Right Honourable Edmund Burke, Occasioned by His Reflections on the Revolution in France*.[10] After hearing William Pitt speak in Parliament, and feeling he had deserted the cause of religious toleration, Priestley published an open letter to Pitt, saying, "I take the liberty . . . to suggest what appear to me to be clearer ideas than you seemed to be possessed of, and such as may be the formulation of a better policy than you have adopted."[11] He published letters to the citizens of Birmingham, setting them right on Unitarianism,[12] and to the citizens of Northumberland, defending himself against various charges.[13] He spoke against slavery, supported French republicanism, religious toleration, abolition of religious tests acts in schools and offices, and the cause of the American colonies. In America his sympathies were with the Jeffersonian Democrats and against the Federalists.

Priestley's was one of the great voices of eighteenth-century enlightenment. He was a bridge between the metaphysical philosophers of that century and the philosophical radicals, such as

Bentham and Mill, of the nineteenth century. In his essay, "Of Political Liberty," he anticipated the Utilitarians when he wrote: "the good and happiness of the members [of society] that is the majority of the members of any state, is the great standard by which everything relating to that state must finally be determined."[14] His distinctions between civil liberty of the individual and political liberty became working definitions in the nineteenth century, especially in the works of John Stuart Mill. Although Priestley's life barely touched the nineteenth century, his ideas about scientific inquiry, educational reform, religious toleration, civil liberties, political reform, improvement of the material conditions of life, were to be major concerns of the period. Joseph Priestley was in the long line of brilliant English eccentrics.

BACKGROUND *and* EDITIONS *of the* LECTURES

PRIESTLEY EXPLAINS in the Preface that the lectures were composed when he was a tutor at Warrington, and were first delivered in 1762; he was then twenty-nine. He evidently felt no need of publishing them at the time, although he could have done so easily enough; the celebrated Warrington printer, William Eyres, was "at his beck and call."[15] In the Warrington period he had printed for his own use but did not publish *A Course of Lectures on the Theory of Language and Universal Grammar* (1762). A sermon, *On the Duty of not Living to Ourselves,* was published in 1764. Other publications while at Warrington were: *An Essay on a Course of Liberal Education for Civil and Active Life, with Plans of Lectures on the Study of History and General Policy, on the History of England, and on the Constitution and Laws of England* (1765); *A Chart of Biography* (1765); *The History and Present State of Electricity, with*

Original Experiments (1767). The six years at Warrington were sufficiently productive without the lectures. In recognition of his *Chart of Biography* Priestley received an LL.D. degree from Edinburgh University in 1765. His election to the Royal Society, June 12, 1766, is generally reported as having been for his work in electricity. W. Cameron Walker has shown, however, that the fellowship was "for literary ability"; the Society's Journal Book reads, "JOSEPH PRIESTLEY of Warrington LL.D., author of Divers works, particularly a Chart of Biography. . . ."[16]

Despite Priestley's facility in writing, as he explains in his Preface to these lectures, he never composed the part on elocution. "Instructions were given as occasion required," he says, and "great pains were taken to form the pupils to a habit of just and graceful delivery." A student testified that "though no [*sic*] proficient in oratory himself, Dr. Priestley contrived to render himself very useful in the promotion of it among the students. His observations on their defects in speaking, and his directions how to remedy them, were very judicious."[17] Since it was "my province to teach elocution," he wrote, and "finding no public exercises at Warrington, I introduced them there, so that afterwards every Saturday the tutors, all the students, and often strangers, were assembled to hear English and Latin compositions, and sometimes to hear the delivery of speeches, and the exhibitions of scenes in plays."[18]

The immediate reason for publishing the lectures fifteen years after they were prepared is explained in the Preface and the Dedication. Priestley wanted "to draw some degree of attention" to Dr. Hartley's "doctrine of the *association of ideas*, to which there is constant reference through the whole work." Similarly, in the Preface of *An Examination of Reid* (1774), his attack on the Scottish philosophy of common sense, Priestley says: "It appears to me that the subject of criticism admits of the happiest illustration from Dr. Hartley's principles; and accordingly, in the composition of those lectures [*On Oratory and Criticism*], I kept them continually in view."[19] He makes a similar statement in his *History and General Policy* (1788), in acknowledging his reliance upon Hartley when dealing with criticism:

> I have made great use of Dr. Hartley's doctrine of *association of ideas*, which appears to me to supply an easy solution of almost all the difficulties attending this curious subject, and gives us solid maxims, instead of arbitrary fancy. In this extensive application of the doctrine of association to the business of criticism, I think I have some claim to merit.[20]

A second motive for publishing was his desire to dedicate them to Lord Shelburne's elder son, John Henry Petty Fitzmaurice (1765–1809), who later sat in Commons for twenty years as a member for Chipping Wycombe before succeeding to the title and becoming the second Marquis of Lansdowne. The boy was twelve years old when the lectures were published. Priestley was much interested in John Henry and his younger brother by three years, William Granville, and although the boys had a tutor, spent much time with them, especially in chemical experiments. The younger boy contracted a fever and died suddenly in the year after publication of the lectures. He and his brother had been collecting gases in a swamp for experiments with mice shortly before he took ill.

Priestley explains in the Preface that he deleted from his original lectures passages "more trite than the rest." The manuscript was sent to the printer in 1776; he wrote to a friend on October 6 of that year: "My 'Lectures on Oratory and Criticism' are got half through the press."[21] How much revision was done he explained in a letter, April 13, 1777, after publication:

> I am afraid you will think I have not taken so much pains to finish the Lectures as you could have wished; but I did as much as I well could, without studying the subject afresh, and I could not bring my mind to it, it is so long since I gave any attention to things of that nature. I struck out a good deal that I thought superfluous.
>
> My manner has always been to give my whole attention to a subject till I have satisfied myself with respect to it, and then think no more about the matter. I hardly ever look into anything that I have published; and when I do, it sometimes appears quite new to me.[22]

These habits of Priestley were not confined to matters of oratory and criticism. He described himself as having "from an early period, been subject to a most humbling failure of recollection." He frequently made experiments he thought to be new, but which he had performed and published before.[23]

The lectures, then, are a young tutor's eager work as revised in tranquility fifteen years later. By this time Priestley was no longer the brash young publicist Brougham scoffed at. He had been to Paris in 1774, had discussed oxygen with Lavoisier, and had mingled in the most sophisticated intellectual London society. He was now established as an author; the advertisement at the back of this book lists thirty-three current works with one publisher.

By the time the lectures were first published in 1777 the mainstream of English rhetoric had passed from faithful and unquestioning reiteration of classical theory to concern for the bases of rhetoric in the laws of human nature revealed by empirical philosophy and science. Lord Kames, in his *Elements of*

Criticism (1762), made one of the first and most successful excursions on this frontier, but it was not until George Campbell's *Philosophy of Rhetoric* (1776) that the frontier was successfully penetrated. This same regard for the origin of rhetoric in the mind which also characterized Priestley's rhetoric earned for the *Lectures* a warm if not highly enthusiastic critical reception. William Enfield, Rector and tutor in belles lettres at Warrington, following Priestley, and author of *The Speaker* (1774), noted for the *Monthly Review* the uniqueness of the *Lectures* and its place in the epistemological tradition in rhetoric fostered by Kames:

> Dr. Priestley, apprehending that the subject [rhetoric and criticism] would receive new light, by referring several principles of which Lord Kaims treats, to one common source, the *association of ideas*, and by explaining the chief facts relating to the influence of oratory and poetry from this principle, here offers to the Public a new theory of human nature grounded on Dr. Hartley's general theory of human nature.[24]

Enfield observed, however, that on the whole the work did not appear very original or thorough, and he could recommend it only as well arranged and perspicuous, showing judgment. Enfield was distressed that Priestley did not include remarks on delivery in the *Lectures*. He was also unsympathetic with the speculative-philosophical tradition in rhetoric, and took the reactionary position that rhetoric and criticism would better be taught by example and precept than by the most accurate philosophical investigation and speculation.[25]

Priestley was pleased, nonetheless, by the general reception of his work, although he did not anticipate time or necessity for an improved edition. In a letter dated the year of publication, he wrote to a friend: "I am encouraged that my 'Lectures on Criticism' gave you any pleasure; but though I much approve of your hints for an improved edition, I fear that I shall hardly be able to give the attention to it that will be necessary to execute them. Besides, I do not imagine that there will be much demand for the work, so as to require a new edition, at least soon."[26] His prediction proved correct, and there was only one English edition during his lifetime.

The first edition of the lectures, 1777, here reproduced, was printed for J. Johnson, No. 72, St. Paul's Church-yard, in a large quarto volume with handsome margins. A reduction of 15 per cent was made in this edition in order to accommodate to the format of the "Landmarks" series.

The work was also published by William Hallhead in Dublin, 1781, in a pirated edition. Priestley's letters and memoirs do not indicate he authorized the Dublin edition or was even aware of it. Dublin editions of his more popular works were common, including *Essay on Government* (1768), *Lectures on History and General Policy* (1788), *Letters to Burke* (1791), and *Lectures on Experimental Philosophy* (1794). The Dublin *Lectures* is identical with the London edition except for an occasional error, such as omission of "not" (p. 90; p. 75 of this edition), which makes the sentence read, "It is enough to say, that plain unadorned style is that mode of expression which is the most natural," rather than "not enough."

A third printing of *Lectures* was made in *The Theological and Miscellaneous Works of Joseph Priestley* (1817–32). Volume XXIII, issued in 1824, contains in addition to the lectures, *English Grammar* and *Universal Grammar*. The editing of the subscription set was done by a wealthy Unitarian and Priestley admirer, John Towill Rutt. He made no substantial changes in the body of the lectures, but relocated Priestley's source references from the text to footnotes, specifically identified literary passages, and added notes of his own. The volume was printed separately in 1826 and 1833.

Since there were only five printings of the lectures—one of these in a volume series—and no American edition, copies are scarce items; particularly as compared with the rhetorics of Kames, Campbell, Blair, and Whately, which went through many English and American editions. In selecting the printing reproduced here, the editors have chosen the original as most nearly expressing Priestley's wishes, and uncluttered by Rutt's comments.

Rhetorical and Philosophical Presuppositions

When Joseph Priestley was asked to assume the duties of Tutor in Languages and Belles Lettres at Warrington Academy in 1761, he had by his own admission no particular fondness for the office, being more inclined at that time to the tutorship in mathematics and natural philosophy. It seems apparent that neither his training nor his affection was particularly suited to the position. Although he was well read in ancient and modern literature, Priestley had no appreciable background in rhetoric and was more disposed to scientific than belletristic studies. Indeed, the sum of his recommendation to the office appears to have been his knowledge of nine foreign languages and his newly composed *English Grammar*. Fortunately there were available in the mid-eighteenth century a number of currently published works which facilitated his preparation of the lectures in belles lettres. Notable among them was John Ward's *System of Oratory* (1759), a faithful and systematic reiteration of classical rhetorical theory uncorrupted by contemporary thought, which, together with John Lawson's *Lectures Concerning Oratory* (1758), marked the culmination of classical rhetoric in the eighteenth century. Equally noteworthy from Priestley's point of view, though in the contrasting intellectual tradition of the Enlightenment, were Alexander Gerard's prize-winning examination of the faculties of taste, *An Essay on Taste* (1759), and Lord Kames's *Elements of Criticism* (1762), an introduction of the experimental method of reasoning into aesthetic subjects after the method of Hume's *Treatise of Human Nature* (1739–40).

Prompted by the pressures of his office, Priestley drew freely from the available works in precept and illustration, presenting a course of lectures on rhetoric and criticism that was admittedly a succinct and systematic view of the observations of others. But the eclectic and derivative nature of the lectures did not in his opinion preclude originality. This view Priestley rested on the belief that he had set traditional rhetorical and aesthetic subjects on a foundation of Hartleian associational psychology never before constructed. Priestley recognized that although the association of ideas plays an important role in the aesthetic theory of other English philosophers, and that he, like previous writers, sought the bases of aesthetics in the nature of the mind, in his course of lectures on rhetoric and criticism the association of ideas was not *a* principle of the mind—as in the works of Hutcheson, Gerard, and Kames—but *the* leading principle.[27] He was well aware that his view of rhetoric was unique because his view of man was so. This "unique" associational view of man he shared with its systematizer, David Hartley, whose *Observations on Man* (1749) Priestley read during his student days at Daventry, and whose opinions shaped every aspect of Priestley's thought and writing from that point forth. The modern reader finds this consistent reference to Hartley's associational psychology the hallmark of Priestley's *Lectures*.

Priestley's concern for the nature of the mind and its effect on aesthetic subjects was sustained by a variety of presuppositions in addition to Hartleian psychology. The most notable of these, and in part an explanation of his associational view of man, was Priestley's unqualified commitment to Newton's first laws of inquiry stated in the third book of *Principia:* admit no more causes of things than are sufficient to explain appearances; to the same effects assign, as far as possible, the same causes.[28] Priestley learned of these laws and Newton's application of them to investigations into Nature, early in his life during that period when he read Gravesande's *Mathematical Elements of Natural Philosophy* (1720–21). In his later years Priestley—like other philosophers following Bacon and Newton—recognized that these laws together with Newtonian analysis and synthesis comprised a method of inquiry universally applicable to investigations in the arts and sciences alike, an investigatory pattern which would reveal with equal facility the nature of chemistry or criticism, man or the universe. Priestley's writings on air, optics, and electricity leave little doubt that although he was no ideal scientist, he did proceed according to the "universally acknowledged rules of philosophizing" (inquiring) in his investigations of physical nature. Similarly, in his investigations of human nature, Priestley was guided by the rules of universal inquiry, assured that the elements revealed by an investigation so conducted would be the true and fundamental principles of man. He employed the universal mode of inquiry to reduce seemingly irreducible phenomena of the mind to their simpler elements in much the same way he reduced common air to simpler gases. In both cases Priestley sought to render given phenomena to as few causes as account entirely for the observed effects. For this reason, his philosophical-scientific methodology may be characterized as "reductionistic," to use the term Hipple applied to Hume's mental chemistry.[29] This method presupposes the Newtonian world-view that elemental and first principles of man explain human nature with the same necessity that basic laws of the universe explain physical nature. This was a commonly held assumption in the eighteenth century; therefore Priestley could so assume with assurance, and employ the rules of philosophical inquiry to discover and prescribe basic facts of human nature which account for a multiplicity of mental phenomena in terms of comparatively few causes. Precisely this simplicity recommended Hartley's associational psychology to Priestley. Hartleian psychology reduces the principles of human nature to their basic element—the association of simple ideas—embracing a number of effects in a single cause. "It wears the face of that *simplicity in causes,* and *variety in effects,* which we discover in every other part of nature."[30]

Priestley was a philosopher in the empirical tradition of Locke and Hume. His distaste for a priority and proliferation of causes set him apart from the pervasive Scottish philosophy of common sense, and made him unsympathetic to the adumbrations of that school in the writings of Shaftesbury and Hutcheson. Indeed, Priestley based his condemnation of Reid's *Inquiry into the Human Mind* (1764) and his criticism of the common-sense school on Reid's postulation of more causes than are necessary to explain the nature of the mind and the Scottish predilection to rooting those causes in irreducible inherent senses. The philosophy resulting from Reid's misguided efforts Priestley dubs an "ingenious piece of sophistry."[31]

To Priestley's way of thinking all of man's intellectual pleasures and pains, all the phenomena of memory, imagination, passion, and reason, and every other mental affection and operation are only different modes or cases of the association of ideas. Compare, for example, the associational and common-sense views of the moral sense. In the latter view, the moral sense is an original (connatural, irreducible) sense born with man, one of many common senses which afford necessary knowledge of self and the outer world. In the contrasting associational view, the sense of morality is not an original principle of the mind, but an acquired coalescence of simple ideas of right and wrong so closely united throughout life by repeated association as to appear to be an original sense. This appearance, Priestley believed, misled Reid and his school, causing them to err in their view of the mind.

The modern reader of Priestley must be mindful that although he was the leading exponent of associational psychology in the eighteenth century, he was bound to that body of orthodox assumptions which comprised the generally held view of the mind. In the eighteenth century the predominant view was that human nature is composed of a number of faculties—memory, judgment, passion, imagination, will—which, working independent of one another or together according to a unifying principle like association, constitute the basic capacities of the mind. Priestley's writings provide ample evidence that his, too, was a faculty oriented view of the mind, amended by his understanding of the effect of association on the creation and function of the faculties. In the *History and General Policy*, when speaking of the virtues of studying history, Priestley refers to the beneficial effect historical precepts have on the judgment, and how such precepts engage the passions and affect the imagination when vividly represented by an artistic historian. Witness further that the greater part of his lectures on oratory and criticism are arranged according to what devices of style affect the passions, judgment, and imagination. Further, Priestley's major psychological work, *Hartley's Theory of the Human Mind* (1775), is written from the assumption that human nature is made up of a number of faculties, each with its particular capacity serving the mind.

More to the point than Priestley's position in one psychological camp or another is recognition that his associational psychology was reasoned from a typically eighteenth-century faculty orientation. Priestley believed the mind to be composed of distinct faculties, which, though they function according to the association of ideas and constitute intermediate states between gross mental phenomena and their basic elements, are faculties nonetheless, possessing distinct capacities and susceptible to particular appeals, which, when properly addressed, bring about fixed and necessary effects.

In light of Priestley's application of the rules of universal inquiry and the association of ideas, two leading ironies of his thought are noteworthy. The first and least explicable is that to his death he supported the Phlogiston Theory—that phlogiston was a material substance which caused inflammability—a theory Lavoisier disproved by using Priestley's discovery of oxygen. The second is that Priestley drew the major portion of his rhetorical and critical theory from writers in the common-sense school—Kames and Gerard—whose basic view of man if not of rhetoric was repugnant to him. This is particularly the case with Kames, whose proliferation of innate causes for rhetorical effects is pre-eminent even in the Scottish school. Apparently Priestley was a victim of certain presuppositions which neither science nor association could eradicate.

Analysis of *A* Course *of* Lectures *on* Oratory *and* Criticism

IT SHOULD be noted, first of all, that the lectures as printed are not fully developed. They are "a short, though connected *text,* from which to discourse *extempore,*" the author explains in The Preface. He recommends this practice as "a method which engages the attention unspeakably more than formally reading every thing from notes." He reviewed the previous lecture, he says, and then gave the current lecture "with more copious *illustrations,* and a greater variety of *examples,*" than are presented in the text.

The lectures are arranged under two heads, "Lectures on Oratory," and "Lectures on Criticism." The first, short section deals with the theory of rhetorical invention and arrangement, and shows Priestley's awareness of the traditions in these subjects. The second, much longer section concerns style, figurative language, the principles of aesthetics and human nature, and taste, illustrating the widely held eighteenth-century view that these are elements of criticism. Oddly enough, since Priestley was much aware of memory, and invented several mnemonic systems to aid his own, he ignores this canon in the lectures except in connection with invention. Although, as he explains, "The last part of the work, relating to *elocution,*" he never composed, there are evidences of his theory scattered through the lectures, and the last three lectures are basically elocutionary; so at least an abbreviated statement of his theory of delivery can be postulated.

LECTURES *on* ORATORY

Recollection, or Rhetorical Invention

Priestley's treatment of the first office of rhetoric is not a traditional one. His typically eighteenth-century concern for the sources of knowledge in the phenomena of the mind, and his commitment to the method of the new science made intolerable to him the classical view of *inventio* as an independent system of rhetorical investigation and discovery. In his view, the source of "what to say" is found in application to the matter of the subject in question, prior to and independent of the function of rhetoric. Invention in his rhetorical scheme aids the mind not in discovering materials that it is wholly unacquainted with, as in the classical view, but only in recollecting and judiciously selecting what—of the information previously furnished by extra-rhetorical investigation—is proper to the desired end of the speech. His rhetoric and theory of invention thus arise as managerial, not investigatory; a rhetoric and invention more concerned with the manner in which speech materials may be handled once acquired, than with the literal discovery or acquisition of them.[32]

To this end Priestley offers a system of topics, commonplaces or general heads, derived from the natural association of ideas prompted by examination of the relation which the parts of a proposition bear to one another. These apparently traditional *topoi* have in the *Lectures* an untraditional function. Notwithstanding their similarity to the topics treated by classical rhetoricians and collected in Ward's *Oratory,* in Priestley's *inventio* these topics serve only to promote recollection of speech materials already supplied to the mind by prior investigation of the subject, not literally to invent or discover materials as in the ancients and Ward. Priestley's treatment of the topic "of definition" is a case in point, as it is essentially the same as the classical stasis *quid sit.* But where in Cicero the "question of definition" is a device for investigating and discovering whether Milo murdered Clodius or killed him in self-defense, in Priestley it serves only to lead the mind to the material regarding the case which it already possesses, but cannot readily recollect, by considering the terms "murder" and "self-defense." Definition serves the mind of the speaker by facilitating recollection and management of what it already possesses, not by discovering what to say (p. 11).

The apparent similarity of Priestley's theory of recollection to Lord Bacon's view that invention in rhetoric is no real invention "but a *Resemblance* or *Suggestion* with application" is readily recognized by scholars in rhetoric.[33] Priestley does not acknowledge Bacon as the source of his view, but presuppositions common to both men indicate that the resemblance is probably more than coincidental. Priestley's commitment to the new organon of science proposed by Bacon and adopted by Newton, and his constant attention to the universal mode of inquiry made it almost inevitable that in his view of rhetoric, literal investigation and discovery of subject-matter should be beyond the scope of rhetorical invention; rhetorical invention, not being true invention, should be restricted to recollecting and suggesting materials to the mind which it has obtained by other than rhetorical means.

This basic similarity in point of view does not, however, warrant the conclusion that Priestley drew his theory of invention primarily or directly from Bacon, since the role of his associational psychology in shaping that view must also be considered. The more appropriate conclusion would be that Priestley's concern for the universal method of investigation and his associational view of the mind disposed him to Bacon's theory of invention and made him sympathetic to the view of rhetoric presented in the *Advancement of Learning*. Priestley found in his copy of Peter Shaw's *Philosophical Works of Francis Bacon*[34] a system of rhetorical invention he could subscribe to with little qualification and from which he could draw the leading premises of his own view. He could not find in Bacon's exposition a detailed topical system or a psychological rationale supporting it.

These details and rationale he drew from the works of Hartley and Ward. Following Hartley's lead, Priestley reasoned that every proposition may be considered simply as a concurrence between a subject and an attribute; assent to such propositions proceeds, in turn, from the close association of ideas suggested by the proposition with truth as it is known. As our idea of Alexander concurs with our idea of his being the conquerer of Darius, we assent to the proposition "Alexander conquered Darius."[35] Were such concurrence not clear or in need of support, recourse would have to be made to a third or middle term demonstrating the concurrence. This function of the middle term Priestley found in Ward's *Oratory*. As a logical concept, the middle term was by the eighteenth century a commonplace. Although evidence indicates that Priestley drew the concept from Ward, he might just as easily have drawn it from Watt's *Logic* (1725), an extremely popular work in the dissenting academies, which Priestley read in his youth and taught from at Warrington.[36] Presumably borrowing, nonetheless, from Ward's discussion of the middle term the proposition illustrating it—*"Whether virtue is to be loved?"*[37]—and from Hartley's view of assent and the proposition, Priestley formulated a scheme of topical analysis that is the basis of his *inventio* of recollection and fills the vacuum created by his exclusion of invention and discovery from the province of rhetoric. He observes that recollection is psychologically and rhetorically merely the introduction of one idea into the mind by means of another with which it was previously associated; if the truth of the proposition "Every good man is a wise man" is not readily apparent or if supporting material is wanting but cannot be remembered, consideration of the implicit relation of "good" and "wise" (cause-effect, means-end) or of the definition of the terms may provide the necessary associational links to prompt the memory or gain the assent (pp. 7–8).

In the stream of eighteenth-century inventional theory, Priestley's view of invention as recollection places him between Ward's mechanical *inventio* of topics and discovery on the one hand, and Hugh Blair's later theory of invention based on the power of natural genius on the other. By grounding the theory of the middle term on Hartleian psychology, Priestley made a notable contribution to rhetoric, offering for the first time a psychological rationale for topical theory. More important, he made clear as part of his rhetorical and inventional theory that distinction in Bacon between the investigatory and communicative function of rhetoric echoed in the works of Campbell, Blair, and Whately.

Method, or Rhetorical Arrangement

In much the same fashion, Priestley's view of the second office of rhetoric is shaped by his associational-scientific orientation. Consistent with his psychological point of view, he suggests that narrative discourse may be arranged to its greatest effect by attention to the strongest and most usual associations of ideas in the mind (p. 35); the propensity of human nature to follow the path of repeated association warrants this suggestion. Regarding method in argumentative discourses—the second of Priestley's untraditional species of composition—his advice becomes more complex. Reasoning from the force they demonstrate in logic and mathematics, Priestley concludes that used separately or mixed, analytic and synthetic patterns of arrangement contribute greatly to the effect of an argumentative discourse. Synthetic method, proceeding in the necessary fashion of a mathematical demonstration from what is granted to what must be granted, has an obvious persuasive effect. Similarly, analytic method, by rendering an accurate description of the actual process of investigation, leads the reader to the same conclusion as the investigator.[38] This method Priestley employed in his six volumes of *Observations on Air*.

Underlying his view of the rhetorical uses of analysis and synthesis as patterns of arrangement is Priestley's inclination to the universal mode of inquiry. Priestley was convinced that analysis is the method of inquiry drawn from logic (p. 56). He confirms his commitment to the Baconian-Newtonian view of inquiry which shaped his inventional and rhetorical theory by observing that inquiries and discoveries made by modern writers on morals have proceeded in the analytic or scientific method of investigation and reporting. He refers, of course, to Hume's "attempt to introduce the experimental method of reasoning into moral subjects" in the *Treatise of Human Nature;* to Hutcheson's search in the *Introduction to Moral Philosophy* (1747) "into the constitution of our nature to see what kind of creatures we are"; and to Hartley's adherence to Newton's analysis and synthesis—"the proper method of philosophizing"—in the *Observations on Man* in order to reveal the nature of man and morality. His understanding of analysis also helps explain the enigmatic aside in the section on invention that what will be advanced on the subject of method "will tend greatly to help the invention" (p. 22). By this he means that review of the analytic process in which a subject was investigated will aid in recollection of materials on the subject discovered by the inquiry. Much the same rationale accounts in part for Priestley's exclusion of ethical and emotional appeals—traditionally generic modes of invention—from what is essential to rhetoric. He reasons that in a scheme of rhetorical invention and arrangement which derives its materials and patterns from the subject matter of the speech and the method of investigation, ethical and emotional proofs which have no origin in the subject per se have no place in the scheme, and must be relegated to accessory or ornamental roles. Extended studies of human nature, logic, and grammar are likewise extra-rhetorical concerns which function not coincidental with but prior to the *art* of rhetoric (pp. 2–4).

The theory of rhetoric one would expect from Priestley's given sources does not arise. Certainly the pressures of his new tutorship and varied duties at Warrington made Ward's compendium attractive to Priestley, as well as Lawson's *Lectures Concerning Oratory*, another summary of classical rhetoric with which he shows a reading acquaintance. Priestley was, in addition, well read in the classical authors, and had in his library at the time of his death Aristotle's *Rhetoric*, Cicero's *Opera*, Demosthenes' *Orations*, Isocrates' *Orationes Et Epistolae*, Quintilian's *Institutes of Oratory*, and two copies (French and English) of Longinus's *On the Sublime*.[39] Furthermore, the orientation of Mr. Aikin's tutor-

ship in "Classics and Polite Literature" which immediately preceded Priestley's was classical, the students reading among other
works Aristotle's *Rhetoric* and *Poetic*, Longinus, and the debates
of Aeschines and Demosthenes.

With the exception of his partition of the *Lectures* into the
Ciceronian four offices, his use of traditional nomenclature, and his
consideration of a number of subjects common to the long
tradition of rhetoric, however, one would not say that Priestley's
general view of rhetoric or his view of invention and arrangement
are classical in precept or spirit. Arguments for his classicism could
not be drawn from his denial of investigatory powers to rhetoric,
his view of invention as recollection, his exclusion of ethos and
pathos from invention, his view of topics as artificial mnemonic
devices, or his *dispositio* of analysis and synthesis. The subjects he
borrows from the ancients through Ward, Priestley alters signifi-
cantly as is illustrated by his view of method and recollection.
Regarding his debt to Bacon, Priestley's associational view of man
and his commitment to new science made the Elizabethan's
concept of the communicative function of rhetoric and the
remembering function of invention acceptable to him with little
alteration, and may have acted either as the source of Priestley's
rhetorical-inventional theory or as substantiation of it if that
theory arose independent of Bacon from Hartleian psychology.

Priestley's notion of rhetorical invention and arrangement was,
then, shaped more by contemporary scientific-psychological theory
than by traditional rhetoric. In keeping with the dominant
psychological mood of the eighteenth century, Priestley looked to
the elemental processes of the mind for his system of rhetoric.
This epistemological analysis together with his commitment to the
experimental method which contemporary philosophers were

applying to moral and aesthetic subjects made classical views of
rhetoric, not so derived, repugnant to him, and inclined him to the
managerial view of rhetoric that his analysis and method dictated.
In distinguishing between the communicative and investigatory
function of rhetoric, Priestley focused his attention not on the first
traditional question of rhetoric—"What may be said on behalf of
a cause?"—but on the second—"How may it best be said?"[40]
Priestley's theory of rhetoric is, in this respect, like George Campbell's. The similarity is coincidental in that neither theorist seemingly had any direct effect on the other. It is less than coincidence,
however, that they should arrive at similar conclusions; both
Campbell and Priestley employed the psychological-scientific
method of critical introspection to arrive at that epistemology of
the human mind which was in their day the radical source of
rhetoric. In this approach they had a common model in *Elements
of Criticism* by Kames, to whom they both acknowledged a debt.
It is not a paradox, therefore, that although they reasoned from
different psychological assumptions (Campbell in good measure
from a psychology of common senses, Priestley from one of
association of ideas), and did not see eye to eye on epistemology,
they should arrive at common conclusions about rhetoric: that the
theory of rhetoric should be drawn from the nature of the mind by
the experimental method of investigation; that rhetoric should be
concerned with the effect of rhetorical devices on the mind; that
the just province of rhetoric is more the effective management of
ideas according to human nature than the discovery of them. The
last of these common conclusions, the seemingly Baconian distinction between inquiry and transmission, Richard Whately carried
to its logical conclusion in the *Elements of Rhetoric* (1828) in his
differentiation between the "method of inquiry" and the "method

of proof," an analysis which is one of his important contributions to rhetoric. Campbell's famous criticism that the later critics (Ward, Lawson) only clothed ancient theory in modern dress could not be leveled at Priestley, who attempted a thorough re-analysis of rhetorical theory.

LECTURES *on* CRITICISM

The Nature and Range of Style

By the mid-eighteenth century the field of rhetoric and criticism had been surveyed repeatedly by neo-classical and epistemological writers in belles lettres. Ward and Lawson had reported faithfully the classical view of the connate arts; and Gerard reviewed traditional rhetorical-critical principles in terms of contemporary psychology. For this reason, Priestley's theory of style and criticism—the concern of over two-thirds of the *Lectures*—is not a wholly new one reasoned deductively from his scientific-psychological orientation, but more a re-examination and reinterpretation of traditional rhetorical and critical principles governed by that frame of reference. Priestley's regard for the facts of human nature as they relate to style fixed him in the stream of eighteenth-century belletristic writers after Bacon, Newton, and Locke, and included among others Addison, Hutcheson, Gerard, Kames, Campbell, and Blair. Like the philosophical method of his predecessors, the logic of Priestley's epistemology is both inductive and deductive. He induces principles of style from the observable phenomena of human nature (generally by critical introspection), and in turn verifies such principles by deducing them from commonly established facts of human nature as he knew them.[41] Like most English writers, he considered many of the common principles of belles lettres—novelty, uniformity, grandeur, sublimity—which were then universally acknowledged elements of rhetoric, taste, and criticism. In addition to the influence of generally held aesthetic precepts, Priestley's notion of style was, of course, also framed by his predisposition to associational psychology, his faculty orientation, and his pervasive reductionistic mode of inquiry adapted from scientific investigation.

Owing to such influences and presuppositions and to his restricted view of invention and arrangement, Priestley's treatment of style is broader than the traditional embellishment of materials. His epistemologist's concern for the origin of stylistic devices in the mind and the effect of these devices on the mind extended his conception of the third office of rhetoric to all such ornamentation as gives life, force, and beauty to thoughts and expression according to the principles of human nature which account for the effect of rhetorical devices on the passions, judgment, and imagination (pp. 71–72). In Priestley's rhetoric the scope of style is broadened in proportion to his narrowing of invention and arrangement. As content and arrangement are in his managerial view determined primarily by the subject and mode of investigation proper and therefore only susceptible to a minimum of assistance from the art of rhetoric, so style, which is exclusive of the subject proper and simply ornamental to it, is the area of greatest artistic latitude, the area of what may be expected from the *art* of rhetoric exclusive of previous application to science. Ethical and emotional modes of appeal, improper to the realm of invention because they are not derived from the subject per se, are proper to the realm of style, which in Priestley's view is concerned with giving thoughts their most favorable appearance according to the dictates of human nature. Similarly, analysis of those finer feelings which account for the influence of style and the pleasures of the imagination is proper to the art of rhetoric in that it ascertains the effect of ornamentation on the mind. To the end of explaining what in man's nature makes him susceptible to rhetorical ornaments and how ornaments affect the mind, Priestley divides the major portion of his rhetoric into what "affects the passions, judgment and imagination." Inherent in this distribution are the remnants of the artistic means of persuasion as they are understood traditionally. Although Priestley ostensively relegates such means merely to the role of devices to gain attention, they serve in fact as means of persuasion exclusive of or supplemental to the speech matter. The use of such rhetorical devices as present tense and vivid representation, for example, more than gains the attention, and more than persuades; it sways the mind, convincing it that what in reality it is only hearing is in fact what is actually taking place. Priestley's distinctions among the three faculties affected by rhetorical ornamentation are also more apparent than real, owing in part to his faculty view of the mind as composed of distinct capacities susceptible to particular modes of persuasion. As they function in his notion of style, the ornaments of rhetoric—what affects the passions, judgment, and imagination—do not influence each faculty separately but any or all of them simultaneously. Priestley, like Campbell, whose rhetoric is also reasoned from a faculty orientation, saw the mind not as an amalgam of exclusive capacities but as an interrelated heirarchy of faculties mutually interdependent and interacting. To Priestley, naturally, the principle of human nature accounting for this unity is the association of ideas. His faculty psychology must be read simply as an orientation not as a working principle of his theory of human nature. Indeed, in Campbell and Priestley, as well as in many of the eighteenth-century belletristic writers reasoning from traditional views of the mind, the apparent faculty orientation is more an underlying presupposition and mode of expression than a critical principle or working element of their psychology.

This same caution must be kept in mind in considering Priestley's faculty oriented view of the ends of rhetoric (pp. 68–69). Despite his differentiation among the ends of rhetoric according to the faculties they affect—a notable point of similarity with Campbell owing perhaps to Baconian origins—Priestley's concern is merely to distinguish between the proper end of rhetoric (informing the judgment, the regard of recollection and method) and the accessory ends of rhetoric (moving the passions and affecting the imagination so as to persuade, the regard of style). In Priestley's rhetoric these ends integrate so as to be practically indistinguishable. This unified concept of the ends of rhetoric Priestley offers in his *Hartley's Theory of the Human Mind*, where he proposes that the end of rhetoric is "to convince the judgment, excite and gain the affections." In the "Lectures on Criticism" he offers many of the leading principles of eighteenth-century rhetoric freshly underwritten by his associational psychology as means to that end.

What Affects the Passions

Vivid representation is in Priestley's rhetoric the element of style that affects the passions and effects persuasion. He argues that since vividness and strong emotions are tied throughout life to reality, the associated idea of reality should recur when the mind is stimulated artificially by such stylistic devices as vivid representation, ideal presence, or use of the present tense. These devices are, Priestley acknowledges, more than mere factors of attention in that they affect the mind—the judgment as well as the passions and imagination—to the point of convincing it that what is really past is present, what is fiction is fact, thereby affording the rhetorician a sure and effective means of rousing men to action without the slow intervention of reason (p. 80). Although not a theory of "pathos" in traditional sense, in that there is more concern with the origins and effects of passions than with appeals to particular emotions, Priestley's view of the ornaments of rhetoric does embrace a theory of persuasion which has the same effect as traditional pathetic appeal if not for the same reasons or by the same means. This similarity in effect does not warrant, however, application of the term pathos to that theory. Priestley's understanding of the devices of style as ornaments accessory to rhetoric, not as generic modes of persuasion drawn from invention, and his discussion of the means of persuasion, are not traditional in mood or precept. His view is, on the contrary, drawn from prevailing eighteenth-century notions of human nature and the elements of rhetoric, and is for this reason a significant step forward from Ward's reactionary and unimaginative catalogue of the passions as Aristotle understood them two thousand years before. But as would be expected, it is more the psychological rationale underlying vivid representation than the theory proper that is original with Priestley. He drew the concept of vivid representation virtually intact from Lord Kames's discussion of the causes of the passions, their susceptibility to fiction, and the influence of passion with respect to our perceptions, opinions, and belief—essential principles of Kames's rhetorical theory. The notion that distinct images afford such vivid representation of thought and sentiments as to effect "transportation"—or to sweep the audience into "'ideal presence'" as Kames puts it—had its origin in Longinus's ideas of the effect of the sublime in language. Proceeding from the ancient's lead, Kames and Priestley had only to re-examine and reinterpret ideal presence in terms of their own particular psychological point of view (associational in Priestley and common-sense in Kames) to bring the theory in line with contemporary thought. Moreover, despite their psychological differences, Priestley drew a number of other particular theorems and illustrations regarding vivid representation from Kames as a comparison of the *Lectures* with the *Elements* will indicate.[42] The uniqueness of Priestley's remarks on vivid representation is limited to the unprecedented associational foundation for this common element of style which he offered in place of Kames's psychology of connate senses.

Although the possibility is remote that Priestley's vivid representation had any effect in shaping Campbell's notion of "vivacity," the apparent similarity of the two views is an arresting and noteworthy, if only coincidental, point of resemblance in their theories of style. In fact, though Campbell was familiar with Priestley's works, as his references to the *Examination of Reid* and the *English Grammar* indicate,[43] there is no evidence that Campbell even heard of Priestley's lectures on rhetoric during the period when he was composing the *Philosophy of Rhetoric*. The similarity has an explanation. The influence of the *Elements of Criticism* on contemporary writers makes it possible that, just as Priestley found in Kames's remarks on the passions and ideal presence a theory of vivid representation that was attractive to him and consonant with his psychological-rhetorical views, so Campbell (be the origin of his vivacity Hume's philosophy or not) may have found in his reading of Kames an analysis of the origins and effects of rhetorical vividness which was in keeping with his own view of the subject, and which pointed up the dependence of rhetorical effectiveness on psychological vividness.

What Affects the Judgment

Several "forms of address adapted to engage belief," as Priestley terms them, affect the judgment. Since such forms— unpremeditated expression, demonstration of conviction, mastery of the subject, marks of candor and the like—are linked throughout life by association with states of mind which induce belief, they produce similar belief when used artistically by the rhetorician to convey these states. The intimate association of strong conviction in a matter with the truth of the matter, for example, insures that when such a conviction is demonstrated naturally or —as in the case of rhetoric—artistically the long associated idea of truth will be introduced in the mind. To this idea of truth, the judgment will confidently give its assent because it has previously been associated with what one may safely assent to. By manifesting the signs of such states of mind, the rhetorician may not only ornament his thoughts to give them a more favorable appearance, he may augment the persuasive effect of the thoughts by affecting the judgment in addition to informing it (p. 109). Like vivid representation, this second mode of persuasion is not essential to the subject but ornamental to it; it has no origin in the matter of the subject proper, only in the manner of presenting it. Also like vivid representation, the forms of address have clear persuasive powers to be used when persuasion is properly the end.

Priestley's forms of address adapted to gain belief appear to be similar in effect though not in precept to "ethos," the third generic mode of persuasion in classical rhetoric. If and to what degree they are ethos in the traditional sense is problematic. The forms of address demonstrate to some degree the good sense, good will, and good character of the speaker and thereby fulfill the Aristotelian requirements for ethos. They do so only indirectly, however, by indicating that the speaker knows his subject, is convinced of its merit, and is candid.

The source of Priestley's notion of these accessory modes of persuasion is evidence that to his way of thinking the classical term ethos would be misleading if applied to this aspect of his rhetoric. Despite his reliance on the forms of address catalogued in the classically oriented *System of Oratory*, Priestley does not draw them from Ward's chapter on "the Character and Address of an Orator" (his discussion of traditional ethos) but rather from the chapters on the figures of speech suited for proof, suited to move the passions, and suited to express the passions—chapters which redound the figurist rhetoric of the sixteenth century.[44] Priestley saw in these forms of address a mode of speaking more emphatic than the ordinary, the effect of which—the assent of the judgment—he could explain in terms of the associational composition of the mind. The unique and significant aspect of Priestley's theory is that judgment is influenced through the artistic association of ideas.

What Affects the Imagination

In the eighteenth century no element of rhetoric and criticism was examined with greater frequency and rigor by philosophical writers in belles lettres than the so-called pleasures of the imagination. From the first rumblings of philosophical aesthetics in Addison's papers in the *Spectator* (1712) to its final echoes in Archibald Alison's *Essay on the Nature and Principles of Taste*

(1790) the concern of epistemological writers in "philosophical criticism"—a study embracing the psychological bases of taste, rhetoric, criticism and aesthetics—was with the principles of human nature which account for the finer pleasures afforded such subjects by the imagination. "Reactionary" writers like Lawson and Ward notwithstanding, the majority of philosophical critics offered analyses of these pleasures in keeping with their particular point of view. Addison, Hutcheson, Hume, Akenside, Gerard, and Kames all based their explanations of these phenomena on human nature after the method of Newton and Locke, each building upon and amending the views of the others. All the major schools of psychology were represented in the effort in one combination or another—the common sense, the empirical-analytic, and the associational. Following the path set out by Kames and Gerard, Campbell and Blair too turned their attention to the effect of rhetoric and human nature on the imagination. It was in keeping with an eighteenth-century tradition that Priestley devoted over one-half of the "Lectures on Criticism" to the principles of human nature that explain how the effect of composition is heightened by those finer feelings and ornaments of rhetoric which afford pleasure to the imagination.

Priestley suggests two sources of the principles of human nature and pleasures of the imagination which explain the efficacy of rhetorical devices. The first is the mental principle responsible for the formation and growth of all of man's intellectual pleasures and pains, the association of simple ideas. The second, derived in part from association but an independent principle no less, is a moderate exertion of the faculties (p. 136). Both of these principles were by 1777 well established in philosophical criticism. Moderate exertion of the faculties had its immediate origin in the writings of Addison and Gerard, and the association of ideas in the writings of Locke, Hutcheson, Gerard, and Kames, although their use of the term was in some respects pejorative. It is clear that in the *Lectures* association has a propitious not pejorative connotation, and is derived from Hartley's mechanical view of the connection of ideas, not from Hume's view of association derived from the philosophical relationships of causation, resemblance, and contiguity as in many of the eighteenth-century theorists. Both the association of ideas and the pleasures of the imagination so derived play a major role in Priestley's theory of style. What is less well recognized is the influence of the notion of "moderate exertion of the faculties" on Priestley's view of rhetorical style. Priestley understands this principle of the mind (detailed in Gerard, and attractive to Priestley because of the impact of association in Gerard's account of it) to be one essential to all of the pleasures of the imagination. He employs it to explain most of the principles of human nature that account for the efficacy of stylistic devices, even those views he borrows from Kames, who recognized no such basis for the elements of style.

Priestly enumerates the numerous species and properties of the pleasures of the imagination in terms of association and moderate exertion, pointing up the relation of these properties to the ornaments of rhetoric. The properties he offers are commonplaces in the eighteenth century: novelty, uniformity, variety, sublimity, and grandeur. Nor is his view of them new. They are derived from Kames's and Gerard's treatment of them, as Priestley acknowledged (p. iii).[45] These same phenomena of the mind also appear in Hartley's *Observations on Man,* a source that could be the origin of Priestley's initial acquaintance with them and the role of association in creating them, as well as the origin of his view of the influence of such pleasures on music, art, poetry, and oratory. So derivative is his account that Priestley's theory of the elements of style based on the operation of the imagination is little more than a patchwork of debts and amendments to the views of Gerard and Kames. Only his Hartleian association as *the* principle of the mind underlying their effect provides Priestley with a measure of originality.

Priestley's understanding of the function of such properties of the mind and pleasures of the imagination, as well as his view of them, is also derivative. As in Gerard these properties constitute the basic elements of taste, and in Kames they comprise the elements of criticism, so in Priestley they serve as the principle underlying the pleasures of the imagination afforded by rhetorical style. In Priestley's rhetoric novelty, sublimity, grandeur, uniformity, variety, comparison, and contrast and the devices of style derived from them, metaphor, allegory, antithesis, metonymy, hyperbole, and personification are properties of the mind affording pleasures of the imagination, and elements of style deriving such pleasures from the natural effect of these properties. Priestley's treatment of comparison is a case in point. Drawing efficacy in part from moderate exertion of the faculties, but primarily from the association of ideas, uniformity and variety afford pleasure to the imagination because the mind is familiar with these qualities conspicuous in the natural world. Exclusive of the light they shed on the subject, considered solely in terms of their ornamental value, such rhetorical devices as comparison, metaphor, and simile (based on uniformity and variety) ornament thoughts and sentiments by demonstrating the resemblance between the ideas they exhibit and the thoughts the writer wishes to communicate. To the degree in which such resemblances afford uniformity and variety these figures of speech are pleasurable, heightening and enlivening the composition. Reasoning from this acknowledged fact of human nature, Priestley offers a rule of style based on the nature of the mind and the pleasures which affect it: the chief excellence of a comparison (and for the same reason of a metaphor and allegory) depends on the proportion there is between the degrees of uniformity and variety, or the points of resemblance, between the principle object and the one to which it is compared (p. 168). For this view of comparison, Priestley is indebted to Kames. There are, however, subtle differences between their views. Priestley, as would be expected, substitutes Hartleian associational psychology as the basis of resemblance and comparison in place of the common sense of resemblance which Kames offers. Of more interest, he reduces resemblance, an independent psychological principle in Kames's treatment of comparison, to the rank of an intermediate relation implicit in uniformity and variety, thus altering and abbreviating Kamesian theory, in addition to reasoning from it. After Hume, of course, the influence of resemblance as a psychological principle was pervasive. It appears as an important element in Campbell's theory of vivacity. Kames's conception of resemblance may also have originated in Hume's views, with which he was familiar. Hume is a possible source of Priestley's view of resemblance, though the influence was more likely indirect through Kames and in keeping with Priestley's associational view of man. Priestley's substitution of associational psychology as the basis of style for Kames's proliferation of common senses is, nonetheless, the hallmark of his critical theory and the sum of his original contribution regarding comparison and figurative language.

On the basis of their psychological dissimilarity, it is almost paradoxical that Priestley should draw so heavily from Kames.

Kames's psychology of original senses, which numbered almost as many causes as rhetorical effects, was not compatible with Priestley's inclination to that simplicity in causes and variety in effects which recommended Hartley's associational psychology (pp. 72–73). Aspects of Kamesian theory were attractive to Priestley, notably Kames's scientific-epistemological approach to the subject of criticism, his sweeping treatment of the common elements of human nature and style, and his repeated reference to the succession of ideas as they affect the mind and rhetorical style. Regarding succession of ideas, it should be noted that most of the theories and principles Priestley borrows are implicitly and explicitly related to association in some way by Kames; this is particularly true of the views of figures of speech drawn from Kames. Apparently Priestley was able to bear with those aspects of Kames's theory repugnant to him for the sake of principles of the mind and elements of style with which he was sympathetic. The *Lectures,* then, because of Priestley's application of the single principle of association, demonstrates a unity of conception extending to such diverse areas of rhetoric as invention (recollection), the principles of human nature underlying style (sublimity), and figurative language (metonymy).

From the foregoing, the most evident features of Priestley's view of style or what is ornamental to rhetoric appear to be four: his distinction between subject matter and the manner of presenting it; his faculty-oriented view of the mind; his concern for the effect of rhetorical devices on human nature; and his near total dependence on Kamesian rhetoric and Hartleian psychology. The theory of style arising from these features is not a traditional one concerned solely with verbal embellishment, but an epistemological one concerned with the properties of the mind and the principles of expression which affect the major faculties of the mind—the passions, judgment, and imagination. It is a theory of style similar to Kames's and Campbell's, focused on the effect of rhetorical devices on the mind and the origin of those devices in the mind according to the elements of human nature which philosophical investigation reveals are characteristic of man. It is a theory based on orthodox principles of belles lettres, drawn from authors attractive to Priestley for the role association played in their views. The originality of the theory derives not from a new view of style based on Priestley's psychological-scientific orientation, but from a re-examination and reinterpretation of traditional belletristic subjects in terms of that orientation.

Elements of Delivery

Priestley's scattered remarks on delivery, and the incidental treatment in the last three chapters, are given to illuminate his remarks on criticism rather than to present a coherent theory. What he says on delivery, however, reveals him as a thoroughgoing "naturalist," without any suggestion of mechanical approaches. Consistent with his position that judgment is fundamental in oratorical appeals, he maintains that the communication of sense is the primary concern of delivery: "the true art of pronunciation [delivery] . . . is governed wholly by the sense" (p. 300). Even in verse, he taught, "a pause in the sense ought to be made to coincide with the metrical pause" (p. 305). "Let your primary regards be always to the *sense* and to *perspicuity*," he advocated. "If no methods can be found to reconcile" sense and metrics, "let the harmony be sacrificed without hesitation." The last words in the book read: "Propriety of sentiment and expression will better cover a defect of harmony, than the harmony will cover a defect of propriety."

The unit of communication consists of "those words . . . which together present but one idea" (p. 310), what we now call a rhetorical phrase. Comprehension of sense is best managed and communicated when the speaker is "expressive of *earnestness*" (p. 115); "we [must] feel the sentiment" (p. 296). "The external expressions of passion, with all their variations . . . are too complex for any person in the circumstances of a public speaker to attend to them" (p. 115). Only an audience "wholly illiterate" could be aroused by "mechanical communication" (p. 114). Not only in delivery, but also in composition, "the more vivid are a man's ideas" (p. 127), the better will he express them. In describing, one "should almost forget that he is only describing, and should feel himself" (p. 172).

To develop a strong, natural delivery, the speaker should be "himself strongly convinced of the truth and importance of what he contends for" (p. 108). This not only gives him a natural delivery, but by the laws of association, suggests belief; "we are, in all cases, more disposed to give our assent to any proposition, if we perceive that the person who contends for it is really in earnest, and believes it himself" (p. 109). Although not using the word, Priestley recognizes the theory of *empathy*. The players in a game of bowls, he notes, when they have a vivid sense of what is happening, "lean their own bodies, and writhe them into every possible attitude, according to the course they would have their bowl to take" (p. 127). Although Priestley taught the values of sincerity, he allowed a place for art in suggesting spontaneity in delivery. The speaker should use devices such as retracting a statement and then modifying it, and connecting what he had previously prepared with the speaking situation and remarks made by others. Such practices suggest *"unpremeditated discourse, in which the sentiments are supposed to be natural and sincere, preceding directly from the heart"* (p. 111).

Priestley recognizes the values of delivery in full communication. "The *tone of voice*, the *gesture*, and a variety of other *circumstances*, may sufficiently indicate a man's real meaning, without regard to words," he says. Indeed, physical expression is so significant, one may say one thing, and by gesture indicate the opposite, as in irony (p. 218).

Although Priestley's remarks on delivery bear his original imprint, there is indication that other authors influenced him. He acknowledges in the Preface his reliance on Kames and the use of examples from John Ward's *A System of Oratory*. Priestley's "just and graceful delivery" (p. iv) resembles John Mason's "just and graceful Pronunciation."[46] One of Mason's devices is used and acknowledged (p. 299), and a sentence of his is cited as imperfect (p. 312). Two sentences from Sheridan's lectures are also used as examples of poor composition (pp. 288, 312). North notes in his dissertation on Priestley that Enfield's *The Speaker* must have been drawn upon, the main evidence being that "twenty-one of the quotations or references which Priestley makes to other authors . . . also appear in *The Speaker*," and that there are echoes from John Lawson's *Lectures Concerning Oratory*.[47] Priestley gives no attention to reading, as did Sheridan, Mason, and Enfield, because his concern was for the extempore method.

In his treatment of delivery, Priestley is a tributary to the Whately-Curry-Winans stream of "natural method" — in contrast to "mechanical" methods. Manner in extemporary delivery

should be "natural to a person who is greatly in earnest" (p. 116);
"all his gestures, the air of his countenance, and his whole manner,
should correspond" with the speaker's "great earnestness and
vehemence" (p. 114).

SUMMARY

PRIESTLEY'S, THEN, is a theory of rhetoric written by a man of
science who was more an "index scholar" in rhetoric than original
thinker. The derivative and eclectic nature of *A Course of
Lectures on Oratory and Criticism* is evident in light of its
dependence upon the rhetorical literature of the eighteenth
century. Priestley's rhetorical debts, both classical and epistemological, are to those writers who shaped prevailing notions of
rhetoric, taste, and criticism between 1748 and 1776. A number of
presuppositions and inclinations did, however, render his theory
unique in the history of rhetoric. Most evident is his attention to
the role of Hartleian association in aesthetic subjects, but equally
important in shaping his rhetoric was his commitment to the
scientific method of Newton and Bacon, and the psychological
method of Hume, Kames, and Gerard. As a result of these
influences, although Priestley was familiar with classical rhetoric,
his view is managerial and epistemological, not classical. His
concern, like that of Campbell and Kames, is more with the
epistemological origins and psychological effects of the elements
of rhetoric than with their use in a particular rhetorical situation.
In the history of rhetorical thought, Priestley is most noteworthy
for his Baconian distinction between inquiry and transmission, and
his psychological reinterpretation of traditional rhetorical principles in terms of associational psychology. It cannot be said

that his rhetoric is a highly original one, but considered as a succinct and systematic view of the observations of others, interspersed with original observations drawn from his scientific-psychological orientation, the *Lectures* will not disappoint the modern reader of Priestley.

SELECTED BIBLIOGRAPHY

Brown, Ira V. *Joseph Priestley: Selections from His Writings*. University Park: Pennsylvania State University Press, 1962.

Fulton, John F., and Peters, Charlotte H. "An Introduction to a Bibliography of the Educational and Scientific Works of Joseph Priestley," *The Papers of the Bibliographical Society of America*, XXX (1936), 150–67.

North, Ross Stafford. "Joseph Priestley on Language, Oratory, and Criticism." Unpublished Ph.D. dissertation, University of Florida, 1957.

> A study of Priestley's *Rudiments of English Grammar, A Course of Lectures on the Theory of Language and Universal Grammar*, and *A Course of Lectures on Oratory and Criticism*.
>
> Abstract of the dissertation was published in *Speech Monographs*, XXV (June, 1958), 111.
>
> The dissertation is in University Microfilms, Mic 57–1850.

Priestley, Joseph [son]. *Memoirs of Dr. Joseph Priestley, to the Year 1795, Written by Himself; with a Continuation . . . by His Son, J. Priestley; and Observations on His Writings, by Thomas Cooper . . . and . . . the Rev. William Christie*. 2 vols. Northumberland, Pa.: J. Binns, 1806.

> Reprinted by J. Johnson, London, 1806.

Rutt, John Towill (ed.). *The Theological and Miscellaneous Works of Joseph Priestley, LL. D., F.R.S., etc.* 25 volumes in 26. [London] Hackney: George Smallfield, 1817–32.

> Vol. 1 was issued in two parts, bound separately: (1) *Memoirs and Correspondence, 1733–1787* (1831); (2) *Life and Correspondence, 1787–1804* (1832). They were also published separate from the set the same years.

Biographical Materials

Aykroyd, W. R. *Three Philosophers (Lavoisier, Priestley and Cavendish)*. London: William Heinemann, 1935.

Brougham, Henry Peter. "Priestley," *Lives of Men of Letters and Science, Who Flourished in the Time of George III*. London: Charles Knight, 1845. Vol. 1, 402–28.

Caven, Robert Martin. *Joseph Priestley, 1733–1804*. London: Institute of Chemistry of Great Britain and Ireland, 1933.

Corry, John. *The Life of Joseph Priestley, LL. D., F.R.S.* Birmingham: Wilks, Grafton, & Co., 1804.

Fitzmaurice, Lord Edmond. *Life of William, Earl of Shelburne.* London: Macmillan and Co., 1876. Vols. II, III.

Fulton, John F. "Joseph Priestley," *Dictionary of American Biography,* XV, 223–26.

Gillam, John Graham. *The Crucible—The Story of Joseph Priestley, LL.D., F.R.S.* London: Robert Hale, 1954.

Gordon, Alexander, and Hartog, P. J. "Joseph Priestley," *Dictionary of National Biography,* XVI, 357–75.

Holt, Anne. *A Life of Joseph Priestley.* London: Oxford University Press, 1931.

Thorpe, T. E. *Joseph Priestley.* London: J. M. Dent & Co., 1906.

Walker, W. Cameron. "The Beginnings of the Scientific Career of Joseph Priestley," *Isis,* XXI (1934), 81–97.

EDITIONS OF A Course of Lectures

Priestley, Joseph. *A Course of Lectures on Oratory and Criticism.* London: J. Johnson, 1777.
     The edition here reproduced.

———. *A Course of Lectures on Oratory and Criticism.* Dublin: William Hallhead, 1781.

Rutt, John Towill (ed.). Vol. XXIII of *Works,* above, contains *The Rudiments of English Grammar; A Course of Lectures on the Theory of Language; Universal Grammar; A Course of Lectures on Oratory and Criticism* (1824).
     This volume was reissued with fresh title page and notes on the grammar by Dr. Kippis, London, 1826 and 1833.

NOTES

1 "Memoirs and Correspondence," *Works,* I, 1, 8.
2 *Ibid.,* p. 25.
3 Brougham, *Lives,* I, 408.
4 Walker, p. 86.
5 *Works,* I, 2, 306.
6 Corry, pp. 43–44.
7 *Works,* I, 1, 27.
8 *Ibid.,* p. 33.
9 *Ibid.,* pp. 62, 63n.
10 Birmingham, 1791; *Works,* XXII.
11 *A Letter to the Right Honourable W. Pitt . . . on the Subjects of Toleration and Church Establishments . . . Occasioned by His Speech Against the Repeal of the Test and Corporation Acts . . . the 28th of March, 1787* (London, 1787); *Works,* XIX, 114.
12 *Familiar Letters, Addressed to the Inhabitants of the Town of Birmingham* (Birmingham, 1790); *Works,* XIX.
13 *Letters to the Inhabitants of Northumberland and Its Neighbourhood, on Subjects Interesting to the Author and to Them* (Northumberland, Pa., 1799); *Works,* XXV.
14 *An Essay on the First Principles of Government; and on the Nature of Political, Civil, and Religious Liberty* (London, 1768); *Works,* XXII, 13. Jeremy Bentham acknowledged his debt to Priestley in later editions of his first book, *A Fragment on Government* (1776): "Priestley was the first (unless it was Beccaria) who taught my lips to pronounce this sacred truth—that the greatest happiness of the greatest number is the foundation of morals and legislation."
15 Fulton and Peters, p. 152.
16 Walker, pp. 92, 95. As an example of the confusion, see Holt (p. 65), who, although he had consulted papers of the Royal Society, says Priestley's *The History and Present State of Electricity, with Original Experiments* was "the immediate cause of his election." The *History* was not published until 1767, a year after the election.
17 *Works,* I, 1, 54n.
18 *Ibid.,* p. 53.
19 Priestley, *An Examination of Dr. Reid's Inquiry into the Human*

Mind on the Principles of Common Sense, Dr. Beattie's Essay on the Nature and Immutability of Truth, and Dr. Oswald's Appeal to Common Sense in Behalf of Religion, (London, 1774), p. xii; *Works,* III, 6.

20 Priestley, *Lectures on History and General Policy* (London, 1793), I, x; *Works,* XXIV, 6.

21 *Works,* I, 1, 294.

22 *Ibid.,* p. 298.

23 *Ibid.,* p. 345.

24 [William Enfield], "A Course of Lectures on Oratory and Criticism," *The Monthly Review,* LVII (August, 1777), 89–90.

25 *Ibid.,* pp. 98–99.

26 *Works,* I, 1, 307.

27 Samuel H. Monk, *The Sublime* (Ann Arbor: University of Michigan Press, 1960), p. 117.

28 Priestley, "Disquisitions Relating to Matter and Spirit," *Works,* III, 221.

29 Walter J. Hipple, Jr. (ed.), *An Essay on Taste,* by Alexander Gerard (Gainesville: Scholars' Facsimiles and Reprints, 1963), p. xv. Hipple refers to the attempts of eighteenth-century aestheticians such as Hume and Gerard to reduce the phenomena of beauty to their basic elements in ideas, sensations, and passions.

30 Priestley, *Hartley's Theory of the Human Mind* (London, 1775), p. xxiv; *Works,* III, 184.

31 Priestley, *Examination of Dr. Reid's Inquiry,* p. vii; *Works,* III, 4.

32 Douglas Ehninger (ed.), *Elements of Rhetoric* by Richard Whately (Carbondale: Southern Illinois University Press, 1963), p. xxvii.

33 Karl R. Wallace, *Francis Bacon on Communication & Rhetoric* (Chapel Hill: University of North Carolina Press, 1943), pp. 55, 223–24.

34 (London, 1733), I, 125–27.

35 Priestley, *Hartley's Theory,* pp. xxvi–xxvii; *Works,* III, 186.

36 Isaac Watts, *Logic: or, the Right Use of Reason* (London, 1745), p. 307. Watts observes that it is the custom of those who teach rhetoric to direct their students to the use of topics. He admits their use only in exceptional occasions, but advises: "Enlarge your general Acquaintance with things daily in order to attain a rich Furniture of Topics, or middle Terms, whereby those Propositions which occur may be either proved or disproved;

but especially meditate and enquire with great Diligence and Exactness into the Nature, Properties, Circumstances and Relations of the particular Subject about which you judge or argue. Consider its Causes, Effects, Consequences, Adjuncts, Opposites, Signs, etc. so far as is needful to your present Purpose" (p. 329).

37　John Ward, *A System of Oratory* (London, 1759), I, 47. Priestley appears to have drawn his remarks on topics from a number of Ward's lectures on the subject, including Lecture VI, "Of the State of a Controversy."

38　Regarding analysis and synthesis in Priestley, see also Wilbur Samuel Howell, "The Declaration of Independence and Eighteenth-Century Logic," *The William and Mary Quarterly,* 3rd Ser. XVIII (October, 1961), 468–69.

39　*Catalogue of the Library of the Late Dr. Joseph Priestley . . . for sale by Thomas Dobson* (Philadelphia, 1816). This list is from his library in America.

40　Ehninger (ed.), *Elements of Rhetoric,* p. xxvi. See also his "Selected Theories of *Inventio* in English Rhetoric, 1759–1828" (Ph.D. dissertation, The Ohio State University, 1949), chap. v.

41　Hipple, p. xvii.

42　Henry Home, Lord Kames, *Elements of Criticism* (5th ed.; Edinburgh, 1774), I, 88–105.

43　George Campbell, *The Philosophy of Rhetoric,* ed. Lloyd F. Bitzer (Carbondale: Southern Illinois University Press, 1963), pp. 38n, 149.

44　Ward, II, chaps. xxxii, xxxiii.

45　In a reference to Gerard (p. 130), Priestley shows his acquaintance with the *Essay on Taste.* On Priestley's debt to Kames and Gerard, see North's dissertation on Priestley, pp. 223–35.

46　John Mason, *An Essay on Elocution, or, Pronunciation* [1748] (3rd ed.; London, 1751), p. 36.

47　North, pp. 259, 261. He observes that "Mason was the first to write a book with the word 'elocution' in the title" (p. 155), and notes that Priestley "is the first and almost only major writer [on rhetoric] to use this term as a name for the canon of delivery" (p. 238).

LECTURES

ON

ORATORY

AND

CRITICISM.

A

COURSE OF LECTURES

ON

ORATORY

AND

CRITICISM.

By JOSEPH PRIESTLEY, LL.D. F.R.S.

Et rerum causas, et quid natura docebat. OVID.

===

LONDON:

Printed for J. JOHNSON, No. 72, St. Paul's Church-yard.

M DCC LXXVII.

ERRATA.

Page						
Page 8,	l. 9,	*for* cause	*read* course.
23,	23,	*for* purfuing	*read* perufing.
30,	20,	*for* properties	*read* proprieties
40,	7,	*for* the notes	*read* notes
56,	11,	*for* procefs. As	*read* procefs; as
72,	5,	*for* attitude	*read* attitudes
107,	2,	*for* himfelf	*read* to himfelf.
136,	4,	*for* transferring	*read* by transferring.
192,	1,	*for* whoever	*read* who.
202,	6,	*for* terms	*read* the terms.
205,	18,	*for* excites;	*read* excites:
217,	1,	*for* parody	*read* a parody
239,	2,	*for* pelagi	*read* pelago
243,	8,	*for* where	*read* when
256,	4,	*for* myriæ	*read* myricæ
261,	9,	*for* from hence	*read* hence
262,	6,	*for* an original	*read* the original
268,	16,	*for* pleafures	*read* pleafure
273,	8,	*for* fhort ones	*read* long ones
	9,	*for* recurring	*read* or recurring
292,	20,	*for* trouble	*read* any trouble

TO

THE RIGHT HONOURABLE

LORD VISCOUNT

FITZMAURICE.

MY DEAR LORD,

AS your Lordſhip is now of a proper age to
underſtand many particulars in the following
Lectures, and will ſoon be capable of a regular ſtudy
and a thorough comprehenſion of the whole ſubject,
I was ambitious to dedicate the work to you; as
a mark of my attachment, and of my earneſt

wiſh

wiſh to contribute whatever may be in my power, towards your improvement in every thing that is uſeful or ornamental, and thereby to the diſtinguiſhed figure that, I flatter myſelf, your Lordſhip will one day make in this country.

To act an uſeful and honourable part in the community to which we belong, is an object of laudable ambition to every man, in proportion to the rank which he holds in it; and your Lordſhip cannot but be fully apprized, that the only foundations for a reſpectable figure in life, are *good principles* and *good diſpoſitions*, joined to a *cultivated underſtanding*. Eminence in theſe reſpects is what, in ſtricteſt right, may be expected of thoſe whom their fellow-citizens, naturally their equals, are, by the conſtitution of their country, made to look up to, as their ſuperiors. It is a *debt* due for that diſtinction. For it is univerſally true, that the *obligation* to do good is of the very ſame extent with the *power* and *opportunity* of doing it.

This, my young Lord, is an age in which every thing begins to be eſtimated by its real *uſe* and *value*.
The

THE DEDICATION.

The fame maxims of good fenfe which regulate all other things, will finally new-arrange whatever belongs to the affairs of fociety and government; and thofe diftinctions which mere *force,* mere *fuperftition,* or mere *accident* will be found to have eftablifhed, and to which *public utility* does not give its fanction, will gradually fink into *public difefteem :* and this, long continued, will make part of that *fpirit of men,* of *nations,* and of *times,* which muft finally bear down every thing that oppofes it. Confequently the only method of *perpetuating* any order of men whatever, is to make it truly *refpectable* and *ufeful :* This was the original foundation of honour, and it cannot finally ftand upon any other.

I muft add, that the world will expect the more from your Lordfhip, on account of your relation to a nobleman who is eminently diftinguifhed for his *private,* as well as his *public virtues,* and for nothing more than his attention to the *education of his children,* and his liberality of fentiment in the conduct of it.

That

THE DEDICATION.

That your Lordſhip may, in riper years, fully re-
ward the care and attention that have been beſtowed
upon you, confirm the hopes which your friends
have formed from your preſent improvements and
diſpoſitions, and eminently contribute to ſupport the
dignity of the rank to which you were born, by
adding to the real *luſtre* and *value* of it, is the ſincere
prayer of,

My Lord,

Your Lordship's

Moſt devoted

Humble Servant,

Nov. 20, 1776.   J. PRIESTLEY.

THE

THE

PREFACE.

THIS Courfe of Lectures was compofed when I was Tutor in the *Languages* and *Belles Lettres* in the Academy at Warrington, and was firft delivered in the year 1762. The *plan* is rather more comprehenfive than any thing that I have feen upon the fubject, the *arrangement* of the materials, as a fyftem, is new, and the *theory*, in feveral refpects, more fo.

For this reafon I have been frequently urged to make the Lectures public; and having poftponed it fo long, I have been induced to do it at this time, partly with a view to the illuftration of the doctrine of the *affociation of ideas*, to which there is a conftant reference through the whole work (in order to explain facts relating to the influence of Oratory, and the ftriking effect of Excellencies in Compofition, upon the genuine principles of human nature) in confequence of having of late endeavoured to draw

b   fome some degree of attention to those principles, as advanced by Dr. Hartley. Another reason for publishing these Lectures at this time is, for the sake of the young Nobleman to whom they are dedicated, to whose improvement my best services are, on many accounts, due.

Considering the nature of the work, it will not be expected, by the candid and judicious, that every thing in it should be original. It is, on the contrary, the business of a *Lecturer*, to bring into an easy and comprehensive view whatever has been observed by others : and in this respect I hope it will be thought that I have not acquitted myself ill ; few works of criticism, of any value, having escaped my attention, at the time that I was engaged in those studies. But I own, that of the later publications of this kind I can give less account than might have been wished ; having been generally engaged in pursuits of a different nature. But, notwithstanding there may be some things in common between this work and other publications of the kind, it is probable that many of the observations will be peculiar to myself, because my general theory of human nature is very much so. I have shewn myself willing to contribute what I may be be able to the illuftration of my fubject. If my endeavours have been attended with fuccefs, the friends of literature will not be difpleafed ; and if, in their opinion, I have contributed nothing to the common ftock of ufeful obfervations, this work, they will conclude, will not ftand long in the way of better.

The moft confiderable work on the fubject of criticifm, that was extant at the time of my compofing thefe Lectures, was that of *Lord Kaims*, to whom I am indebted for a very great number of my examples, efpecially thofe from the dramatic writers, and fometimes for the obfervations too ; but with refpect to this fubject, on which fo many able men have written, it is hardly poffible to fay to whom we are *ultimately* obliged for any very valuable remark.

Several of the examples in the firft part of this work are borrowed from Dr. *Ward's Oratory*, and fome from other works of the fame nature ; but many of the inftances are of my own collecting. I would have been more particular in making my acknowledgments, if I had been better able to recollect them, and had thought it at all neceffary. Let my reader confider this work as a fuccinct and fyftematical view of the obfervations of others, interfperfed with original

ginal

ginal ones of my own; and he will not, I hope, think that the perufal of it has been time ill-beſtowed.

A conſiderable part of what I had compoſed for the uſe of my pupils in the *firſt part* of this work, which is, in its own nature, more trite than the reſt, I have here omitted; retaining only as much as was neceſſary to preſerve the appearance of an uniform *ſyſtem* in the whole, and thoſe parts which were the moſt original.

The laſt part of the work, relating to *elocution*, I never compoſed, though I ſhould have done it, if I had continued longer in that employment. The reaſon of this omiſſion was, that it was my cuſtom (as I believe it is ſtill that of my ſucceſſors in that department of the academy, and it is certainly a moſt uſeful one) to have lectures appropriated ſolely to the buſineſs of elocution, which all the ſtudents who were deſigned for public ſpeakers conſtantly attended, at leaſt once a week. At theſe lectures great pains were taken to form the pupils to a habit of juſt and graceful delivery; and the inſtructions were given as occaſion required; ſo that the reduceing of them to writing was by no means neceſſary.

It

It may be thought by some, that these lectures are much too *short*, and too concisely written, for the purpose of public instruction : but they should be apprized, that it was my custom to write down only the *outlines* of what I delivered in the class ; that, for the benefit of my pupils, I used to attend them provided with more copious *illustrations*, and a greater variety of *examples* ; and, besides, always spent a considerable part of the time appropriated to every lecture in examining them on the subject of the preceding lecture, hearing their remarks or objections, and explaining more distinctly what they appeared not to have clearly understood.

Upon this plan (which I found by experience to be a very useful one, and which I mention so particularly here, with a view to recommend it to other tutors) it was not necessary for me to write out more than a short, though connected *text*, from which to discourse *extempore* ; a method which engages the attention unspeakably more than formally reading every thing from notes. It was my custom also to leave a fair copy of what I wrote in the lecture-room, that the pupils might have recourse to it, and study it at their leisure, so as to be

better

better prepared for examination at the enfuing lecture. What I now publifh is the *text* above mentioned, with fome improvements which have fince occurred to me.

The fame method I took with refpect to every other fubject on which I gave lectures; with this difference, that thofe on the *Theory of Languages* and *Univerfal Grammar* were *printed* for the ufe of the pupils. This work I have promifed, in the preface to my *Englifh Grammar*, to revife, and publifh at my leifure; and if thefe fhould have the good fortune to give fatisfaction, I may, in due time, proceed to publifh another Courfe of Lectures, viz. on the *Study of Hiftory* and *General Policy*; which, indeed, I have promifed to publifh, in the preface to my *Effay on the firft Principles of Government*. The public may be affured, that, as I have not hitherto, I fhall not, in future, obtrude upon them any work, that fhall not appear to myfelf, however miftaken I may be in my judgment, both confiderably *original* and *ufeful*.

THE

THE CONTENTS.

PART I.

LECT.

THE CONTENTS.

LECTURE

LECTURE I.

The INTRODUCTION, *and the* DISTRIBUTION *of the Subject.*

THE ufe of fpeech is common to all mankind. For we find none of the human race but who are capable of expreffing their ideas, fentiments, and intentions to others, in a more or lefs adequate manner, by words: and this capacity was neceffary to that mutual *intercourfe*, and free communication, without which beings of our focial nature could not be happy.

It is the province of *art* to improve upon *nature*, by adding to her powers and advantages: and, for the exercife of our intellectual and active powers, all the gifts of nature are little more than the bare unwrought materials of thofe accomplifhments, from which refult the dignity and refined happinefs of focial life.

Thus ORATORY is the natural faculty of fpeech improved by art; whereby the ufe of it is perfected, facilitated, and extended; and confequently its *value* and *influence* greatly increafed. And the excellence of this art is the more generally acknowledged, and its effects the more admired, becaufe, language being common to us all, all men can the more eafily conceive both

B the

the importance, and the difficulty of the improvements of which
it is capable.

Very few perfons ever find themfelves at a lofs to deliver a
fingle fentence or two at a time; becaufe they are able to fee at
one view the whole of what they intend to fay. But it is not
common to find a perfon able to acquit himfelf with propriety in
a fpeech of confiderable length, even though he prepare himfelf
by digefting beforehand all that he intends to fay; becaufe the
order and *connexion of fentiment*, and variety of *diction*, neceffary
in a continued fpeech, are not eafily carried in memory: and it
requires a very extraordinary invention and recollection to fpeak
long, in a proper and graceful manner, quite *extempore.*. Nor can
a perfon, without the affiftance of art and inftruction, even com-
pofe a fet difcourfe upon any fubject; becaufe it requires greater
exactnefs in the ufe of words, more accuracy of method, and
variety of tranfition than perfons uninftructed and unufed to *compofition* can be mafters of. For this reafon we fee many perfons
who make a good figure in converfation, by no means able to
make a fpeech, or a compofition of any confiderable length.
It is in this refpect, where the powers of nature fail us, in expreffing our fentiments to advantage, that we have recourfe to
the *art of Oratory.*

It may not be amifs, at the entrance upon thefe Lectures upon
Oratory and Criticifm, to premife one caution; which is, that
we muft not expect too much from the *art*; fince this can do
little for us in comparifon of what muft be the fruit of our own
previous application to *fcience.* The art of oratory can only
confift of rules for the proper ufe of thofe materials which muft
be acquired from various ftudy and obfervation, of which, therefore,

fore, unlefs a perfon be poffeffed, no art of oratory can make
him an orator.

In order to fpeak, or write well upon any fubject, it is neceffary that that fubject be thoroughly underftood, that every argument which is to be ufed be previoufly collected, and the value
of it afcertained. How abfurd, for inftance, would it be to
imagine that a perfon, who had never ftudied law, government,
and hiftory, fhould be enabled, by the art of oratory, to make a
political harangue, or write a differtation upon the conftitution
of a ftate? With what fuccefs would an orator, who had not ftudied the Law, undertake the defence of a client? or a perfon
wholly unacquainted with morals or theology, attempt to fpeak
from the pulpit? Whatever fubject, therefore, any perfon intends
to write or fpeak upon, he muft, by applying to the proper
fources, acquire a perfect knowledge of it, before he can expect
any affiftance from the art of oratory, as fuch.

Moreover, let a perfon be ever fo perfect a mafter of his fubject, he could not be taught to fpeak or write about it with propriety and good effect, without being previoufly inftructed in the
principles of GRAMMAR, i. e. without a knowledge of the in-
flection of words, and of the ftructure of fentences, in the language he makes ufe of.

It is neceffary, likewife, as far as *reafoning* is concerned, that
a perfon be, in fome fenfe, a *logician* before he be an orator;
fince it is by the rules of LOGIC that we judge of every thing
relating to *arguments*, their perfpicuity or confufion, their fallacy or their force. More efpecially is it of confequence to every
orator whofe bufinefs is with *men*, to be well acquainted with
human nature; that knowing the paffions, prejudices, interefts,

and views of thofe he hath to do with, he may know how to addrefs them accordingly.

But notwithftanding this be treated of in many books written
on the fubjeÅ of oratory, and particularly by Ariftotle; there is
no more reafon why we fhould encumber a fyftem of oratory
with it, than that we croud into it the elements of any other
fcience, or branch of knowledge, that the orator may have occafion for. Befides, thofe plain principles of human aÅions with
which the orator hath to do, are obvious to common refleÅiòn, and
muft have occurred to every perfon before he hath lived to the
age in which he has any occafion for the art of oratory.
For this part of the furniture of an orator, therefore, let the
ftudent have recourfe to *Ethical treatifes*, as far as they unfold the
principles of human nature; let him ftudy authentic hiftories of
human charaÅers and conduÅ; and let him principally attend to
the emotions of his own heart. However, that knowledge of
human nature, which is neceffary to underftand the *rationale* of
the ornaments of ftyle will not be excluded a place in thefe Lectures, but will be explained pretty much at large in the third
part of the courfe.

Suppofing a man, therefore, to be perfeÅly acquainted with
the fubjeÅ on which he propofes to fpeak or write, that he is not
deficient in the knowledge of grammatical propriety, and that
by logic, natural or artificial, he can judge of the force or fallacy
of any argument that occurs, or is propofed to him; it is afked
what affiftance he may expeÅ from the art of oratory, in carry-
ing his defign into execution in the moft advantageous manner?
In this cafe, all that remains to be done is,

First,

First, to affist him in the habit of *recollection*, or to direct him which way to turn his thoughts, in order to find the arguments and illustrations with which his mind is already furnished; and likewise, when a general topic, or head of difcourfe, is found, in what manner to confirm or illuftrate it, in order to have materials for the bulk or body of the difcourfe. In this manner oratory may affift the *invention*; but it is not in finding things with which the mind was wholly unacquainted, but in readily recollecting, and judicioufly felecting, what is proper for his purpofe, out of the materials with which the mind was previoufly furnifhed.

Secondly, the art of oratory teaches in what *order* to difpofe of thofe topics. It fhews what difpofition of the materials of a difcourfe will give them the greateft force, and contribute the moft to produce the effect intended by it.

Thirdly, to contribute ftill farther to the effect of a difcourfe, the art of oratory teaches what *ftyle*, or manner of expreffion, will beft become, adorn, and recommend it.

Fourthly, if the difcourfe is to be pronounced, the art of oratory teaches what tone of voice, or what geftures of the body, will beft become, and add grace to the delivery of it.

The four great objects, therefore, that fall within the province of the orator are RECOLLECTION, METHOD, STYLE, and ELOCUTION. Of thefe I fhall treat in the order in which they are here mentioned.

LECTURE

LECTURE II.

Of the Nature and Use of Topics.

ALL the kinds of compofition may be reduced to two, viz.
NARRATION and ARGUMENTATION. For either we
propofe fimply to relate *facts*, with a view to communicate information, as in *Hiftory*, natural or civil, *Travels*, &c. or we lay
down fome *propofition*, and endeavour to prove or explain it.

With refpect to *Narration* of any kind, it is fuperfluous to fay
much about it under the firft head of *Recollection*, or *Invention*,
except fo far as facts are wanted for the purpofe of *argumentative
difcourfes*. The chief affiftance that thofe who compofe only in
the narrative ftyle can expect from the art of oratory, is in
digefting and *adorning* their compofitions; and thefe articles will
be confidered in the fecond and third parts of thefe lectures.

The whole bufinefs, therefore, of artificial recollection muft,
in a manner, be confined to the ufe of thofe who compofe *argumentative difcourfes*, whofe minds are previoufly furnifhed with
every argument and obfervation proper to be introduced into
them; but who may not be able to find them fo readily as they
could wifh. To fuch perfons the following directions and obfervations may not be unufeful.

                                                    RECOL-

RECOLLECTION comprehends whatever is proper to be said upon any fubject; that is, all the thoughts or fentiments that make up the body of a difcourfe. Thefe, which may be called the nerves and finews of a compofition, may all be confidered as *arguments* in proof of what is advanced. Now every argument that can with propriety be brought as a proof of a propofition, fhould bear fome kind of *relation* to both the terms of it. For, according to logicians, every propofition afferts the agreement or difagreement of two ideas, or things, which are called the *fubject* and *predicate*, or *attribute* of the propofition. If the agreement or difagreement of thefe do not appear at firft view, we make ufe of another idea, called a *middle term*, which, being feverally applied to them both, will, by informing us of the relation they both bear to it, enable us to judge of the relation they both bear to one another. But unlefs this third idea bear fome relation to both the others, it will be impoffible to compare them together by the help of it.

I fhall illuftrate thefe obfervations by the example of the following propofition: *Every good man is a wife man.* It may not be apparent, at firft view, that the *fubject* and *attribute* of this propofition do really coincide, as is afferted in it. In order to fhow that, notwithftanding this, they really do agree, I introduce another idea, viz. *the making ufe of the means of happinefs*; and by confidering that a good man is one who lives and acts in fuch a manner as will fecure his *greateft happinefs*, which is alfo the object of the trueft wifdom; I fee that the defcription of a *good man* intirely agrees with that of a *wife man*, and that they are *the fame perfon*, which the propofition afferts. But I could not have made ufe of this *intermediate idea*, in order to fhew the relation of the terms to one another, unlefs it had borne fome re-

I

lation to them both, and had thereby been capable of being compared with them.

In this cafe, the relation that *means of happinefs* bears to *goodnefs* is that of *effect*; goodnefs being the fource of thofe actions which tend to produce true happinefs; as the relation that the idea of the means of happinefs bears to *wifdom* is that of *means*, or *inftrument*, which wifdom employs to effect her purpofe. And it is not improbable but that if a perfon had confidered the natural *effects* of virtue and goodnefs, and what caufe of actions a wife man would be led to adopt, he would have hit upon this idea, which furnifhes fo clear an argument in proof of the propofition in queftion. Or again, the fame idea might have occurred to a perfon who had carefully confidered the *definitions* of the terms of his propofitions; fince he would have found that property of goodnefs connected with thofe ideas which form the characteriftic of wifdom. So that either the relation of *caufe and effect*, that of *means and end*, or the *definition of terms* might have led the mind of the compofer to the idea he wanted. Thefe are called COMMON PLACES, TOPICS, or GENERAL HEADS, under which arguments of all kinds may be claffed, and an attention to them may fuggeft the arguments that fall under them.

It belongs to the art of oratory to point out thefe topics, common places, or general heads to which all arguments may be reduced; that, whenever we undertake to prove any thing, by running over the titles of them in our minds, our thoughts may be directed to what fuits our purpofe. To make the ufe of thefe topics ftill more intelligible and eafy, I fhall illuftrate each of them by an example or two.

All propofitions, or things to be proved, metaphyfically confidered, may be reduced to the fame form; as being a declaration
of the coincidence of the fubject and attribute of them. Thus
if I fay, that *man is mortal*, I mean that my idea of *man* coincides with my idea of a *mortal being*, or a being *fubject to death*;
or if I fay, *Alexander conquered Darius*, I mean that my
idea of Alexander, and of the perfon who conquered Darius,
are the fame. We fhall, however, find it moft convenient,
in the bufinefs of popular oratory, to quit this general idea, and
confider all propofitions, or fubjects of difcourfe, as fubdivided
into two kinds, viz. *univerfal*, and *particular* propofitions.

Univerfal propofitions are thofe which have no relation to particular perfons, times, or places, but are at all times, in all places, and with regard to all perfons, true or falfe; as thefe, *man
is mortal*; *virtue makes the happinefs of man*; *the three angles of
every right-lined triangle are equal to two rectangles.* This head
includes all *metaphyfical* and *mathematical* fubjects.

Particular propofitions are thofe which have relation to, and are
limited by, particular perfons, times, or places; as *Alexander
conquered Darius*; *France is larger than England*; *Carthage was
founded before Rome*, &c. This head comprehends all hiftorical
debates, geographical, and chronological knowledge, confulta-
tions about the intereft of particular ftates at particular times,
judicial inquiries into the actions of particular perfons, and all
perfonal panegyric, or invective.

I divide all fubjects of difcourfe into thefe two kinds, becaufe
the topics of argument fuited to each are very confiderably diftinct; though things which relate to particular perfons, times,
or places, may often, with propriety, be introduced into a difcourfe
upon a propofition that is univerfally true, or univerfally falfe,

　　　　　　　　　　　　　　　　　　　　　　　　without

without refpect to any particular perfon, time, or place; and, fince every thing that is *particular* is comprehended in that which is *univerfal*, arguments relating to particular perfons, places, and times, may be fetched from thofe topics, which are peculiarly adapted to univerfal propofitions.

Convenient topics for univerfal propofitions are the following: *Definition, Adjunts, Antecedents, Confequents, Means, Analogy, Contrariety, Example* and *Authority.*

Before I explain thefe topics, I would obferve, that it is not very material, with refpect to the real ufe of them, whether the diftribution be metaphyfically exact; particularly, whether fome of them, ftrictly fpeaking, be not fuperfluous, as being comprifed under others; as, for example, whether it might not have been fufficient to have comprifed *example* under the head of *confequents.* It is fufficient if, by attending to them, the mind be led to proper arguments. The table may be too fcanty, but can hardly be too full. Notwithftanding this, a great deal of the redundancy of other tables is retrenched in this.

LECTURE

L E C T U R E III.

Of UNIVERSAL TOPICS.

I. *Of* DEFINITION.

DEFINITION fuggefts arguments in all cafes in which a controverfy refts upon afcertaining the precife *meaning of words*. Thus in order to prove a perfon, whofe actions are well known, to be guilty of any particular crime; as *facrilege*, *burglary*, &c. we merely define what thofe particular crimes are. If the definition be allowed, the proof is complete; as it fhews that the action in queftion and the crime are the fame.

In a great number of metaphyfical, moral, and religious controverfies, the difputants appeal to the definition of *terms*; and could thefe be agreed upon, the controverfies would be at an end. The unhappinefs is, that, in things of an abftrufe nature, few perfons affix precifely the fame ideas to the fame terms: from whence it often happens that they fancy they differ, when, in reality, they are agreed, and all the difpute is, at the bottom, about *words*, and not *things*.

The greateft attention is neceffary to be paid to this topic by thofe who write treatifes upon any intire art or fcience; as *Grammar*, *Logic*, *Oratory*, &c. fince definition comprehends the

diftri-

diftribution of things into their parts, which muft be difcuffed in their order. Thus a perfon who writes a grammar muft confider that grammar confifts of *Orthography, Etymology, Syntax,* and *Profody*; and difcufs what relates to each of them in their order.

II. *Of* ADJUNCTS, *or the* properties *of either of the terms of a propofition.*

Divines and moralifts argue from this topic when, demonftrating that *man ought to obey* GOD, they urge that man is an *intelligent, dependent,* and *obliged* creature; that GOD is his *maker, governor,* and *judge*; and that his *laws are reafonable*, founded on wifdom and goodnefs: becaufe each of thefe adjuncts, or properties of the terms of the propofition, fuggefts an argument for the truth of it.

Moralifts likewife argue from this fame topic, that *the rich ought to relieve the poor*; becaufe they are both *fellow-creatures,* liable to a reverfe of fortune, and that the one hath to fpare what the other is in want of.

In a very ftrict fenfe, every argument might be referred to the topic of *Adjuncts*; becaufe every argument we can ufe muft be fuggefted by fome property, or adjunct, of one or other of the terms of the propofition. But the examples above given fhow that the term need not be taken in fo ftrict a fenfe, and that an attention to this topic in a loofer fenfe, may afford a diftinct and ufeful head of arguments; efpecially to divines and moralifts.

III. *Of*

III. *Of* Antecedents.

It is of fervice fometimes to look back into what, in the order of nature, preceded either the fubject or attribute of the propofition we are demonftrating.

Thus divines prove that *Chriftianity is probable*, becaufe the circumftances of mankind previous to the publication of it, were fuch as made a revelation highly expedient and defirable.

Upon this principle Hiftorians argue that the hiftory of Greece, prior to the times of Cyrus the Great, is not much to be depended upon, becaufe writing and records of any kind were not common in Greece before that time.

In political and civil affairs, a people are more eafily perfuaded to commit an important truft to a perfon, when his advocate can fhow that, in former fituations, he behaved with ability and integrity.   And political writers argue againft any fcheme by fhowing that it was engaged in from bad principles, that the advocates for it had been bribed, and that their particular previous connexions and fituations obliged them to enter into it : as it is a great argument in favour of any fcheme, that the views with which it was undertaken were upright and honourable.

To this topic is alfo to be referred whatever is faid in praife of a perfon, on the fubject of his birth, family, &c.

This topic alfo includes all corollaries or inferences from truths before demonftrated : for a propofition muft be admitted as true, if it can be fhown to be a neceffary confequence of another acknowledged truth.

IV. *Of*

IV. *Of* CONSEQUENTS.

Moralifts argue from this topic when, demonftrating the *excellence of virtue*, they difplay the many happy confequences of it on a man's *frame*, *connections* and *expectations*; or when, afferting the evil of vice and wickednefs, they paint the frightful confequences of it, both in this, and a future world.

Divines make ufe of this topic when they prove the *being and perfections of God from the frame of nature*, and the admirable proportion and ufes of its feveral parts; when they prove that *chriftianity is true*, from the *miracles* that were wrought to prove it, and from the numbers that were actually thereby converted to the faith of Chrift; and who adhered to it under very confiderable temporal difadvantages.

In like manner, mathematicians refute a propofition, by fhowing that the confequences of it are abfurd.

On this topic, likewife, we declaim againft a *law*, or fcheme of policy, by fhowing the confequences of it to be prejudicial to the ftate; or plead for it, if the confequences of it be beneficial.

V. *Of* MEANS.

As arguments may be fuggefted by confidering what is *antecedent* or *confequent* to things, or the *caufes* and *effects* of them, fo it is poffible that the topic of the *means* whereby caufes produce their effects, may be of fome ufe to the fame purpofe.

Thus a divine, demonftrating the regard that the Supreme Being hath for virtue, might expatiate upon the means he hath

ufed

ufed to bring men back to the practice of it after they had apoftatifed from it, in his various interpofitions in the ftate of the world in favour of virtue and religion, in his commiffion to the prophets to be preachers of righteoufnefs, and in fending Chrift to redeem mankind by his precepts, example, and obedience unto death.

In confidering the nature and ufefulnefs of any fcheme of policy, it is of ufe to examine the means that muft be ufed to bring it about; and from the nature of the means, arguments may be fetched for or againft the fcheme propofed.

It is an argument againft *popery*, that it is obliged to have recourfe to *perfecution*, and the horrid inquifition, as the means of bringing men back to the profeffion of that faith, and of keeping them in it.

VI. *Of* ANALOGY.

This head comprifes every thing that is *fimilar* to what is advanced in a propofition.

Writers in defence of chriftianity make excellent ufe of this topic when, anfwering objections againft any thing that appears difficult or myfterious in revealed religion, they fhow that the fame difficulty occurs on the fubject of natural religion. For example, when it is objected that, in the fcriptures, we meet with frequent inftances of innocent perfons fuffering with the guilty, and fometimes on the account of the guilty, they reply, that the like frequently happens in the courfe of *common providence*; as when children fuffer through the extravagance of their parents, who, by more œconomy, might have made a better provifion for them; and when tempefts and earthquakes overwhelm, in un-
distinguifhed

diftinguifhed deftruction, perfons of all conditions and characters, &c.

In all branches of fcience it is of the greateft importance to
fhow the *analogy*, or mutual correfpondence, of the feveral propofitions ; and it is always deemed an argument in favour of a
new difcovery, if it be analogous to others already made, and if
that analogy be wanting, we require much ftronger evidence of
other kinds.

Lawyers argue from this topic when they urge, in favour of
their client, *precedents* of the determination of other caufes.
Since the uniformity of the proceedings in law, and the *famenefs
of right* in the fame circumftances, require that every perfon be
intitled to the fame juftice that another had done him, in a cafe
nearly like, or analogous to his own. *Comparifons* alfo belong to
this head.

VII. *Of* CONTRARIES.

It is, upon many fubjects, no lefs ufeful to confider what
things are *contrary*, or *oppofite* to the terms of the propofition,
than what are connected with them. As when moralifts, in order to demonftrate the *advantages of a virtuous life*, defcribe the
fatal effects of vicious courfes upon the minds, the bodies, the
reputation and fortunes of men ; or, on the contrary, in order to
fet the hatefulnefs of vice in a ftronger light, they contraft it
with a view of the amiablenefs of virtue. In all fuch cafes as
thefe this argument concludes in a very ftrong manner : for virtue and vice, being directly oppofite to one another, it is very
obvious to reflect, that all their effects and influences muft be the
very reverfe of one another.

VIII. *Of*

VIII. *Of* EXAMPLE.

It greatly illuftrates and confirms even moral maxims to fhow them exemplified in real hiftory, in the characters and lives of men. Thus the fatal effects of *ambition* will be made much more fenfible, if, after examining the nature and tendency of that paffion in general, the writer fubjoin the example of *Alexander*, *Julius Cæfar*, *Charles of Sweden*, &c.; and the value of *wife and good princes* will be greatly enhanced by a view of the amiable characters, and ufeful lives of *Titus*, *Trajan*, *Antoninus*, &c.; and it is of particular ufe to divines, to fupport all their maxims by examples from the fcriptures.

It is likewife a happy confirmation of a principle in mechanics, mathematics, and philofophy, if it can be brought to an *experiment*, be fubjected to the *fenfes*, and *reduced to practice*.

IX. *Of* AUTHORITY.

It is a great confirmation of our belief of even univerfal propofitions, which have no connexion with particular perfons, places, or times, to have a *teftimony* in favour of them from perfons whofe opinions are generally allowed to be juft.

A confiderable part of that ftrong affent which we give to truths of an abftract nature, as to mathematical theorems, and philofophical difcoveries, which may be even our own inveftigating, and much more if they be not, is derived from the authority of others, who concur with us in profeffing an affent to them ; which may help us to account for a feeming pa-

D   radox,

radox, viz. why the difciples of fome Greek mafters of philofophy ufually, in a courfe of time, grew more zealoufly attached
to the tenets of their refpective fchools, than the founders themfelves originally were.

Cicero argues from this topic, when, in proof of a future
ftate, he alledges, not only the natural arguments for it; but,
what he feems to lay the chief ftrefs upon, the concurrent teftimony of all the wife ancients.

Lawyers argue from this, when, in favour of a determination,
not fixed by cuftom and precedent, they alledge the opinions of
perfons learned in the law, given without any view to the cafe in
hand.

Argumenta ad hominem, or thofe in which we appeal to a man's
known principles and profeffion, belong to this head. If the authority of others have any weight with a man, much more may
it be prefumed that his own opinion, that is, his own authority,
will weigh with him.

LECTURE

LECTURE IV.

Of Particular TOPICS; *and Objections to the Use of* TOPICS *answered.*

PARTICULAR topics are those which furnish arguments
for *particular propositions*; or those which relate to particular
persons, *times*, and *places*. Of these I shall do little more than
give distinct tables. The tables will, likewise, be very *general*;
so that each article may be subdivided again and again, without
end. But what is here done is abundantly sufficient for a treatise on the art in general, and it will be very easy for any person
to carry the division as far as he pleases for his own use.

Topics of arguments for limited propositions, viz. such as relate to particular FACTS. With respect to these we may
consider

    The Person,
    The Time,
    The Place,
    The Motive,
    The Manner,
    The Instrument,
    The Evidence,
    The Law concerning it,
        &c. &c. &c.   I shall

I ſhall give an example of the ſubdiviſion of one or two of
theſe heads.   With reſpect to *perſon* we may conſider

    The Sex,
    The Age,
    The perſonal Qualifications,
    The Fortune, as rich or poor,
    The Education,
    The Capacity or Ability ; as Senſe, Learning, &c.
    The Profeſſion, or Employment in Life,
    The Nation, Tribe, Family, &c.
    The Offices of public Life,
    The Relations of private Life,
    The Connexion, Company, Party, &c.
    The general Character, &c.

Laws may be conſidered as to

    Their Preciſion or Ambiguity,
    Their Intention,
    Their cuſtomary Forms, &c. &c.

It is obvious that it may be convenient to have recourſe to theſe
topics in any kind of diſcourſe or compoſition in which any particular fact or perſon is introduced ; as, whether a fact be *proved*,
or *diſproved* ; whether a perſon be *accuſed*, or *defended* ; whether
a writer make a *panegyric*, or an *invective* ; or ſimply compoſe
a *hiſtory*.
    To give an idea of the uſe of a few of theſe topics, it may be
obſerved, with regard to *ſex*, that a *woman* is not ſo likely to be
                                                                guilty

guilty of *robbery* as a *man*; but perhaps more likely to be concerned in *poison*.   With respect to *age*, that an *old man* would most
naturally have recourse to *fraud*, a *young man* to *violence*: with
respect to *nation*, that *drunkenness* would not so easily be believed
of a *Spaniard*, as of a *German*; and that an *Italian* would more
easily be actuated by outrageous *jealousy* than a *Frenchman*.
With respect to *fortune or condition* in life, that it is natural to
believe that a *rich man* is the most likely to be the aggressor in a
quarrel with a *poor man*; and lastly, with respect to *education*,
that a person educated at *St. Omer's* would be much more justly
suspected of being disaffected to the English government, than a
person educated at *Oxford* or *Cambridge*.

But I would refer the person who is desirous of seeing a spe-
cimen of the most excellent declamation upon a great variety of
these topics, to *Cicero's accusation of Varres*, and *defence of Milo*;
also to his invectives against Cataline and Antony, and to *Pliny's
panegyric upon the emperor Trajan*.

As materials for discourse may occur to us from considering
the general heads to which they may be referred, so it is possible, likewise, that we may take hints of arguments from the
manner in which they are generally introduced, or the *form* into
which they are thrown.   One form of argument, for instance, is
from *greater to less*, or from *less to greater*.   Thus a person will be
more easily believed to have committed a *less* infamous action,
who is known to have committed a *more* infamous one; as, on
the other hand, if a person have never been known to be guilty
of a small transgression, it will not easily be believed that he hath,
all at once, been guilty of a great and flagrant one.

Matter

Matter for difcourfe may alfo occur to a perfon who confiders what may be faid by way of *objection* to what he hath advanced, and what *conceffions* he may make to his opponent. His invention may alfo be affifted by confidering whether he can, with propriety, introduce any thing in the form of *irony*, of a *queftion*, of an *exclamation*, and of every other poffible form of addrefs. Moreover, what will be advanced in thefe lectures upon the fubject of *method*, will tend greatly to help the invention.

I am aware that this whole bufinefs of topics is objected to by fome as altogether ufelefs, and what no perfons, who are capable of compofing at all, ever ftand in need of, or have recourfe to. To this I reply, that, in fact, no perfon ever did, or ever can compofe at all without having recourfe to fomething of a fimilar nature. What is *recollection* but the introduction of one idea into the mind by means of another with which it was previoufly affociated? Are not ideas affociated by means of their connection with, and relation to one another? And is it not very poffible that *particular ideas* may be recollected by means of *general ideas*, which include them?

It is impoffible to endeavour to *recollect* (or, as we generally fay, *invent*) materials for a difcourfe, without running over in our minds fuch general heads of difcourfe as we have found by experience to affift us in that operation. It is even impoffible to conceive in what other manner a *voluntary effort* to invent, or recollect, can be directed. A perfon may not have recourfe to any particular lift, or enumeration, of topics; or he may never have heard of the artificial diftribution of them by rhetoricians; but if he compofe at all, though he may be ignorant of the *name*, he muft be poffeffed of the *thing*. And if a perfon have any *regular method* in his compofitions, he muft, moreover, have ar-

ranged

ranged thofe topics in his mind in fome kind of order ; the feveral
particulars of which, being attended to fucceffively, furnifhes him
with *a plan for compofition.* Now is it not better to fit down to
compofition provided with a tolerably complete lift of thofe topics,
digefted with care and precifion, than make ufe of fuch an one
as we cafually and without any defign form to ourfelves from
general reading only, or a little practice in compofition, which
cannot but be very imperfect, and inadequate to the purpofe to
which it is applied ?

After previoufly running over fuch a table, a perfon would be
much better able to form an idea of the *extent* of his fubject,
and might conduct his compofition accordingly ; or perufing it
after reading the compofition of another, he might with much
greater certainty know whether any thing of importance had
been left unfaid upon the fubject ; or whether, if the difcourfe
were neceffarily limited to a few arguments, the writer had fe-
lected the beft.

I cannot help being of opinion that thofe perfons, in particular, whofe profeffion obliges them frequently to compofe *moral
effays* and *fermons,* in which the thoughts are not expected to be
original (in which, therefore, their chief bufinefs is merely to
recollect, and *digeft* the moft valuable materials upon each fubject)
would fpend a few minutes to good purpofe in purfuing a well-
digefted table of topics, before they fat down to write. By this
means they could feldom be at a lofs for matter ; they would
more eafily felect what was moft important ; and with lefs trouble arrange it in the moft advantageous manner. For want, or
through neglect of this, as well as for other reafons, we often
hear noble and copious fubjects treated in a jejune and trifling
manner, fome parts exceffively overdone, others of equal importance

portance wholly omitted, and the whole put together in a moſt perplexed order; which exhibits the appearance rather of random indigeſted thoughts, than of a compoſition which was the reſult of a previous ſtudy of the ſubjeſt, and an acquaintance with the whole extent of it. And this previous acquaintance with the whole extent of a ſubjeſt can be acquired no other way ſo eaſily as by the peruſal of a judicious ſet of rhetorical topics.

If we pay any regard to the practice of the famous orators of antiquity, we cannot but be diſpoſed to think favourably of topics; for it is certain that they made great uſe of topics, as appears in the writings of Cicero and Quintilian. Too much may be expeſted from any thing, and an improper uſe may be made of any thing; but this is no argument againſt the judicious and proper uſe of it.

It were abſurd for any perſon ſlaviſhly to oblige himſelf to borrow ſomething from every topic of diſcourſe; much more to ſet it down in the order in which they may happen to be enumerated; but, having glanced the whole, let him take what is moſt to his purpoſe, and omit every thing that would appear far-fetched, or to be introduced for the ſake of ſwelling the bulk of a diſcourſe.

I am very ready, however, to acknowledge, that rhetorical topics are more uſeful in the compoſition of *ſet declamations on trite ſubjeſts*, and to *young perſons*, than in the communication of original matter, and to perſons much uſed to compoſition. Original thoughts cannot but ſuggeſt themſelves, ſo that all the aſſiſtance any perſon can want in this caſe, is a proper manner of *arranging* them. And a perſon much uſed to compoſition will have acquired a habit of recollection, without any expreſs attention to topics; juſt as a perſon uſed to the harpſichord, or

any

any other inftrument of mufic, will be able to perform without
an *exprefs attention* to rules, or even to the manner of placing his
fingers.   His idea of the tune in general, is fo clofely affociated
with all the motions of his fingers neceffary to the playing of it,
and thefe motions are alfo fo clofely affociated together, that they
follow one another mechanically, in what Dr. Hartley calls a
fecondarily automatic manner, which is almoft as certain as a motion *originally* and *properly automatic*.

E   LECTURE

LECTURE V.

Of AMPLIFICATION.

HAVING confidered the proper *topics of argument* for the proof of any propofition, it remains that I confider what makes the bulk of a difcourfe, under the head of *Amplification.*

In general, whatever may with propriety be faid upon any topic, fhould tend to *confirm*, or *illuftrate* that topic; and be longer or fhorter as the cafe requires: and, fince any particular argument may require *proof* or *confirmation*, it muft be confidered in every refpect as the original propofition itfelf, and be fupported by arguments fetched from the topics which are proper to it. In a regular difcourfe, the amplification, or enlargement, is nothing more than a collection of fuch arguments and obfervations as tend to confirm or illuftrate the fubject of it; and therefore not a fentence, or a word, fhould be inferted that doth not improve the fenfe, and tend to make the apprehenfion of the reader, or hearer, either more *juft*, or more *ftrong* and lively.

More particularly, the precife nature of amplification, with refpect to argumentative difcourfes, confifts either in supplying fuch *intermediate arguments* as might have been fuppreffed, or in a more copious *induction of particulars.*

A demon-

A demonstration may be given in such a manner as may be sufficiently full and conclusive to a person who is pretty well versed in the science to which it belongs, or such as are similar to it, and yet may want a great many intermediate steps, and mediums of proof, necessary to make it intelligible to a person who is not so well prepared. When a person writes for the *learned*, it is superfluous to use more words than will enable them to see the force of what he advances, and it is impertinent to mention those intermediate ideas which he knows are quite familiar to their minds. But if this discourse be made intelligible to the *bulk of mankind*, and especially if it must be adapted to the capacities of *children* and *young persons*, it must be *amplified*, by inserting in it those intermediate steps, and mediums of proof, which before were omitted as unnecessary. Because it would be absurd in any writer, and would defeat the purpose of his discourse, to take any thing for granted that his reader was not acquainted with, or to omit any thing that he was not able to supply.

Newton's Principia is a remarkable instance to the present purpose. The demonstrations in that treatise are extremely concise, a great number of intermediate steps being omitted; and therefore but few, even of mathematicians, are capable of understanding it without a comment. The commentary *amplifies*, by supplying the steps that were suppressed by the author; and thus the book may be fitted for more general use.

When the proof of a general proposition consists of the *induction of particulars*, it may be sufficient in some cases, to mention only a few of the particulars. In other cases, it may be convenient to amplify, or swell the demonstration by a more copious enumeration.

A nar-

A *narration* or *defcription* is concife, when only a few of the moft important particulars are mentioned, and amplified and enlarged by a more minute detail. The former is fufficient, where it anfwers a writer's purpofe barely to inform his reader of the *reality* of an event; the latter is neceffary, if he be defirous that the reader be *interefted* in it, and *affeted* with it.

Addifon (Spetator, No. 519.) obferving how full of life are thofe parts of nature which are fubjet to our obfervation, amplifies it in the following beautiful manner : " Every part of " matter is peopled, every green leaf fwarms with inhabitants. " There is fcarce a fingle humour in the body of a man, or of " any other animal, in which our glaffes do not difcover myriads " of living creatures. The furface of animals is alfo covered " with other animals, which are, in the fame manner, the bafis " of other animals, that live upon it. Nay, we find in the moft " folid bodies, as in marble itfelf, innumerable cells and cavities, " that are crouded with fuch imperceptible inhabitants, as are " too little for the naked eye to difcover. On the other hand, " if we look into the more bulky parts of nature, we fee the " feas, lakes, and rivers, teeming with numberlefs kinds of liv- " ing creatures. We find every mountain and marfh, wildernefs " and wood, plentifully ftocked with birds and beafts; and every " part of matter affording proper neceffaries and conveniencies " for the livelihood of multitudes which inhabit it."

It is likewife ufual to amplify narration and defcription by *obfervations* or *refletions* intermixed. By this means Polybius greatly fwelled the bulk of his hiftory, and for want of this kind of amplification, hiftorical abftracts are generally very dull and infipid. All books of *meditation,* as Mr. Hervey's, contain a mixture of narration and reflection; and the pleafure with

which

which such books are universally read, demonstrates the propriety and happiness of such a mixture.

These two kinds of amplification are used in the *body of a discourse*; but it is often requisite that, previous to the confirmation of a topic by arguments, it should be explained very minutely, and the parts of which it consists be expressed in more, or plainer terms, and mistakes concerning it be pointed out, and guarded against, to prevent misconstruction. This very usefully enlarges a discourse.

It may happen that the nature and conclusiveness of an argument may not be evident at the first view. In this case, it may answer a very good purpose to amplify, by shewing, either before or after the proof of the proposition, the nature and strength of the arguments brought in support of it, and by stating with some exactness the degree of influence they are intitled to.

Lastly, it contributes to swell a discourse, to point out the *connexion of the sentences* that compose it more particularly than by single conjunctives, in the manner explained in the *Lectures upon Grammar* *.

These are the principal sources from whence materials for amplification are drawn. It will be to the advantage of a composition that they do not succeed one another in the same order, but that they be introduced with great variety. This will give the discourse the greater appearance of *ease*. It will be more pleasing, and in every respect better adapted to answer the end proposed by it.

All the *faults* which properly belong to amplification, are the following. It is absurd to introduce any thing under any topic

* This is a work which has been printed for private use, and will in due time be laid before the public.

which

which has no relation to it, not tending either to confirm or illuſtrate it. It is, likewiſe, a fault to attempt to illuſtrate what is too plain to need any illuſtration. In this, regard muſt be had to the hearers or readers : for, to a mixed multitude, or to a ſet of pupils, a *copious illuſtration*, a *diverſified expreſſion*, or a mere *repetition*, may be proper, which would be abſurd before a learned aſſembly. But it is a greater fault not to advance what is ſufficient to confirm or illuſtrate any argument; ſince without that, the end of the diſcourſe, which was conviction or perſuaſion, cannot be attained.

Other faults in the body of a diſcourſe belong to other heads than that of amplification.

It is of ſome importance to obſerve, on the ſubject of amplification, that perſons of a very exact judgment are generally the leaſt copious in compoſition, and notwithſtanding they have the greateſt knowledge, compoſe with peculiar difficulty; their nicer diſcernment, which makes them attend to all the relations and connexions of things, rejecting every thing that doth not in every reſpect ſuit their purpoſe. Whereas thoſe perſons who are unattentive to the minuter properties of things, find no difficulty in admitting a great variety of thoughts that offer themſelves in compoſition; a ſlight aſſociation of any ideas with the ſubject in hand being ſufficient to introduce them. In general, the latter are more proper for public ſpeakers, and the former for writers. The want of cloſe connexion, ſmall improprieties, or even inconſiſtencies, paſs unnoticed with moſt perſons when they hear a diſcourſe. Beſides, no perſon can ſo well depend upon his memory in comparing one part of a diſcourſe that he has only *heard*, with another. But all theſe little inaccuracies are expoſed to obſervation,

tion, when a good judge of compofition hath the whole difcourfe before him in *writing*.

It may, likewife, be of fervice to add, that it is very poffible a writer may cramp his faculties, and injure his productions, by too great a *fcrupulofity* in the firft compofition. That clofe attention to a fubject which compofition requires, unavoidably warms the imagination : then ideas crowd upon us, the mind haftens, as it were, into the midft of things, and is impatient till thofe ftrong conceptions be expreffed.   In fuch a fituation, to reject the firft, perhaps loofe and incorrect thoughts, is to reject a train of juft and valuable thoughts, that would follow by their connexion with them, and to embarrafs and impoverifh the whole work.   Whenever, therefore, we begin to feel the ardour of compofition, it is moft advifeable to indulge it freely, and leave little proprieties to be adjufted at our leifure.

Befides, if we would wifh to communicate to our readers thofe ftrong fenfations that we feel in the ardour of compofition, we muft endeavour to exprefs the whole of our fentiments and fenfations, in the very *order* and *connexion* in which they actually prefented themfelves to us at that time.   For, fuch is the fimilarity of all human minds, that when the fame appearances are prefented to another perfon, his mind will, in general, be equally ftruck and affected with them, and the compofition will appear to him to be natural and animated.   Whereas, if, in confequence of an ill-judged fcrupulofity and delay, we once lofe fight of any part of that train of ideas with which our own minds were fo warmed and interefted, it may be impoffible to recover it : and perhaps no other train of ideas, though, feparately taken, they may appear to be better adapted to the fubject, may have the fame power to excite thofe fenfations with which we would wifh

the

the compofition might be read. Whatever thefe fenfations be, they will be the fame with thofe with which the compofition was written; it being almoft impoffible to *counterfeit* fuccefsfully in fuch a cafe as this. As, therefore, we wifh to affect and intereft the minds of our readers, we fhould endeavour, without lofing time in examining every thing with a minute exactnefs, to exprefs the *whole ftate of our own minds* while they are thus affected and interefted. Correction will be employed with more advantage afterwards.

PART

P A R T II.

OF

M E T H O D.

L E C T U R E VI.

Of METHOD *in* Narrative Difcourfes.

THE orator being furnifhed with proper materials for his difcourfe, from the topics of argumentation and amplification, explained under the laft general head of *recolleƈtion,* his next care is to difpofe of them to the beft advantage, in the moft regular and convenient METHOD; the rules of which I now proceed to lay down. This I fhall do with refpeƈt to both the kinds to which every compofition may be reduced, viz. the *Narrative* and *Argumentative.*

If the view of the hiftorian be fimply to communicate *informa-tion,* and he be defirous to do it in fuch a manner as to give it the

F   eafieft

eafieft admiffion into the mind, and leave the moft lafting impreffion upon the memory, his general endeavour muft be to give as
clear and juft an idea as poffible of the moft ftriking relations
that the ideas he exhibits bear to one another; fince it is by
means of their *mutual relations* that ideas introduce one another,
and *cohere*, as it were, in the mind.

In general, the *order of nature*, or of their *real exiftence*, will
be found to be, at the fame time, both the eafieft, and, in every
refpect, the beft manner of reciting them, viz. the order of *time*
for *events*, and that of *place*, for the fubjects of what is called
natural hiftory.

Thus the chronological fucceffion of events hath generally fupplied the writers of civil hiftory, biography, and travels, with
the moft natural and ufeful method of communicating information. The *geographer*, having finifhed one country, naturally
thinks of paffing into a neighbouring one; and, in natural
hiftory, we always expect an intire and unbroken account of fome
one of the animal, vegetable, or mineral kingdoms, before we
be led to another.

This is making thofe tranfitions which our minds are moft ac-
cuftomed to, and therefore make with the moft eafe. It is taking advantage of the ftrongeft affociations by which the ideas of
things cohere in our minds; on account of which every particular of the narration both gains the eafieft admiffion into our
minds, and is beft retained when admitted: whereas the mind
is greatly difgufted with unufual, and confequently unexpected,
and, to us, unnatural connexions of things. Such connexions
not being analogous to any other pre-exifting and eftablifhed in
the mind, the things fo connected will not coalefce, and recal
one another, fo as to be remembered in their order.

How-

However, thefe very fame reafons, drawn from the nature of things, and the ftate of the human mind, to which thefe relations are addreffed, will often dictate particular deviations from the general order of narration; will admonifh the hiftorian to quit the order of time for a while, and the geographer that of proximity of fituation. The relations of events to one another, by way of *caufe and effect*, will fomctimes unavoidably, and very juftifiably, oblige an hiftorian to trace an important event back to the *caufes* that gave birth to it; and again to purfue it through its diftant *confequences*, far beyond the æra in which it commenced. In *biography*, the confideration of the effects of education, the influence of a ruling paffion, the confequences of an extraordinary and critical incident, and the like, may render an occafional tranfition from a man's birth to his death, or from his death to his birth, to be by no means a difagreeable or unprofitable digreffion. And if the relation of fimilarity, or even of contrariety, in natural productions, cuftoms, climates, &c. give occafion to it, we willingly follow the geographer and natural hiftorian in their moft fudden and rapid excurfions, to parts of the world the moft diftant from thofe they are profeffedly defcribing.

In all thefe and the like cafes, a writer can never be blamed if he difpofe the materials of his compofition by an attention to the ftrongeft and moft ufual *affociations of ideas* in the human mind. We are not fond of purfuing any uniform track long without interruption: fo that the natural connexions of ideas not quite foreign to the fubject, with others which occur in the courfe of a narration, may, in the hands of a judicious hiftorian, give occafion to *digreffions* from his principal fubject, which fhall greatly relieve the attention, pleafe the imagination, refrefh and affift the memory.

The

The danger is, left thefe excurfions from the principal fubject, which are fo inviting to a writer, and often agreeable to the reader, fhould lead them too far : fince it is very poffible to pur-fue a natural and proper digreffion, till we find ourfelves at a lofs for tranfitions equally eafy and natural, by which to return to the principal fubject : and no digreffion can be faid to be unex-ceptionable, that doth not connect equally well at both ends with the piece in which it is introduced.

If a digreffion be continued till we quite lofe fight of the prin-cipal fubject, the uniformity of the whole piece is broken, and at the end of fuch digreffion the reader hath, as it were, to be-gin again ; and he may be under a neceffity of looking a confi-derable way back, before he can recover the train of ideas he had loft, and without which he cannot proceed with the work. For no chain of events can be underftood, unlefs they be feen in their connexion with others on which they depend. Every writer, therefore, fhould, by all means, take care, if poffible, fo to dif-pofe of his materials, as that nothing interrupt or keep out of fight, any train of ideas, till the perception of them be of little or no confequence to any thing that is to follow. If fuch di-greffions, however, be unavoidable, it is abfolutely neceffary that, after fuch digreffion, the writer *repeat*, or recapitulate, which is by no means graceful.

I fhall exemplify thefe obfervations on the excellencies and faults of methodical narration, by an account of the manner of fome of the moft confiderable writers in that way, ancient and modern.

The generality of hiftorians, with *Xenophon*, *Livy*, *Salluft*, *Tacitus*, and fome others, aim at the moft agreeable method of writing hiftory, viz. by obferving the order of *time* in general ;
but

but by no means fuffering a regard to it to interrupt the account of any *intire tranfaction*, or prevent their looking either backward or forward for an incident that would throw light upon any character or event.

This method all writers of *fiction* and *romance*, without exception, aim at, as the moft agreeable and perfect: and fuch writers are the more at liberty to follow it, as they are under no conftraint from fuch a variety of confiderations as the writers of true hiftory muft attend to, and which do not always leave them the mafters of their own choice. If the matter, or manner, of a true hiftorian do not pleafe us, it may be the *fubject* that is in fault; if a romance do not pleafe us, we juftly blame either the invention, or judgment of the *writer*.

Thucydides, out of his extreme regard to truth, hath adhered too fcrupuloufly to chronological order; fo as frequently to pafs, in a very abrupt and difpleafing manner, from the midft of an important and interefting tranfaction, to a very diftant and trivial one; and he never begins or completes any tranfaction but in its proper year. Being the firft among the Greeks who paid much attention to *exactnefs in chronology*, he is the more excufable in following it fo clofely as he did; fince he could have no example of any inconvenience attending it.

Herodotus rambles from his fubject much more frequently than Thucydides, but on a very different, and lefs juftifiable account: for his digreffions from an interefting narration are fo far from being intended to keep us nearer to chronological order, that they throw us farther from it; when frequently, upon barely naming a perfon or nation, in the midft of an event, of which we are impatient to know the iffue, he ftops to give an account of, perhaps, the whole hiftory of that nation or perfon, or fome parti-

cular

cular relating to them quite foreign to the action that is depending, and without the leaſt regard to the time in which what he thus digreſſes to relate happened. But to the *father of hiſtory*, and an *old man*, every indulgence ought to be made. With all his defects of method, there are few hiſtorians more pleaſing upon the whole.

Xenophon, though, in general, an excellent hiſtorian, yet in his *expedition of the ten thouſand*, when he comes to relate the death of *Cyrus*, in the battle with his brother, goes back to relate at large the intire hiſtory of his private life, manners, and ſchemes, &c. leaving the minds of his readers in a ſtate of the moſt anxious ſuſpenſe, to know what was the fate of the *Greeks*, who were the proper heroes of his hiſtory. The only inducement that one could imagine a writer could have to make ſuch digreſſions as theſe, muſt have been to give the hiſtory of the ſame perſon in the ſame place, though at the expence both of the *order of time*, and of the *unity of action*.

The digreſſions of *Tacitus*, to give an account of the origin, and early hiſtory of any people or country, immediately before an account of the wars the Romans had with them, have the beſt effect; as they both tend to intereſt us in the progreſs and event of the war, and, conſidering the ſubject of his hiſtory, contribute to relieve the mind, in the moſt agreeable manner, from an attention to a ſcene which was in itſelf too uniform and diſguſting. The ſubject of the *Annals of Tacitus* was of ſuch a nature as to occaſion little or no inconvenience from ſtrict chronological order; the unity of action being no where broken in upon by it, as it is by the annals of Thucydides.

The writer of a *ſingle hiſtory* hath no embarraſſment in compariſon of a perſon who undertakes to give an account of two or

more

more nations, whofe hiſtories are intermixed with one another. The former is at liberty to take as much of any foreign hiſtory as he hath occaſion for to illuſtrate his own; the other is in a manner under a neceſſity, either of making repetitions, or of leaving chaſms in one or other of the hiſtories. The former expedient is tedious and ungraceful, the latter makes one of the hiſtories very imperfect and uninterefting.

The writers of the *Univerſal Hiſtory* found themſelves in this dilemma, and their very valuable work bears too many marks of it. To avoid *repetitions*, they have left almoſt all the hiſtories imperfect, which obliges a reader to look into ſeveral, before he can find a perfect account of any.   They have likewiſe made the modern hiſtory of the *Arabians* and *Turks*, in particular, unneceſſarily and exceſſively tedious, by inſerting in the text ſeveral different accounts of the ſame event; when it would have occaſioned no more trouble to the writer, and have been vaſtly more agreeable to the reader, to have retained only the moſt approved account of any event in the *text*, and have left the other accounts to the *notes*.

By the uſe of *notes* the moderns have a conſiderable advantage over the ancients, who had no idea of ſuch a convenience.   By the help of notes a hiſtory may go on without interruption, and yet a great variety of *incidental things*, worth recording, and which cannot be introduced with eaſe into the body of a work, may have a place aſſigned to them, where they may be attended to at the reader's leiſure.

Bayle hath made the greateſt uſe of notes of any of the moderns.   Indeed, the text of his *Biographical Dictionary* ſeems to have been compoſed for the ſake of the notes; which were ſuch *miſcellaneous remarks* upon men and opinions, as could not have
been

been incorporated into any regular work, or have been publiſhed conveniently in any other form.

What Bayle did, in a manner, through neceſſity, ſome others (and particularly *Harris*) have adopted through choice; and have thereby made their works nothing more than *unconnected anecdotes*, to which the text only ſerves as an index. Whereas the moſt proper uſe of the notes in biographical writings, is to ſerve as a repoſitory for the more *minute particulars* of a perſon's life, which, though of great uſe to illuſtrate the character, are yet too inconſiderable to make a figure in the body of the work.

The lives of *Suetonius* conſiſt, chiefly, of ſuch curious and uſeful particulars as tend to give us an idea of the real *characters* of the *Twelve Cæſars*, and were by no means deſigned to be a complete hiſtory of their lives and actions.

Tacitus's life of Agricola, and *Quintus Curtius's life of Alexander the Great*, are works of a very different nature, being regular hiſtories of the actions of thoſe great men. *Plutarch's lives* are a moſt judicious mixture both of private characterſtic incidents, and of public tranſactions.

Tacitus's tract concerning the *manners of the Germans* is an excellent model for that kind of narrative; giving a moſt diſtinct account both of the general policy and particular inſtitutions of that people.

All *didactic treatiſes* belong chiefly to this head of narration; the writer having little to do with argumentation, and being concerned chiefly to give as intelligible and diſtinct an account as poſſible of all the *precepts of the art*, or of every thing that is requiſite to be done in order to ſucceed in it.

Whether

Whether a writer difcourfe of the *mechanic*, or the *liberal arts*, fuch as *grammar*, *oratory*, &c. the nature of the thing will direct him, in general, to divide the fubject into its proper diftinct parts, and to give an account of what is moft effential in the firft place, and what is only ornamental afterwards.

G   LECTURE

L E C T U R E   VII.

Of METHOD *in* Argumentative *difcourfes*; *of* ANALYSIS *and*
SYNTHESIS; *and of* GEOMETRICAL DEMONSTRATION.

THE greateſt difficulty, in point of method, is found in properly arranging the parts of an *argument*, ſo as to give
them the moſt weight, and encreaſe the degree of evidence re-
ſulting from the whole, by the aptneſs of their order and connexion.

Logicians ſpeak of two kinds of method in argumentative diſcourſes, the *analytic* and the *ſynthetic*; and the diſtribution is
complete and accurate. For, in all ſcience, we either proceed
from particular obſervations to more general concluſions, which
is *analyſis*; or, beginning with more general and comprehenſive
propoſitions, we deſcend to the particular propoſitions which are
contained in them, which is *ſyntheſis*.

In the former method we are obliged to proceed in our *inveſti-*
gation of truth : for it is only by comparing a number of particular obſervations which are ſelf-evident, that we perceive any
analogy in effects, which leads us to apprehend an uniformity
in their cauſe, in the knowledge of which all ſcience conſiſts. In
the latter method it is generally more convenient to explain a
fyſtem of ſcience to others. For, in general, thoſe truths which

2   were

were the refult of our own inquiry, may be made as intelligible
to others as thofe by which we arrived at the knowledge of them;
and it is eafier to fhow how one geneial principle comprehends
the particulars comprized under it, than to trace all thofe particulars to one that comprehends them all.

On the other hand, the analytic method is properly to communicate truth to others in the very manner in which it was difcovered; and firft difcoveries are generally the refult of fuch a
laborious and minute examination, as is, in its own nature, a
flow and tedious procedure. Is it not much readier to take the
right key at firft, and open a number of locks, than begin with
examining the locks, and after trying feveral keys that will open
one or two of them only, at laft to produce that which will open
them all?

Notwithftanding this, in theories not perfectly afcertained, or
with regard to fentiments not generally admitted, it may be advifeable to inform others in the method of analyfis; becaufe
then, beginning with no principles or pofitions but what are
common, and univerfally allowed, we may lead others infenfibly,
and without fhocking their prejudices, to the right conclufion.
It is as if the perfons we are inftructing did themfelves make all
the obfervations, and, after trying every hypothefis, find that
none would anfwer except that which we point out to them.
This method is more tedious, but perhaps more fure. Before
we admit any hypothefis, we naturally confider whether it will
agree with every obfervation previoufly made, and every propofition previoufly admitted; and therefore in a method of communication borrowed from that cautious method of inquiry, we
are of courfe led diftinctly to confider, and very particularly to
obviate all kinds of objections.

In fact, almost every branch of science (except some parts of pure mathematics, capable of the strictest demonstration) hath been delivered at first by the investigators of it in this method of analysis; and it hath not been till after some time that the patrons of it have digested it into a synthetic, or systematic form.

This latter method, however, is absolutely necessary when any branch of science is introduced into *schools*, where there is occasion for the most concise and compendious methods of instruction. It is only the elements of science that can be learned in schools, and it would take up too much of the little time that youth can give to their studies, to lead them through all the slow processes of analysis in every thing they learn. Analytical discourses are, therefore, more properly addressed to those persons who have gone through their preparatory studies, and who have leisure for *new speculations*.

These two methods are seldom used absolutely unmixed in any work of considerable length, except by mathematicians; and for the greater variety, in *long discourses*, a method sometimes partaking more of the analytic, and sometimes leaning more to the synthetic, is adopted, as best suits the taste of the writer.

A method the most properly analytic is pursued by mathematicians in all kinds of algebraic investigations, in approximations, and in experimental philosophy: whereas the geometric method of proposition and demonstration is of the synthetic kind.

A great variety of modern treatises upon moral subjects, in which mankind are far from being agreed, have lately been written in the analytic method, as best suited to the infant state of the science. The science of theology hath been, perhaps, too precipitately handled in the method of synthesis, or systematically;

and

and feveral ingenious perfons, being aware of it, have gone
back, and have begun again in the more cautious method of
analytical inquiry.

Having thus given a general idea of the nature of the methods
of fynthefis and analyfis, and of the proper ufe of both, I proceed to confider them feparately and more particularly.

Since the fubject of every fynthetic difcourfe is fome *propofition*,
or *theorem*, which is to be proved, and the bulk of the difcourfe
a kind of *demonftration*, it may be of confiderable fervice to a
compofer to have in view the methods of demonftration ufed by
mathematicians.

Truth, whether geometrical, metaphyfical, moral, or theological, is of the fame nature, and the evidence of it is perceived
in a fimilar manner by the fame human minds. Now it is univerfally allowed that the form in which evidence is prefented by
Euclid, and other geometricians of reputation, is that in which
it gains the readieft and moft irrefiftible admiffion into the mind;
and their method of conducting a demonftration, and difpofing
of every thing preceding it, and fubfequent to it, hath been fo
generally approved, that it is eftablifhed and invariable. Such
a fuccefsful method of procedure with refpect to mathematical
truth, certainly deferves the attention and imitation of all who
are defirous to promote the interefts of any kind of truth.

In order, therefore, to give the moft perfect rules of fynthetic
demonftration, I fhall explain the method of geometricians, and
endeavour to fhow how far it may be adopted, or imitated with
advantage, by writers in general, and particularly by divines and
moralifts.

Every

Every propofition is, by geometricians, demonftrated either from *axioms*, that is, felf-evident truths ; or fuch as have been elfewhere demonftrated from thofe which are felf-evident.

In like manner, whatever we propofe to demonftrate, the laft appeal lies to *felf-evident truths* ; in moral fubjects, to confciouf-nefs, or internal feelings ; and in matters of revelation, to the plain fenfe of fcripture : and it is very expedient and advifeable, in difcourfes upon important fubjects of any kind, after the manner of geometricians, to premife thefe felf-evident truths, beyond which no appeal can be admitted.

Moreover, left there fhould be any difagreement or difpute about the ufe of the words employed in the argument, it is, likewife, convenient that, after their manner, thefe axioms be preceded by *definitions* explaining the fenfe in which all the im-portant words which reprefent complex ideas are ufed. When, in this manner, it is determined in what fenfe words are to be ufed, and what are the allowed uncontroverted principles we are to go upon, they may be applied with great eafe and certainty in the remainder of the difcourfe ; and the demonftration in which they are introduced, will be freed from that confufion and em-barraffment which would otherwife attend it.

Befides, this method is, in a manner, the very *touchftone of truth* ; and therefore, if our views really be to promote the in-tereft of *truth* (and fooner would I teach the art of poifoning than that of *fophiftry)* this method hath another great advantage to recommend it. For if thefe definitions and axioms be laid down with due accuracy and circumfpection, they not only in-troduce the eafieft, the moft natural, and cogent method of de-monftrating any propofition, but lead to an eafy method of ex-amining the ftrength or weaknefs of the enfuing arguments. If

the

the argument in fuch a methodical difcourfe be not conclufive, it contains within itfelf the principles of its own confutation. Such a difcourfe muft be evidently *inconfiftent with itfelf*. On the other hand, if the definitions and axioms be admitted, the propofitions that are demonftrated from them, by the fimple rules of reafoning, muft be next to felf-evident, and carry the ftrongeft poffible conviction along with them.

I am not, in thefe and the following obfervations, pleading for the geometrical TERMS, *axiom* and *definition*, or for the very exact and precife method in which geometricians place them. It is not the *name*, but the *thing* that I recommend; and only fo far as reafon directs to fimilar methods in fimilar cafes. A regard to *perfpicuity* would direct us (if we would be underftood) to explain diftinctly the meaning of every word we ufe, that is of the leaft doubtful fignification, and to introduce the definitions, if not formally, at the entrance of a difcourfe, yet as foon as they become neceffary. It is manifeftly convenient likewife, upon feveral occafions, to refer exprefsly to maxims which are univerfally allowed or felf-evident, in order to fhow diftinctly upon what foundation an argument refts. The more diftinct we keep our own propofitions, or thofe which, in any difcourfe, we profefs to maintain, from thofe, by the help or medium of which, we prove them, the better. We can much more eafily examine any fentiments when we fee in what place to begin, and are fhown their mutual connexion, and the dependance that one part hath upon another.

LECTURE

LECTURE VIII.

Of the several parts of a proper DEMONSTRATION.

AFTER thefe ufeful preliminaries, viz. afcertaining the ufe of terms, and premifing what is univerfally known, or taken for granted, with refpect to a fubject, the geometrician proceeds to his *propofition*, in which he lays down, in the plaineft terms, what he hath farther to advance. This either conftitutes a fingle propofition, or is refolvable into feveral heads, each of which are diftinct propofitions, and muft be demonftrated feparately. Moreover, the principal propofition is fometimes preceded by one, or feveral others, which are called *lemmas*, and are defigned to prepare the way for the principal propofition, by proving the truth of fuch other propofitions as may be made ufe of to demonftrate it.

In like manner, if, when we have taken a view of the whole of a fubject, in all its extent, and have confidered every argument which we intend to bring in proof of it, we fufpect that any of the intermediate propofitions, upon which the demonftration principally depends, may themfelves want proof, or illuftration, it may be extremely convenient to difpatch it in the introduction, previous to our naming the principal propofition ; becaufe it may prevent its occafioning any interruption in the courfe

3   of

of the demonſtration. Such doubtful poſitions muſt otherwiſe be
propoſed by way of anſwering *objections*, after the demonſtration,
which may not always be quite convenient; becauſe the difficulty
may have occurred to the mind of the hearer, or reader, from the
firſt; and his keeping it in view through the whole of the demonſtration, may have prevented the arguments from being heard
with that attention, and freedom from prejudice, with which they
would have been heard, if that objection had been obviated by
way of lemma, in the introduction. The geometrician wiſely an-
ticipates all *objection*.

In ſome caſes, indeed, it may be impoſſible to anticipate all objections; as they may be of ſuch a nature as that they could not
be *underſtood* till the demonſtration had been heard. In that caſe
the objections not only may come after the demonſtration (as of
neceſſity they muſt, if they be mentioned at all) but alſo may do
ſo without any inconvenience. Becauſe if the objection could not
be underſtood before the demonſtration, it could not have occurred to the hearer or reader before, ſo as to lay any bias upon his
mind in the courſe of it.

Objections being thus, as far as poſſible, anticipated, and the
truth of every intermediate propoſition that we ſhall have occaſion for, proved, the way is properly cleared for the *principal
propoſition*, which muſt be propoſed without any ornament, in the
moſt intelligible terms. If the propoſition be complex, the whole
extent of it muſt be ſhown in the moſt commodious diviſion of it
into its proper parts : alſo the order in which each part will be
diſcuſſed muſt be pointed out diſtinctly, that the whole proceſs of
the demonſtration may lie with the greateſt clearneſs before the
minds of thoſe to whom it is addreſſed ; and that, in the progreſs
of the diſcourſe, they may perceive the connexion of all the

H

parts,

parts, and may fee all along what progrefs the fpeaker or writer hath made in his argument.

In cafes relating to matters of *fact*, it may require a long and circumftantial *narration* before the point to be proved can be underftood. Whatever narration, therefore, is requifite to fet a queftion in difpute in a clear light, belongs to this part of a difcourfe, and is properly referred to the propofition.

The geometrician, when he hath laid down his propofition, proceeds, by a feries of fteps which terminate in a fingle proof, to fhow the agreement or coincidence of the terms of it: and as one demonftration, in fubjects that will admit of it, is decifive, a multiplicity and redundancy of proofs is feldom affected by mathematicians. But in this the moralift and divine muft content themfelves with following them at a great and very humble diftance. As the fubjects they treat of are not always capable of ftrict *demonftration*, they are obliged to have recourfe to a variety of arguments, each of which may add fomething to *probability*, (which in its own nature admits of degrees) till the united ftrength of them all be fufficient to determine the affent.

In this cafe, it is of fome confequence that attention be paid to the *order of the proofs*, fuppofing them to be of different natures, and different degrees of ftrength. Arguments of a fimilar nature, that is, drawn from fimilar confiderations, as from reafon or fcripture, obfervation or experience, &c. fhould be ranged together; becaufe in that pofition they confirm, and throw light upon one another. And though arguments which have no weight ought by no means to be ufed at all, and one that hath but little weight had better be fpared, where there are a fufficient number of fubftantial and ftriking arguments, yet in fome cafes it may

be

be requifite to take notice of every circumftance that may tend to throw light and evidence upon a doubtful fpeculation.

In fuch an enumeration of arguments, it is not advifeable to place a flight probability in the fame rank with arguments which are much ftronger and more conclufive. Rather, fince there are fo many ways in which, with a little addrefs, it may be introduced to more advantage, in an *indirect manner*, let it be hinted at in fome other place. Very often an argument, difguifed in the form of an epithet, a metaphor, a comparifon or illuftration, &c. is more pleafing, looks more like a redundancy of argument, and in every refpect hath a better effect, than if it were placed in an equal rank with arguments of more weight. Indeed, in fuch a fituation, it might be conftrued to look like a diffidence of our caufe, and a folicitude to make the moft of every argument favourable to it.

If the arguments be nearly equal in weight, no order drawn from their *comparative ftrength* is to be preferred to that *natural order* which is fuggefted by the fubjects from which they are derived.

After the demonftration of the propofition, the geometrician, if there be occafion, makes mifcellaneous remarks, ferving to throw light upon the fubject, under the name of *fcholia*. And fuch like obfervations, particularly fuch as illuftrate the nature and force of the evidence, or point out fimilar proceffes in other fubjects, throw an agreeable variety into a compofition, and tend, in an indirect manner, to ftrengthen the preceding arguments.

Laftly, in the form of *Corollaries*, the geometrican deduces from his propofition, now fully proved, other truths which flow from it, if the dependance be fo ftrict that it would have appeared trifling to make them formal propofitions.

H 2   In

In like manner, when there is no danger of too greatly multiplying the objects of attention, it may have a good effect to fhow the extenfive and happy influence of the principle we have been maintaining, by tracing its beneficial confequences, and fhowing the connexion it hath with other acknowledged truths; particularly when thofe confequences, and thofe connexions with other truths, are of fuch a nature, that they could not conveniently be introduced into the body of the difcourfe, by way of arguments in favour of the propofition we maintain.

Having explained pretty much at large how all the proper parts of an argumentative difcourfe, calculated to inform the underftanding, fhould be difpofed, in order to produce their proper effect, I fhall fubjoin the following brief fummary of the procefs.

The meaning of the terms of the propofition fhould be accurately fixed, principles made ufe of in the demonftration diftinctly noted, and, if there be occafion, proved; the queftion ftated in the moſt intelligible manner, with a circumftantial relation of every fact that may contribute to fet it in the cleareft point of light, and the fubject divided into the diftinct parts of which it confifts. The order of nature muft chiefly be confulted in arranging the arguments brought to fupport each of them, and flight probabilities fhould be introduced in an indirect manner. Obfervations relating to the nature of the proof that is made ufe of, with the connexion and mutual influence of the feveral arguments, and other mifcellaneous remarks that may naturally occur, come next; and the whole difcourfe clofes with a view of the extent of the doctrine, in all the valuable inferences and ufes that may be drawn from it.

The

The principal *faults* in the feveral parts of this kind of difpofition, may be feen in the following brief enumeration of them.

As it is highly requifite to define ftrictly every term in the
propofition, when the meaning of it is in danger of being
miftaken; fo it is affected and trifling to define thofe that, it is
morally certain, will not be mifunderftood.

We cannot be too cautious what principles we take for granted
in order to argue from.   Thefe *axioms* are the foundation of
our whole fuperftructure.   We ought, therefore, very rarely,
and not without the moft urgent neceffity, to have recourfe to
argumenta ad hominem; being fenfible that though fuch arguments
may lead fome particular perfons into a right way of thinking, the
connexion between *truth* and *falfehood* cannot be natural, and
promifes out ill to be lafting; and that whenever fuch perfons
begin to be aware that the principles from which you argued
with them were falfe, they of courfe give up the fentiments
which were deduced from them.

Diftribution is the moft faulty when the parts are not of the
fame nature and order, and not fufficiently diftinct; and by no
means fhould any one of them comprehend any of the reft.
Rather fubdivide the principal heads of a difcourfe into fubordi-
nate ones.

It is a capital fault in the difpofition of an argumentative
difcourfe, to divide the fubject in fuch a manner, as that the
writer fhall have occafion for the fame amplification in different
parts of it.   This is the confequence of making the heads of
difcourfe too much fimilar to one another.   It is more advifeable to make fewer heads, and thofe more diftinct.

In

In a difcourfe, in which a great variety of arguments are. ufed, it hath a good effect both to give a general view of them before they be feparately enlarged upon, and to give a diftinct recapitulation of them after the amplification; as it makes the evidence more intelligible, and unites the force of all the arguments.

Introductions to difcourfes admit of great variety, according to the nature of the fubject, the circumftances of the fpeaker, and of the perfons he addreffes. Since the end that is propofed by every thing that is faid, previous to our entering upon any fubject, is to procure us a more favourable hearing, and thereby prepare the way for the arguments that we intend to advance, we may, with advantage, introduce a fubject by a variety of general remarks concerning it, particularly fuch as tend to fhow the *ufe* and *importance* of it; or by fhewing the propriety of treating it at that particular time, in that particular place, in that particular manner, &c. It may alfo be very expedient to introduce an obnoxious fubject, by removing preconceived prejudices, and anfwering popular objections.

Introductions may likewife be fuggefted by a variety of temporary circumftances, impoffible to be defcribed beforehand, but which naturally occur to a fpeaker, or writer, in the circumftances proper for them. See Cicero's introductions to his philofophical and rhetorical difcourfes, and alfo thofe to his orations. In the latter there is generally the greateft propriety; but the former have no peculiar relation to the pieces to which they are prefixed. Indeed, he acknowledges that they were compofed before he knew what ufe he fhould make of them. The introductions to the two hiftories of Salluft are juftly to be found fault with on the fame account.

LECTURE

L E C T U R E   IX.

Of the ANALYTIC METHOD.   *Of Locke's Essay on the Human Understanding, and Hutcheson's Moral Philosophy.*

THE regular and unmixed synthesis is best adapted (as was observed above) to subjects, the theories of which are ascertained, or systems for the use of learners; who, in general, have occasion to be taught in the most expeditious manner. In fact, we find very few treatises drawn up in this method, except *elementary* ones, for the use of students, and particularly in pure mathematics and philosophy.

The generality of writers deliver their sentiments to the public upon subjects of speculation in a looser and very different method. Far from always laying down propositions, and then entering upon the proof of them, they as frequently begin with observations or experiments, and show how they lead to the principles they intend to establish: or, in a treatise of a considerable extent, they use sometimes the one, and sometimes the other method, naming the proposition before the proof, or the proof before the proposition, as they imagine the one or the other will introduce their sentiments with the most advantage, and make their performance the most agreeable to their readers.

As

3

As the *analytic* method of communicating any truth is, properly speaking, nothing more than a copy of the method of its *investigation*, the more minute delineation of this procefs is beft referred to logic, which treats profeffedly of the nature of thofe inveftigations. Little, therefore, needs to be added here to what was faid in the comparifon of the two methods, and the cafes in which they are each of them beft applied. A few obfervations in this place fhall fuffice.

Notwithftanding the analytic method of communicating truth be properly a copy of the method of inveftigation, it is manifeftly fuperfluous to relate every ftep of any *actual procefs*. As it could not but happen that, in the courfe of every inquiry, a variety of obfervations muft have occurred which were foreign to the purpofe, and many hypothefes have fuggefted themfelves which fubfequent obfervations obliged us to reject. Thefe abortive notions, contributing nothing to the illuftration of the fubject, it is moft advifeable, in general, to omit; unlefs, in confequence of confiderable ftrefs having been previoufly laid upon them, it be requifite to fhow that fuch ftrefs was unreafonable; that particular facts and obfervations, which had been urged in treating upon that fubject, had no relation to it, and that particular hypothefes, advanced and contended for by others, were ill founded. Much more, therefore, may often, with advantage, be introduced into an analytic inquiry, which is made after other unfuccefsful inquiries, and particularly when popular prejudices have been adopted upon any fubject, than would be neceffary or proper, in a difcuffion intirely new, and with refpect to which there were, confequently, few prejudices to obviate, and few objections to anfwer.

In

In this latter cafe, that fet of obfervations is the beft chofen
which leads moft directly to that only hypothefis which we have
in view, and intend to eftablifh ; and the moft pleafing, as well
as the moft fatisfactory method of conducting fuch an inquiry is,
that which is as near an imitation as poffible of the method of
approximation, in feveral of the mathematical fciences. Let the
final difcovery be opened by degrees, by advancing, in the firft
place, fuch obfervations as make our hypothefis only probable, or
which conclude equally in favour of it and fome others. Let the
probability grow ftronger by degrees, by fubfequent obfervations
excluding, in their turns, more and more of the remaining hypothefes ; and let the *experimenta crucis*, which abfolutely ex-
clude all others whatever, be referved for the laft.

When writers do not difpofe their arguments in this manner,
" they lofe," as Dr. Hartley well obferves, " much of their clear-
" nefs and force. *Sir Ifaac Newton's Optics, Chronology*, and
" *Comment on Daniel*," he fays, " abound with inftances to this
" purpofe ; and it is probable that his great abilities and practice
" in algebraic inveftigations led him to it infenfibly."

Since *example* contributes as much to inftruction as precept, I
fhall, for the farther illuftration of thefe rules, fubjoin an account of the method in which fome of our moft celebrated and
approved writers have conducted their argumentative difcourfes
upon fome important fubjects.

I fhall only premife one general obfervation, which is, that
treatifes written profeffedly upon the *whole* of any branch of fcience, and which are not taken up with the difcuffion of any fingle
queftion, are neceffarily of a very mixed nature, with refpect to
their method. For, according to the received divifions of fcience, they muft, generally, confift of parts that are of a nature

I   very

very different from one another, and which, therefore, require to be difcuffed in a very different manner. Sometimes a regular demonftration is ufed; in other places the analyfis is preferred, and the practical parts of the fcience are explained in the method of didactic narration, intermixed with the reafons (borrowed from the fcientific parts of the fubject) on which the precepts are founded.

Mr. Locke, propofing, in his excellent *Treatife on the Human Underftanding,* to inquire into the origin, certainty, and extent of human knowledge, together with the grounds and degrees of belief, opinion, and affent; confiders, in the firft place, all the properties and diftinctions of *ideas,* as the elements of all our knowledge, and traces the fources from which, and the channels by which, they are conveyed to our minds. He then confiders in what manner, and with what degrees of accuracy, *words* are made to reprefent all thefe varieties of ideas, with what relates to the proper ufe and abufe of words; and, laftly, from thefe preliminaries, as fo many certain facts and *data,* he draws the conclufions he had in view, concerning the nature and bounds of that knowledge, which refults from the perception of the pro-perties and relations of thefe ideas, and the imperfection attend-ing the communication of this knowledge by words. All, there-fore, that he advances upon the fubject of *ideas* and *words* muft be confidered as *definitions, axioms,* or *lemmas,* to be ufed in the demonftration of the propofition he lays down in the remaining part of the treatife.

In examining the properties of fome claffes of ideas, he is led into large difquifitions concerning fome particular ideas; as thofe of *power, identity, &c.* but whether his opinions concerning

thefe

thefe ideas be juft or not, it by no means affects the truth or ufe-fulnefs of the bulk of his obfervations and conclufions.

His manner of amplification is very diffufe, and his method in the former part, didactic and narrative; relating a feries of obfervations on the properties of ideas, with a tacit appeal to every man's confcioufnefs of the truth of what he advances.

In MR. HUTCHESON's *Treatife of Moral Philofophy*, we are firft prefented with a narrative delineation of the feveral powers and principles of human nature, the juftnefs of which human experience and human actions are fuppofed to avouch. Having delineated the internal frame of man, he defcribes the various ufes to which thefe powers may be applied, and the various plea-fures and enjoyments we receive by their means. The nature of each of thefe fpecies of pleafure he examines feparately, in order to determine which of them contributes moft to human happi-nefs, and thereby conftitutes the chief good of man.

The refult of this analytical inquiry is, that the chief good of man confifts in the gratification of thofe affections which have the happinefs of our fellow-creatures for their object, or are con-nected with it; which affections are termed virtuous.

Virtue, thus explained, he branches out into its feveral kinds, and particularly fhews the extent of it, as refpecting God, man-kind, and ourfelves. Laftly, he demonftrates, more particularly, the various obligations of virtue, in the principal cafes that may occur in a ftate of nature, and likewife thofe which occur in a ftate of civil fociety; the *right*, and the *lawful*, in every cafe being determined by the tendency any action hath to promote the good of mankind in general, or of any particular fociety whofe intereft is confiftent with it.

LECTURE

LECTURE X.

Of the METHOD *of Mr.* Hume's Inquiry into the Principles of Morals, Hartley's Obfervations on Man, Harris's Hermes, *that of* Sermons, *and of* Mifcellaneous Writings.

THE plan of the moſt valuable part of Mr. HUME's *inquiry concerning the principles of morals,* is nearly the ſame with that part of Mr. Hutcheſon's Moral Philoſophy, which correſponds to it, and may moſt properly be termed *analytical.* For, in order to determine *the foundation of virtue,* he conſiders particularly every thing that is acknowledged to gain the eſteem of mankind; examining upon what common property it is that their encomiums turn, and in what meaſure their approbation is beſtowed; and having found that nothing is the object of eſteem but what is *uſeful to ſociety,* and, moreover, that the ſeveral virtues are claſſed in the firſt or ſecond rank of importance, according as they are more or leſs eſſential to the well-being of ſociety, he concludes, that *public utility* is the foundation of all virtue.

This ingenious writer greatly excels in his method of conducting argumentative diſcourſes, and, particularly, we ſee clearly in his writings the advantage of p opoſing ſingular opinions in the method of analyſis. The greater part of his diſcourſes are ſo

exact

exact a copy of the easiest and most perfect method of investigation, that we imagine we see, in every step of the process, the
very manner in which he himself was led to conceive the sentiments he recommends.   To obviate objections, he carefully con-
ceals the result of some of his inquiries, till his reader be prepared
for it, by such a happy gradation of previous observations and
inferences, that he cannot tell how to avoid it; and if, at that
time, he should wish to refuse his assent, and hesitate about it,
as he has, before he was aware, assented to all the premises, he
is at a loss where to found his objection.   This writer ought,
therefore, to be read with very great caution.

Dr. Hartley, proposing a new hypothesis of the principles of the human mind, examines very particularly every
thing relating to, or dependent upon the mind of man, viz. sensations, ideas, muscular motion, the external senses, affections,
memory, imagination, reasoning, dreams, &c. and endeavours to
show that none of the phenomena of any of them contradict his
hypothesis; that many of them admit a peculiarly easy and complete illustration by it; and that the most difficult cases are not
rendered more difficult, but rather easier by the help of it.   And
lest this hypothesis concerning the principles of the human
mind should be suspected to bear an unfavourable aspect upon
a plan of human duty, and human expectations, he considers the
whole of both systematically; showing, whenever he hath opportunity, that the evidences of religion, natural and revealed,
with the rule of life drawn from it, receive additional light and
evidence from it; and, lastly, that it hath a happy influence both
upon our conduct in this life, and upon our expectations after
death.

This

This is the general plan of that immenſe work. The particular method of it is ſtrictly geometrical, and ſynthetical. The author begins with definitions and axioms, lays down formal propoſitions, and advances ſuch proof as the nature of the caſe will admit. He deduces formal corollaries from almoſt every propoſition, and in the *ſcholia* he explains the nature of his proofs, and ſhows in what manner evidence is reflected from one part to another. Interſperſed through the whole of this work is a vaſt variety of curious and uſeful knowledge.

This method may not, at firſt ſight, ſeem ſo well adapted to a theory ſo much *original* as that of Dr. Hartley; and it muſt certainly have been a work of great labour and difficulty to digeſt a ſet of ſentiments, ſo intirely new, into ſo regular and ſyſtematical a form; becauſe in a ſynthetic diſcourſe every thing that is advanced muſt have one particular place, and no other: whereas in the analytic method there is much greater latitude. For that method is a copy of the method of inveſtigation, and the ſame thought may occur to the mind in a variety of connexions. Nevertheleſs, ſo *extenſive* a theory could not eaſily have been delivered without confuſion in any other method. Beſides, it was enough to recommend this method to Dr. Hartley, that, of all others, it is the *faireſt*, and ſhows the greateſt impartiality; as a treatiſe in this form is the moſt commodious for examination, and ſuggeſts the eaſieſt method of ſhowing the fallacy of it, if it be falſe. A perſon would be much more at a loſs how to anſwer Mr. Hume, than Dr. Hartley.

Mr. Harris, propoſing in his *Hermes* to trace the firſt principles of ſpeech, and to ſhow, by an analytical proceſs, in what manner they may be inveſtigated, firſt examines intire *ſentences,*

ces, and confiders what differences, in the forms of expreffions, correfpond to the differences in their meaning. Having thus difcovered the properties of different fentences; he confiders the particular *words* that compofe fentences, and thus having, by degrees, arrived at the fimpleft elements of fpeech, and difcovered how many differences there are in words, or the number of general heads to which they may be reduced, he hath completely accomplifhed his fcheme of analyfis.

It may not be unufeful to obferve, in order to illuftrate the variety of method, that another perfon, intending to draw up a fynthetic or fyftematic treatife upon the fame fubject, for the ufe of learners, would moft naturally take a method the very reverfe of Mr. Harris's. For example, he would, in the firft place, enumerate the feveral claffes into which *words* may be diftributed, and fhow the modifications that each of them admit. After this he would fhow in what manner thefe words, according to their different fpecies, form *fentences*, and how thefe fentences are combined into *periods*. This is the method of the General Grammar of *Meffieurs de Port Royal*, and others.

Divines conduct their inquiries into the fenfe of the facred writers upon any controverted fubject in a method nearly analytical. For, in order to give their readers intire fatisfaction with regard to their impartiality, they produce all the texts of fcripture relating to the queftion in debate, ranging them under fuch proper heads as the nature of the undertaking requires, and afcertaining the meaning of every paffage they quote with all poffible accuracy; and they deduce the doctrine they contend for as an inference fairly drawn from the texts thus collected and compared.

It

It makes no material difference in the method of these inquiries, if the opinion of the writer be advanced in the entrance of the work, and the texts be afterwards produced as proofs of what he advances. All such propositions require to be proved by an *induction of particulars*; and it is a capital thing, in the conduct of these inquiries, that the induction be as complete as possible.

Our best SERMONS, with respect to the method of their composition, are of two kinds. Some are intended to be a demonstration of some doctrine of religion, or a discourse upon some religious duty, with proper inferences, in the regular synthetic method. Others are usually called *textual*, because the writers, assuming some text of scripture, endeavour to extract from it all the useful information and direction it contains. They accordingly, in this latter method, divide their subject into as many parts as their text contains distinct articles, and treat of each separately, according to its nature. The method of this kind of sermons admits of endless variety, but the text cannot be changed.

To the former the text serves only as a *motto*, and may be changed at pleasure; the method being suggested by the *subject*, and not at all by the *text*. It follows, likewise, from the account given in the preceding lectures of the best method of conducting a demonstration, that there must be a great uniformity in the plan of these discourses, and that each will exhaust the whole subject.

To remedy this inconvenience, it is usual, and it introduces an agreeable variety into this kind of sermons, to take only some part of such a scheme of synthesis into one discourse. Some intire discourses, for instance, are usefully taken up in *definition* only, or in determining the sense of terms of considerable consequence; such as *faith*, *grace*, &c. and, where wrong senses

I

have

have been affixed to such terms, it hath a good effect, in giving the sense of them, to do it, as it is usually termed, both *negatively* and *positively*; that is, to explain, in the first place, what the sense is *not*, and then what it *is*. But let every interpretation that is distinctly refuted and rejected be such as either actually *is*, *hath been*, or very probably *may be* adopted. Otherwise the negative definition is superfluous and ridiculous. Indeed, in many circumstances, to take notice of several that do fall within the above-mentioned limitations would be trifling and useless.

Besides, in order to avoid unnecessarily opposing popular prejudices, it is generally advisable to define important words justly, without taking the least notice of other senses that have long been affixed to them. The very mention of them, though with a view to refute them, will very often only tend to strengthen the mechanical association by which the words and the wrong sense have been connected. These strong associations are like *habits*, which require to be treated with great caution, and must not be combated by bringing the ideas belonging to them frequently before the mind. Opposite ideas must be introduced, and they be suffered to disappear, as it were, gradually, and of themselves.

Other discourses present us with the proof only of any doctrine or duty with one distinct set of arguments, or even illustrate one particular proof. Others are employed in answering objections, or only some particular objections. In others again, after a brief explication, we are shewn the *effects* of a doctrine, duty, or habit of mind in speculative or practical *inferences*.

In short, as either a single part, or any combination of the parts of a complete synthesis may be usefully employed to form a discourse, the variety that may be introduced in those discourses, which are not confined to any particular *text*, but which

K   relate

relate to the *subject*, is prodigious. And, in general, it will be found to be much more agreeable to an auditory to hear a subject treated in a variety of discourses, from different texts, and at different times; each of which, by this method of distribution, may appear to be *complete of itself,* than to have their minister make use of the same text, and the same heads of discourse, till the whole subject is exhausted.

The above processes, of *synthesis* and *analysis*, are calculated either to demonstrate truth unknown to others, or to set one that is known in the strongest point of light; and when a person proposes to treat a subject fully, with either of these views, he cannot do better than to take one or other of those methods, according as the nature of the case will direct. But supposing the subject a person writes upon be familiar, and his sentiments be so generally received, that he need be under no concern about the *proof* of them; he may, for the sake of an agreeable variety, adopt almost whatever method he pleases. In such a case there is no part of a discourse, and no sentiment belonging to it, but what may, by the address of the composer, be introduced in almost any place whatever, and the rest of the discourse be so adjusted, as to occasion no sensible confusion or disorder. To see this executed in the happiest manner, consult the *Spectator*, and other celebrated familiar essays.

To illustrate this in one instance. Mr. ADDISON's beautiful essay on *omens*, *Spectator*, No. 7, is introduced by a very diverting account of some incidents that happened in a visit which he made. These occasion a reflection on the folly of adding to the real evils of life by such superstitious fears and supernumerary duties. To confirm this he recites a variety of other instances similar to those that occurred to him upon his visit. These introduce

duce

duce other observations on the folly of that kind of superstition; and the essay closes with the proper method of fortifying the mind against those terrors, and an account of his own temper and practice with respect to them.

The method of this kind of essays is admired in proportion as the turn and succession of thought in them appears easy and natural. Consequently, the only thing to be attended to, with regard to it, is the *transition* from sentiment to sentiment. Let the train be such as that it may be conceived probable that the thoughts would naturally suggest one another in the order in which they are put down; and whatever the piece consists of, whether observations, reflections, arguments, &c. (provided they be in themselves just and striking) the essay will appear natural, easy, and agreeable.

The Ode, and most other poems, which may be analysed into a mixture of narration and reflection, must be allowed the same latitude. Some bounds, however, must be set to the licentiousness of the human imagination, particularly that of poets, which otherwise would ramble from one subject to another by very slight transitions, such as may be forgotten the moment they have been made use of, and consequently wholly omitted in the composition: so that, though a real train of connected ideas transmitted the thoughts of the poet from one subject to another, there remain no traces of that medium of transition, and the reader can perceive no connexion at all between the parts of it.

Something of *unity* ought, undoubtedly, to be preserved through the whole of every intire piece, whether in prose or verse; and to this general design of the whole, every part, wherever situated, ought to bear some relation.　As in a piece of music, not-

K 2

withstanding

withftanding the feeming wild excurfion of the notes, they are all chords to that which is called the key-note.

A want of fufficient connection is manifeft in many of the odes of Horace; the epifode of Eurydice in the laft book of the Georgics, feems to have been introduced rather on account of its own beauty than its relation to the fubject of the book; and it has exercifed the utmoft ingenuity of critics to fhow the propriety of feveral parts of Pindar's poems. In general, the moderns pay more attention to regularity than the ancients.

I would obferve, at the conclufion of this part of the courfe, that the whole ufe of topics and of the difpofition of them, hitherto explained, hath for its object and end the *informing of the judgment*, and *influencing the practice*, and that this is the only direct and proper, at leaft the ultimate end of oratory. The pleafure that a difcourfe may give to the *imagination*, or the emotion it may raife in the *paffions*, are things that are brought about more indirectly, being effected by the *manner* in which things that tend ultimately to *convince* and *perfuade* are expreffed. The orator may, indeed, intend to pleafe or affect his hearers; but, if he underftands himfelf, he only means to influence their *judgments*, or *refolutions*, by the medium of the imagination or the paffions.

In thefe two preceding parts of this courfe, therefore, thofe things have been confidered which are more peculiarly the proper objects of an orator, and *effential* to his views. In what remains will be explained what is, though very greatly, yet indirectly of fervice to him, and an *advantage* rather than a neceffary part of his art. This thought, by the way, fuggefts an important advice, with which I fhall conclude this part.

Let

Let the firft, and principal view of every orator, whether in writing or fpeaking, be to *inform the judgment*, and thereby *direct the practice*; and let him only atttempt to *pleafe*, or *affect*, when it is fubfervient to that defign; when the occafion itfelf, in a manner, prompts to it, and the bent of his own genius leads him to comply with fuch an invitation.

PART

PART III.

OF

STYLE.

LECTURE XI.

Of TASTE, *and the Nature of* FIGURATIVE LANGUAGE.

THE third part into which the art of oratory is diftributed, comprehends whatever is *ornamental* in a difcourfe or compofition. The bare materials, and even the difpofition of them in a difcourfe, are adapted to do little more than make an impreffion upon thofe perfons who, of themfelves, and from a regard to the nature and importance of the fubject, will give their attention to it; whereas the fubject of this laft part is calculated to attract and engage the attention, by the grace and harmony of the ftyle, the turn of thought, or the ftriking or pleafing manner

in

in which fentiments are introduced and expreffed. We have hitherto examined what we may call the bones, mufcles, and nerves of a compofition; we now come to the covering of this body, to defcribe the external lineaments, the colour, the complexion, and graceful attitude of it.

In treating of this part of my fubject, I fhall endeavour to lay open the fources of all the pleafures we receive from this moft refined art, explaining what are the properties, or principles, in our frame which lay the mind open to its influences, as well as defcribe the various forms of expreffion which are found, by experience, to affect our minds in fo agreeable a manner, and give examples of fuch forms of expreffion.

Whatever contributes to adorn a difcourfe, muft either give life and beauty to the *fentiment*, or harmony to the *diction*. I fhall confider each of thefe in their order. By ornament of *thoughts*, I mean that manner of introducing and prefenting them to the mind which will give them the moft favourable appearance. This, therefore, comprehends all the pleafures which may be faid to be perceived by the *mind*; whereas, when I treat of the ornament of *diction*, I fhall confider the language as affecting the *ear* only.

Whatever it be, in the fentiment or ideas, that makes a difcourfe to be read with pleafure, muft either be *interefting*, by exciting thofe grofs and more fenfible feelings we call *paffions*, or muft awaken thofe more delicate fenfations, which are generally called the *pleafures of the imagination*. Each of thefe kinds of feelings are, by fome philofophers, referred to fo many diftinct *reflex*, or *internal fenfes*, as they call thofe faculties of the mind by which we perceive them; whereas, according to Dr. Hartley's theory, thofe fenfations confift of nothing more than a congeries

or

or combination of ideas and sensations, separately indistinguish-able, but which were formerly associated either with the idea it-self that excites them, or with some other idea, or circumstance, attending the introduction of them. It is this latter hypothesis that I adopt, and, by the help of it, I hope to be able to throw some new light on this curious subject.

An enumeration of the *stronger passions* of the human mind, which are roused by the powers of oratory, and the art of com-position, I regard as foreign to my undertaking to attempt : but it may, with reason, be expected that I should describe those *finer feelings* which constitute *the pleasures of the imagination*, and which are seldom attended to in any delineations of human na-ture ; as also some *critical situations of mind* respecting the passions and emotions in general, the knowledge of which is essential to criticism upon works of genius and imagination; and explain those *forms of address* which are *adapted to gain assent*. But, previous to this, I shall give some account of *Taste*, and of the difference between *plain* and *figurative language*.

An exquisite feeling of the finer sensations abovementioned, may be said to constitute a *fine taste :* but no person can be a com-plete *judge* of the merit of a composition unless he perfectly un-derstand the subject of it, so as both clearly to distinguish the character of the *design*; as whether it be great or mean, new or common, &c. and also to judge how far the execution is adapted to the undertaking.

The well-known story of the shoemaker viewing the Venus of Apelles, may assist us to distinguish our ideas in this case. This artisan discovered no strong sense of pleasure upon the sight of so extraordinary an effect of human genius, and therefore could

L   not

not be faid to have *tafte*, but he certainly was a very good judge of the proportions of the foot and of the fhoe.

Judgment is univerfally acknowledged to be altogether acquired, and that *tafte*, too, or the capacity of perceiving the pleafures of imagination, may alfo be acquired, to a very great degree, is evident from the actual acquirement of a variety of fimilar taftes, even late in life. Inftances of this may be given in a tafte for flowers, for gardening, and for architecture, which are hardly ever acquired very early in life.

It is hardly poffible that any perfon who never attempted to fketch out an object himfelf, fhould have a high relifh for the beauties of painting; but let any perfon be inftructed in drawing, let him be much employed in viewing and examining a great variety of pictures, let him be led to converfe much with painters, and other connoiffeurs in that art; and I think one might pronounce, without any great apprehenfion of being miftaken, that he would, infallibly, not only acquire *judgment* in the productions of that art, and be able to diftinguifh a fine defign and execution, but that he would have a *relifh* for it, that what he approved he would *admire*, and that the view of it would affect him with a fenfible pleafure. The fame may be faid with refpect to mufick, poetry, and all the other fine arts.

Befides, it will appear very clearly, in our progrefs through this fubject, that all the *principles of tafte* in works of genius, the very fources from which all thefe fine pleafures are derived, are within the reach of all perfons whatfoever; and that fcarce any perfon can pafs his life in cultivated fociety, where the fine arts flourifh, without acquiring, in a greater or a lefs degree, a tafte for fome or other of them.

In

In fact, since all emotions excited by works of genius consist of such ideas and sensations as are capable of being associated with the perception of such works, nothing can be requisite to the acquisition of taste, but exposing the mind to a situation in which those associated ideas will be frequently presented to it. A great deal, however, depends upon the time of life, and other circumstances, in which such impressions are made upon the mind. Youth, especially, which is favourable to all impressions, is peculiarly favourable to these. But this circumstance makes a difference in *degree* only, and not in the nature of the thing. Some persons may also have acquired a dislike to these, as well as other studies; but as this dislike was produced by an early association of ideas, so it may be overcome by opposite associations. It must not be forgotten, also, that as our bodies in general differ with respect to their *sensibility to impressions*, so the texture of the brain, on which the mental faculties depend, must be subject to a similar difference.

I proposed in this place to shew in what figurative and ornamented style consists. In plain unadorned style every thing is called by its proper name, no more words are used than are apparently sufficient to express the sense, and the form and order of every part of the sentence are such as exactly express the real state of mind of him that uses it; not a question, for instance, being asked when the person who makes it is able to supply the answer. It is not enough to say, that plain unadorned style is that mode of expression which is the most *natural*: for style the most highly ornamented, and enlivened with the strongest figures, is as natural as the plain style, and occurs as naturally, without the precepts of art, and even without design, in proper circumstances.

Style

Style may be said to be figurative when the literal interpretation, according to the usual sense of words, and the construction of them, would lead a person to mistake the sense; as, for instance, when any thing is signified by a term which was not originally affixed to it; when the terms which are used to express any thing would, if interpreted literally, lead a person to imagine it was greater or less than it is; and when the form of the sentence is such as, when explained by the rules of grammar only, doth not truly express the state of mind of him that uses it.

Notwithstanding this, style that is merely figurative and ornamented, is far from being calculated to *deceive*. For whenever it is used, no other language, or mode of speech, could give so true an idea of the state of the speaker's mind, though it is confessed to be by no means *literally* expressive of that state. For instance, when *Virgil* calls the two *Scipios*, *the Thunderbolts of War*, he makes use of an ornamented and highly-figurative expression, not corresponding to his real sentiments; for he would never have replied in the affirmative, if he had been asked seriously whether he really imagined they were two thunderbolts; and yet no plainer terms, though more expressive of their true character, would have given his readers so clear an idea of the *force* and *impetuosity* which he meant to ascribe to those heroes.

Again, when the same excellent and correct poet says that mount *Ætna threw its fires as high as the stars*, nobody taxes him with a designed falsehood; though his expressions be not literally true, and we are sure he could not but have been sensible of it himself at the time that he made use of them: but nothing short of an hyperbole could have given us a true image of the effort of his imagination, to express his idea of the very great height of those flames.

Lastly,

Laſtly, when Æneas, in the ſame poet, in the midſt of the relation of his adventures, comes to mention *Sicily*, inſtead of ſaying, in ſo many words, that *his father died there*, addreſſes himſelf directly to his father, and exclaims, *Hic me, pater optime, feſſum deſeris*; do any of his readers imagine he really conceived his father to be within hearing ? But no ſimple narration could ſufficiently have expreſſed that ſtrong regret, and tender affection, which the revival of his father's memory awakened in his mind. We naturally *perſonify* every thing that cauſes us much pleaſure or pain, and a vivid recollection makes every thing ſeem preſent. Thus this direct addreſs to the dead Anchiſes, though, ſtrictly ſpeaking, without the leaſt foundation, gives us the trueſt idea of the unfeigned grief of Æneas, and of the affecting ſenſe he had of his loſs, and therefore lets us into the true ſtate of his mind ; not, indeed, by a direct interpretation of his words, but in a more certain, though an indirect manner, by means of thoſe *circumſtances* which always accompany that ſtate of mind.

Figurative ſpeech, therefore, is indicative of a perſon's real feelings and ſtate of mind, not by means of the words it conſiſts of, conſidered as *ſigns of ſeparate ideas*, and interpreted according to their common acceptation ; but as *circumſtances* naturally attending thoſe feelings which compoſe any ſtate of mind. Thoſe figurative expreſſions, therefore, are ſcarce conſidered and attended to as *words*, but are viewed in the ſame light as *attitudes, geſtures,* and *looks*, which are infinitely more expreſſive of *ſentiments* and *feelings* than words can poſſibly be.

Since, however, the literal impropriety of figurative expreſſions is excuſed only on account of their being conſidered as indications of thoſe feelings and ſentiments which no words, literally interpreted, could deſcribe, they ſhould never be uſed but

I   when

when the fituation of the perfon who ufes them is fuch as will render thofe feelings and fentiments natural. Otherwife, there being nothing left to excufe and cover the impropriety of the figure, the words prefent nothing but the *naked abfurdity*, and the writer is detected, either in pretending to feelings that could have no exiftence, or in afferting what is apparently falfe and contradictory. This obfervation may be applied to every figure of fpeech; and as it is an obfervation of confiderable confequence, it will be frequently repeated, and applied to the particular figures, when they come to be feparately explained and illuftrated.

LECTURE

L E C T U R E   XII.

The Division of this Part of the Work into what affects the PASSIONS, JUDGMENT, *and* IMAGINATION.

Of the Effect of VIVID REPRESENTATION, *the Use of the* PRESENT TENSE *in describing past Scenes, and of* PARTICULAR NAMES *and* CIRCUMSTANCES.

HAVING considered the nature of taste, and of figurative language in general, I proceed to consider distinctly the several objects that offer themselves to our attention respecting the *ornament* that sentiment admits of. These, as they were before pointed out, are either some of the more remarkable and general affections of the stronger *passions*; those forms of address which are adapted to engage *assent*, or those finer feelings which constitute the *pleasures of the imagination.* Each of these three objects will engage our attention in the order in which they are here mentioned.

The first observation I shall make on *the general affections of the passions*, is, that they are engaged, and we feel ourselves interested, in proportion to the *vividness of our ideas* of those objects and circumstances which contribute to excite them. The genuine

and

and proper use of the paffions undoubtedly is to rouze men to juft and vigorous action upon every emergency, without the flow intervention of reafon. It is, therefore, wifely provided, that they fhould be raifed by the immediate view and apprehenfion of the circumftances proper for their exertion. Being, therefore, blind and mechanical principles, they can only be connected with the view of fuitable circumftances; fo that, whenever thefe are prefented, whether the paffion would, in fact, be ufeful or not, it cannot fail to be excited, and to rife to its ufual height.

This obfervation fupplies us with a reafon why our minds are as fenfibly affected with fcenes of *paft*, or even of *ideal diftrefs*, as with a mere relation of what is *prefent* and *real*. All the advantage that the latter circumftances united have, is, that they engage us to think more intenfely of the cafe, which will confequently make the ideas more vivid, and the fcene more interefting. But that fcenes of *ideal* diftrefs have as much power over the imagination as fcenes of diftrefs that are *paft*, cannot but be allowed, when we confider, that even reafon can plead nothing more in favour of the one than of the other; fince the paffion is equally *unavailing* in both cafes. Why may I not, with reafon, be as much interefted in the adventures of Æneas or Telemachus, as in thofe of Themiftocles, Xenophon, or any of the heroes of Greece or Rome? If the one never had any exiftence, neither have the other any at prefent, which, with refpect to the *final caufes* of our paffions, is the fame thing.

The faithful hiftorian, and the writer of romances, having the fame accefs to the fprings of the human paffions, it is no wonder that the latter generally moves them more forcibly, fince he hath the choice of every circumftance that contributes to raife them; whereas the former hath nothing in his power but the *difpofition*

of

of them, and is reſtricted even in that. I fancy, however, that
no perſon of reading and obſervation can doubt of the fact, that
more tears have been ſhed, and more intenſe joy hath been expreſſed in the peruſal of novels, romances, and feigned tragedies,
than in reading all the true hiſtories in the world. Who ever,
upon any occurrence in real hiſtory, ever felt what he muſt feel
in reading Clariſſa, George Barnwell, Eloiſa, and many other
well-contrived fictions. It is to no purpoſe to ſay to ourſelves,
" This is all a fiction, why am I thus affected ?" if we read, and
form an *idea* of the ſcenes there exhibited, we muſt *feel* in
ſpite of ourſelves. The thought of its being a fiction enables us
to make but a feeble and ineffectual effort to repreſs our feelings,
when the ideas which excite them are very ſtrong and vivid.
Some perſons, however, may have acquired ſuch an averſion to
all works of fiction, that they cannot be prevailed upon to give
that unprejudiced attention to them which this experiment requires.

The uſe of the *preſent tenſe* in the narration of paſt events,
contributes greatly to heighten the ideal preſence of any ſcene.
This form of narration is introduced with the moſt advantage
when a preceding lively and animated deſcription hath already,
as it were, tranſported the reader into the ſcene of action. In
that ſituation of mind, he is ſo far from being ſenſible of the real
impropriety of that ſtyle, that it appears to him the moſt natural;
and indeed no other would correſpond to his feelings : and too
precipitate a return to the proper ſtyle of narration would have a
very bad effect, as it would put an end to the pleaſing *illuſion*,
which makes the ſcene ſo intereſting, and which can continue no
longer than while the reader conceives himſelf preſent with the

M   objects

objects that are prefented to his imagination. In the following poetical defcription of a battle, we have an example of a very *natural*, and therefore (for the reafon given above) *unperceived* tranfition from the preter to the prefent time.

> And now with fhouts the fhocking armies clofed,
> To lances lances, fhields to fhields oppofed;
> Hoft againft hoft the fhadowy legions drew,
> The founding darts an iron tempeft flew;
> Victors and vanquifh'd *join* promifcuous cries,
> Triumphing fhouts and dying groans *arife*.
> With ftreaming blood the flipp'ry field *is* dy'd,
> And flaughter'd heroes *fwell* the dreadful tide.

In the following defcriptions we cannot but feel the ill effect of too precipitate a return to the proper ftyle of narration, and of the ftill worfe effect of paffing from time paft to the prefent, and from the prefent to the paft, as it were alternately in the fame fcene.

> Here all the terrors of grim war *appear*,
> Here *rages* force, here *tremble* flight and fear;
> Here *ftorm'd* contention, and here fury *frown'd*,
> And the dire orb portentous gorgon *crown'd*.

> > ILIAD V. 914.

> Then died Scamandrius, expert in the chace,
> In woods and wilds to wound the favage race:
> Diana taught him all her fylvan arts,
> To bend the bow, and aim unerring darts:
> But vainly here Diana's arts he *tries*,
> The fatal lance *arrefts* him as he flies;

From

From Menelaus' arm the weapon fent
Thro' his broad back and heaving bofom *went* :
Down finks the warrior with a thund'ring found,
His brazen armour *rings* againſt the ground.

ILIAD V. 65.

Since no form of expreſſion can appear natural, unleſs it correfpond to the feelings of the perfon who ufes it, let no writer
adopt the prefent tenfe in defcribing a paſt tranfaction, unleſs the
fcene be fo interefting, that the reader can hardly help realizing
it, and fancying that he actually fees and hears every thing that
is reprefented; otherwife the affectation becomes fenfible, and
cannot fail to give difguſt.

It is a very extravagant ſtretch of this figure when a public
fpeaker reprefents a fcene that is paſt or future as prefent in the
very place of audience; for it requires an illufion capable not
only of affecting the imagination, but of impofing upon the
bodily fenfes too, to cover the abfurdity of fuch language.
Let this obfervation be applied to fome preachers when they defcribe the day of judgment.

Thefe obfervations relating to the vivid reprefentation of objects, ſhow us the importance of a difcreet ufe of fiction, and
works of imagination, for the cultivation of the human heart.
The heart is inſtructed chiefly by its own feelings. It is of confequence, therefore, how they are directed, and it cannot be a
matter of indifference what tales and novels are put into the
hands of children and youth. When once perfons are of an age
to form ideas of fuch defcriptions, and feel the fenfations refulting
from them, reading a romance is nearly the fame thing as their
feeing fo much of the world, and of mankind. Whatever, there-

M 2

fore,

fore, we ſhould think improper for them to *ſee*, it is improper for them to *read* or *hear*; for they have like ſenſations, and retain ſimilar impreſſions from both.

In the ſecond place, I would obſerve, with regard to the conduct of the paſſions, that to repreſent things to the life, in order thoroughly to affect and intereſt a reader in the peruſal of a compoſition, it is of ſingular advantage to be very *cirumſtantial*, and to introduce as many *ſenſible images* as poſſible.

The powers of art have no other means of exciting our paſſions than by preſenting ſuch ſcenes as are found to excite them in real life. Now in nature, and real life, we ſee nothing but *particulars*, and to theſe ideas alone are the ſtrongeſt ſenſations and emotions annexed. General and abſtract names are only ſubſtitutes for the particular, and are therefore farther removed from their connexion with real objects; inſomuch, that when general and abſtract terms are uſed, the imagination muſt be employed to reduce them to particulars, before any real ſcene can be imagined, or any paſſion raiſed. Now ſince general terms do not, without an effort of the imagination, ſuggeſt thoſe determinate ideas which alone have the power of exciting the paſſions, and the very exertion of ſuch an effort muſt, in ſome meaſure, prevent that temporary illuſion, which is requiſite to the ideal preſence of objects, it is proper that the writer, who would thoroughly affect and intereſt his reader, ſhould, as much as poſſible, make that effort unneſſary, by avoiding general and abſtract terms, and introducing the proper names of perſons and things, which have a more immediate connection with ſcenes of real life.

Every body muſt have experienced, in relating any thing that really happened, how difficult it is to avoid mentioning thoſe circumſtances

cumſtances of *time*, *place*, and *perſon*, which were orginally aſſociated with the particulars of the ſtory; and it is evident
(notwithſtanding it be generally eſteemed a mark of greater judgment to *generalize* ſtories, and omit thoſe particulars) that ſtories
told with all thoſe circumſtances, provided they be not ſo many as
to diſtract the mind of the hearer, and too much retard the relation of the principal incidents, are generally heard with more
attention.   In fact, it cannot be but that theſe circumſtances excite more determinate and preciſe ideas; and the more preciſe and
vivid are our ideas, with the greater ſtrength do they excite all
the emotions and paſſions that depend upon them.   The mention
of theſe particulars makes a relation to reſemble real and active
life.

So important is this obſervation, and ſo far is it from having
been thoroughly attended to, that it may almoſt furniſh a criterion
to diſtinguiſh true hiſtory from fable and romance.   Even the
beſt of our modern romances, which are a much more perfect
copy of human life than any of the fictions of the ancients, if
they be compared with true hiſtory, will be found to fall greatly
ſhort of it in their detail of ſuch particulars as, becauſe they have
a kind of *arbitrary*, and, as it were, *variable* connexion with
real facts, do not eaſily ſuggeſt themſelves to thoſe perſons who
attend only to the connexion and ſubordination of the incidents
they have invented, and who, therefore, never introduce more
perſons or things than are neceſſary to fill them up : whereas a
redundancy of particulars, which are not neceſſarily connected,
will croud into a relation of real facts.

It may not be improper to add, in this place, that the mention
of ſo many particular perſons, places, and times, in the books

I

of

of scripture affords, to the curious observers of nature and probability, no small evidence of their genuineness and truth.

The advice I would found upon these observations is, that a writer who would copy nature, and command the passions which are peculiar to the several scenes of it, should, in all narration or description, wherever the circumstances of a discourse will admit of it, prefer a more particular to a more general term; as *father, mother, brother, sister,* &c. instead of *relation*; *justice, temperance, veracity,* &c. and *cruelty, covetousness, deceit,* &c. as the case requires, instead of the more indefinite terms *virtue,* and *vice*; and universally, the proper names of persons, places, and things, rather than more comprehensive terms which are applicable to other ideas besides those that are intended to be conveyed.

Shakespeare interests his readers more than most other dramatic poets, because he copies nature and real life in this respect more closely than most others. It will, perhaps, not appear improbable that Shakespeare's frequent use of particular terms, and his attention to the choice of them, contributed not a little to his peculiar excellence in distinguishing the passions and characters of human nature; whereas dealing much in general terms, leads writers to confound all characters, and not to make those distinctions which nature doth. If it should be rather thought that Shakespeare's happiness in distinguishing characters led him to be so particular and circumstantial in his descriptions, it may be allowed, without contradicting the converse of this 'hypothesis; and it equally confirms the supposition of the connection that is here suggested to subsist between the distinguishing particular characters, and the use of particular terms. Homer abounds more in the minute details of circumstances than Virgil, and his characters are better distinguished. Virgil uses more general terms

2

upon

upon all occaſions, and the ſameneſs of his characters is remarkable.

To exemplify this obſervation, I ſhall ſubjoin a deſcription from
Shakeſpeare, of the manner in which a prodigy was talked of
among the common people, as being particularly excellent in its
kind.

> Old men, and beldams in the ſtreets
> Do prophecy upon it dangerouſly.
> Young Arthur's death is common in their mouths;
> And when they talk of him, they ſhake their heads,
> And whiſper one another in the ear;
> And he that ſpeaks doth graſp the hearer's wriſt,
> Whilſt he that hears makes fearful action,
> With wrinkled brows, with nods, with rolling eyes.
> I ſaw a ſmith ſtand with his hammer thus,
> The while his iron did on th' anvil cool,
> With open mouth ſwallowing a taylor's news,
> Who, with his ſhears and meaſure in his hand,
> Standing on ſlippers, which his nimble haſte
> Had falſely thruſt upon contrary feet,
> Told of a many thouſand warlike French
> That were embattled, and rank'd in Kent.
> Another lean, unwaſh'd artificer
> Cuts off his tale, and talks of Arthur's death.
>   Kɪɴɢ Jᴏʜɴ, Act IV. Scene 4.

The ſacred writings abound with the moſt lively and animating
deſcriptions, which derive their excellence from the notice that is
taken of particular circumſtances. See, among other paſſages,
Iſaiah xxxix. 4. to 15. and Jer. xiv. 15. to the end.

One

One reaſon why philoſophers ſeldom ſucceed in poetry, may be, that *abſtract ideas* are too familiar to their minds. Philoſophers are perpetually employed in reducing particular to general propoſitions, a turn of thinking very unfavourable to poetry. One reaſon, likewiſe, why poetry is generally ſooner brought to perfection than any other branch of polite literature, may be, that, in early ages, the ſtate of language is moſt favourable to poetry; as it then contains fewer abſtract terms. On this account, a poet in an early age has the advantage of a later poet, who has equal ſtrength of imagination. It may be ſaid that, to counterbalance this, the greater progreſs which the art of criticiſm will have made in a more refined age, will be an advantage to a later poet. But perhaps refinement in criticiſm may rather be unfavourable to the genuine ſpirit of poetry, as an attention to rules tends to deaden and diſſipate the fire of imagination.

LECTURE

LECTURE XIII.

Of the Tendency of strong Emotions *to produce* BELIEF, *and the* transferring of Passions *from one Object to another.*

THE tendency of strong emotions and passions to generate belief may help to throw light upon several things which occur upon the subject of criticism, and works of taste and genius. And that we should be prone to conclude, that very vivid ideas, and strong emotions of mind, are derived from external objects, and circumstances really existing, can be no matter of surprize, when we reflect that objects really existing do generally excite such ideas and emotions. *Vivid ideas* and *strong emotions,* therefore, having been, through life, associated with *reality,* it is easy to imagine that, upon the perception of the proper feelings, the associated idea of reality will likewise recur, and adhere to it as usual; unless the emotion be combined with such other ideas and circumstances as have had as strong an association with *fiction.* In this case the absurdity and impossibility of the scene precludes assent; and at the same time, by taking away the associated circumstance, it greatly weakens the original impression. But while the impressions remain vivid, and no certain marks of fiction appear, the idea of reality will occur; that is, the mind will find itself strongly inclined to believe the scene to be real.

N   This

This may help us to account for the satisfaction that is received, and particularly by youth, and all persons of little knowledge and experience, in reading the history of such beings and powers as far exceed every thing human, and which never could have had any existence ; as of *fairies* in European countries, *genies* in the East ; the *heathen gods and goddesses* in the ancient classical ages, and *knights-errant* and *necromancers* in modern story.

It may, likewise, suggest a reason why these stories are read with less pleasure by persons more advanced in years. In youth the vivid and magnified ideas presented by such stories, and the emotions consequent upon them, have a stronger association with *truth* than any improbable circumstances attending them have yet acquired with *falsehood*. In reading them, therefore, there is nothing to prevent the object from being conceived to be *ideally present*, and their unexperienced passions are excited mechanically, as by the presence of the like real objects. Whereas the association which such strange powers and properties have acquired with the ideas of *impossibility*, *falsehood*, and *absurdity*, in the minds of persons of considerable age and reflection, often makes it impossible for them, even in imagination, to conceive such things really to exist.

If, however, the fiction be consistent with itself, and be natural upon any uniform principles, or suppositions, so that it shall require only one single effort of the imagination to conceive the existence of the imaginary beings and powers, and the ideas of inconsistency and contradiction do not frequently occur through the course of the narration, to destroy the illusion ; a reader of a lively turn of mind, though of good discernment, may enter into the scene, and receive great pleasure from the performance. But still, in consequence of a thousand reiterated associations, all representationprefentations of things not founded on *nature* and *truth* will grow lefs and lefs interefting as men advance in life. Even thofe fictions which moft nearly refemble truth, have but little power of amufing perfons of great age and reflection. And that ftories in which are introduced fuch imaginary beings as the heathen gods, fairies, genies, necromancers, and the like, retain their power of amufing perfons of reading and tafte fo long as they do, may be afcribed to the impreffions made by them upon fuch perfons in their very early years; by means of which the fcenes in which they are exhibited are rendered much more vivid, and confequently have ftronger affociations with *reality* than they would have had, if thofe perfons had not been made acquainted with them, till they had been capable of perceiving their abfurdity.

Our pronenefs to verify ftrong fenfations may be feen, in the pleafure we receive from arguments intended to prove that there is fome foundation in true hiftory for thofe ftories which affected us ftrongly when we were young; for inftance, the fabulous hiftory and mythology of the Greeks; the poffibility of Æneas and Dido having been cotemporaries; the favourable hearing which arguments in proof of the reality of apparitions and witches have met with from many perfons of fenfe and experience; and from the pleafure which all perfons of tafte have lately received from the attempt to fhew the real correfpondence there is with nature and truth in the manners, cuftoms, ceremonies, and extravagancies of chivalry. May I not, likewife, appeal to all perfons of reading and imagination, if it would not give them a moft fenfible pleafure to receive certain information, that all the adventures of fuch perfons as *Robinfon Crufoe*, and others whofe fictitious ftories they have read with delight,

N 2   were

were literally true? And whatever we should receive pleasure from believing, we should certainly be *inclined* to believe.

This connexion of vivid ideas and emotions with reality, will easily furnish the mind with pretences for justifying the extravagance of such passions as love, gratitude, anger, revenge, and envy. If these passions be raised, though ever so unreasonably, they are often able, by this means, to adjust the object to their gratification. Besides, since, in consequence of almost constant joint impressions, all ideas are associated with other ideas similar to themselves, these passions, while the mind is under their influence, and as it were wholly occupied by them, will excite, in abundance, all such ideas as conspire with themselves, and preclude all attention to objects and circumstances connected with, and which would tend to introduce, an opposite state of mind.

In the eye of the captivated lover, the object of his affections appears with more charms than first excited his passion: and how apt are we to take offence at those persons who endeavour to give us an ill opinion of those who have shown us kindness or respect? On the other hand, how little merit can any body allow the man that hath affronted him? and how mean and contemptible a figure do those persons sometimes make in our imagination, whose superiority at first excited our envy?

An attention to these affections of our minds will show us the admirable propriety of innumerable fine touches of passion in our inimitable Shakespeare. How naturally doth he represent Cassius, full of envy at the greatness of Cæsar, whose equal he had been, dwelling upon every little circumstance which shows the natural weakness of him whom fortune had made his master. Speaking of their swimming together cross the Tiber, he says,

But

> But ere we could arrive the point propofed,
> Cæfar cry'd, Help me, Caffius, or I fink.
> I, as Æneas our great anceftor,
> Did from the flames of Troy, upon his fhoulder,
> The old Anchifes bear; fo from the waves of Tiber
> Did I the tired Cæfar.

Again, in the fame fpeech,

> He had a fever when he was in Spain,
> And when the fit was on him, I did mark
> How he did fhake. 'Tis true this god did fhake.
> ———————— I did hear him groan,
> Ay, and that tongue of his ————
> Alas! it cried, Give me fome drink, *Titinius*,
> As a fick girl. ————   JULIUS CÆSAR, Act I. Scene 3.

In the fame author, king Lear, expofed to a violent tempeft, with his mind full of the ingratitude of his daughters, to juftify his vexation and impatience, conceives them to have taken part with his daughters.

> ——————— Here I ftand your brave,
> A poor, infirm, weak, and defpifed old man.
> But yet I call you fervile minifters,
> That have with two pernicious daughters join'd
> Your high-engender'd battles, 'gainft a head
> So old, and white as this. Oh! Oh! 'tis foul.
>   Act III. Scene 2.

This is perfectly natural, provided we can fuppofe his mind to have been fo violently agitated as to perfonify, and feel real indig-

nation

nation againſt things inanimate, which (as will be explained ſhortly) is perhaps oftener the real caſe than is commonly imagined.

With equal regard to nature doth he repreſent Hamlet as ſhortening the time that intervened between the death of his father and the marriage of his mother with his uncle, becauſe that circumſtance heightened and gratified his indignation. At firſt he ſays,

> ——————— That it ſhould come to this!
> But two months dead; nay, not ſo much, not two.

Preſently after, in the ſame ſoliloquy,

> ——————— Yet within a month.

Afterwards he calls it a little month; and, at laſt,

> Ere yet the ſalt of moſt unrighteous tears
> Had left the fluſhing of her galled eyes,
> She married——Oh moſt wicked ſpeed, to poſt
> With ſuch dexterity to inceſtuous ſheets.
>
> Act I. Scene 1.

Nearly allied to this laſt obſervation is the following, that all ſtrong paſſions and emotions are liable to be transferred to indifferent objects, either related to the proper object, or thoſe whoſe ideas are accidentally preſent to the mind, at the time that it is under the influence of ſuch emotion or paſſion. This is nothing more than the ſimpleſt caſe of the aſſociation of ideas, but the effects of it are well worthy of our attention. Brute creatures, and even inanimate things, are not exempted from being, in this indirect manner, the objects of ſuch human paſſions, as it were the greateſt abſurdity to ſuppoſe them the *juſt* objects of.

Do

Do not all poets and writers of romance reprefent enamoured lovers in raptures with every thing belonging to the object of their affections, and taking uncommon pleafure in the groves, and every place where they have had their delightful interviews. Pious David envied even the fwallows which had built their nefts and laid their young in the Houfe of God. Aware of this, do not all perfons dread to communicate difagreeable information, and are they not eager to be the meffengers of good news? In the former cafe, the meffenger becomes the object of averfion; in the latter cafe, he is regarded with good-will and friendfhip.

The lofs or abfence of a friend may give fo much uneafinefs, that our impatience for the want of him, fhall produce a kind of indignation, which may, for a moment, fall even upon the object of our affection himfelf. This delicate circumftance, as Lord Kaimes obferves, hath not efcaped the notice of Shakefpeare, who hath given an exact idea of it, in the laft words of the following paffage :

——————————— He is drown'd
Whom thus we ftray to find, and the fea mocks
Our fruftrate fearch on land.   Well, let him go.
                    Tempest, Act III. Scene 3.

It is poffible, however, that the poet might have had nothing more in view than fimply to exprefs *acquiefcence in the event.* For the words, *Well, let him go,* will not exprefs any thing of *indignation,* without a particular tone, and manner, in the pronunciation of them.

With as true a hand hath he copied thefe finer touches of nature in reprefenting King *Richard* as expreffing his indignation

I   againft

againſt a horſe which had formerly been his, but which his enemy
had got poſſeſſion of, and then rode.

> That jade had eat bread from my royal hand;
> This hand hath made him proud with clapping him.
> Would he not ſtumble? Would he not fall down?
> (Since pride muſt have a fall) and break the neck
> Of that proud man that did uſurp his back.
>
> RICHARD II. Act V. Scene 11.

In the ſame maſter of the human feelings we ſee the mind of
Othello, when thrown into a violent perturbation by the firſt ſuſ-
picion of jealouſy againſt his wife, deſcribed as expreſſing its firſt
reſentment in terms of the utmoſt impatience againſt the in-
former.

> Villain, be ſure thou prove my love a whore!
> Be ſure of it, &c.
>
> OTHELLO, Act III. Scene 8.

That theſe ſeeming irregular ſallies of paſſion are, however,
natural, may eaſily be conceived from conſidering, that in our
infancy we never look farther than the neareſt cauſe of
our diſquiet on which to fix our reſentment; that few perſons,
upon ſudden provocation, can forbear expreſſing their reſentment
in the ſame indiſcriminate manner; and that there are many well-
atteſted inſtances of the greateſt imaginable extravagancies of this
kind in perſons of ſtrong paſſions and little reflection. Are we
not credibly informed by Herodotus, that Xerxes, in great wrath
and earneſtneſs, inſulted the Helleſpont, both by words and actions, when he found the bridge he had laid over it broken to
pieces. Nay, did not the Athenians inſtitute a proceſs at law

2   againſt

againſt all inſtruments of murder, by which clubs, axes, ſwords, and the like, were ſtrictly tried, and, if found guilty, expelled the territories of Attica? Nothing like any of theſe inſtances could ever have occurred, nor could any paſſion ever have been expreſſed, or gratified, in ſo abſurd a manner, if the mind had not been under a *temporary illuſion*, during which it actually conceived thoſe things, which were no moral agents, to be the proper objects of paſſion.

Let it be obſerved, that the perſonification of brute creatures and inanimate things is taken notice of in this place, as it accounts for their becoming the objects of the *paſſions* properly ſo called. This ſubject will be conſidered in a future lecture in quite another light, as contributing to excite thoſe *finer feelings*, which have been before ſpoken of, as conſtituting the pleaſures of the imagination.

LECTURE XIV.

Of the Influence of the Passions on each other, and other Circum-
stances relating to strong Emotions of Mind.

ANOTHER obfervation relating to the paffions, and of
confiderable ufe in criticifm, is that they are excited with
more or lefs eafe according to the *ftate of mind previous to them*;
and that when feveral of them are in joint poffeffion of the
mind, they are liable to be greatly affected by their *mutual influ-*
ences upon one another.

Thofe paffions, the emotions belonging to which are fimilar,
eafily introduce, and, as it were, pafs into one another. As Mr.
Hume well expreffes it, " All refembling impreffions are connected
" together ; and no fooner one arifes, than the reft naturally fol-
" low. Grief and difappointment give rife to anger, anger to
" envy, envy to malice, and malice to grief again. In like
" manner our temper, when elevated with joy, naturally throws
" itfelf into love, generofity, courage, pride, and other refem-
" bling affections." *Hume's differtation on the paffions.*

On the other hand, when emotions of a very oppofite nature,
which confift of contrary feelings, are, from independent caufes,
excited in the mind at the fame time, the oppofition, or contraft, ferves to heighten both. Their difference being hereby
                                                    rendered

rendered very fenfible, each of them is more ftrongly felt than either of them would have been, if they had been imprefled fingly.

The former of thefe obfervations admits of the eafieft illuf-tration from the *kindred paffions*, as they may be called, of love and pity. Thefe, having the fame languid tone, the fame fitu-ation of mind is favourable to the introduction of both; and the mind, after having been under the influence of one, is more ea-fily fufceptible of impreffions from the other.

This is finely illuftrated in the fpeech of Othello in Shakefpeare, the following lines of which clofe the account he gives of his courtfhip of Defdemona.

> ———— On this hint I fpake.
> She loved me for the dangers I had paft,
> And I loved her that fhe did pity them.
>   OTHELLO, Act I. Scene 8.

It muft, however, be acknowledged that, in this cafe, a rela-tion of perilous adventures, in which a perfon hath acquitted himfelf bravely, begets a great *efteem* for the adventurer, which is a confiderable ingredient in the paffion of love.

To be fenfible of the effect of the *contrariety* of emotions, let any one but think how impatient of *mirth* muft a perfon be who is oppreffed with *forrow!* how much every appearance of joy heightens his diftrefs! Hence the fentiments which Milton afcribes to Satan in Paradife:

> With what delight could I have walk'd the round!
> ———— But I in none of thefe
> Find place or refuge, and the more I fee

O 2   Pleafures

Pleasures about me, so much the more I feel
Torments within me.

PARADISE LOST, Book IX.

When two states of mind are wholly opposite to one another,
it is pleasant to observe the *fluctuation of mind* occasioned by the
alternate prevalence of each of them. If a *resolution* must succeed
it, as is the case of Meleager's mother debating with herself
whether to destroy her son, or revenge her brother ; the prepon-
derating of the mind to one side in some measure gratifies that
passion, which necessarily abates its violence, and gives a momentary advantage to the contrary inclination. This circumstance may prolong the state of suspense, in which, in this situation, the mind is necessarily kept a considerable time.

If no resolution be depending, as in the mere impression made
upon the mind by good and bad news, the stronger emotion will
at length overpower the less ; and the mind, after having been
subject to the influence of both, will settle in a state which is the
result of their joint impressions. We see a strong conflict of opposite sensations in Osmyn in chains on hearing some unexpected good news. *Mourning Bride, Act III. Scene 2.*

These observations relating to the opposition of emotions and
passions is of great importance, even in the conduct of life. In
no other respect doth men's happiness so much depend upon the
regulation of their passions. Since it is obvious that the sense
we have of our happiness may be increased by comparison with
the misery of others ; and our meanness and wretchedness may,
for the same reason, be made sensible and intolerable, by reflection upon the happiness we do not partake. The passion of
envy hath no other source for its venom ; and hence the delight-

3   ful

ful sentiments of gratitude, and the calm emotions of contentment derive all their pleasures.

In order to raise a very lively and tender sentiment, it is of advantage to describe the circumstances which raise it, in as *few words* as possible. The less time is lost in transition, the nearer is any sentiment brought in contrast with the preceding state of mind, and consequently the more sensibly it is perceived. Besides, when few words are sufficient to present a moving scene to the mind, it approaches nearly to giving a view of the *scene itself*, without description. The writer disappears, and the scene itself is before us : and to apply a general maxim to this particular case, if the principal and leading circumstances in any scene be expressed, the more negligent a writer seems to be to unfold all the particulars connected with them, the more will the reader *imagine*; and instead of his perceiving the effect of every circumstance of the scene separately, they will all croud upon his mind in one *complex sensation*, and affect him with all their powers united.

The following is a moving image in Virgil's description of the return of Eurydice to the infernal regions.

　　　Invalidas tibi tendens, *heu non tua*, palmas.
　　　　　　　　　　　　　　　　GEORG. Lib. IV.

The reader conceives a more lively sensation of a variety of undistinguished emotions from that short parenthesis, *heu non tua*, than if the poet had expatiated upon all the circumstances of the difference of Eurydice's present relation to Orpheus, and that in which they had stood to one another, and which, but the moment before, they had both fondly imagined was going to revive.

　　　　　　　　　　　　　　　　　　The

The fame author gives his readers a more exquifite fenfation, by means of a fingle epithet, in the following paffage, in which he defcribes the attempt that Dædalus made to defcribe the misfortune of his fon, than he could have conveyed in more words, though ever fo proper.

> Bis conatus erat cafus effingere in auro,
> Bis *patriæ* cecidére manus.   Æneid, Lib. VII.

When, under any affection of mind, ftrong fenfations have been affociated with *particular words*, it is natural for a perfon under the influence of the correfponding paffion to repeat fuch words. In thefe cafes, fingle words prefent to the mind intire fcenes with all their moving circumftances.

Inimitably expreffive of tendernefs is the repetition of the name of *Eurydice*, in the affecting hiftory of Orpheus, both in Virgil and Ovid, thus happily imitated by Mr. Pope.

> Yet e'en in death Eurydice he fung,
> Eurydice ftill trembled on his tongue:
>   Eurydice the woods,
>   Eurydice the floods,
> Eurydice the rocks and hollow mountains rung.
>   ODE ON CÆCILIA'S DAY.

In all ftrong paffions, fome one idea being prefent to the mind more eminently than others, perfons under the influence of them naturally exprefs that idea the firft, even though it obliges them to throw the fentence in which it is introduced into diforder. Thus Nifus, in Virgil, expofing himfelf to death for Eurialus,

> Me me adfum, qui feci; in me convertite ferrum.
> Oh Rutuli, mea fraus omnis.   Æneid, Lib. IX.

I   Perolla,

Perolla, in Livy, full of horror and aftonifhment at the inten-
tion of his fon to murder Hannibal, begins his fpeech to him in
the utmoft diforder, with the moft folemn form of adjuration;
" Per, ego, te, fili," &c.

It is a direct confequence of the affociation of ideas, that,
when a perfon hath fuffered greatly on any account, he connects
the idea of the fame caufe with any great diftrefs. This fhews
with what propriety Shakefpeare makes King Lear, whofe fuf-
ferings were owing to his daughters, fpeak to Edgar, difguifed
like a lunatic, in the following manner:

> What, have his *daughters* brought him to this pafs?
> Could'ft thou fave nothing? Did'ft thou give them all?
> KING LEAR.

And Macduff,

> ————— He hath no children.   MACBETH.

Writers not really feeling the paffions they defcribe, and not
being mafters of the natural expreffion of them, are apt, without their being aware of it, to make perfons under the influence
of a ftrong emotion or paffion, fpeak in a manner that is very
unfuitable to it. Sometimes, for inftance, they feem rather to be
defcribing the *paffion of another*, than expreffing their own.
Sometimes the language of perfons, in interefting circumftances,
fhows fuch an excurfion of mind from the principal object, as
demonftrates that their minds were not fufficiently engroffed with
it. And fometimes, aiming to ftrike and aftonifh, they make
their heroes ufe fuch language as is expreffive of no paffion
whatever, but is quite extravagant and abfurd.

The

The French dramatic writers are moft commonly guilty of the
firft impropriety.   Seldom conceiving the force of a real paffion,
they declaim upon the fubject in fuch a ftyle as an *obferver* might
poffibly ufe, but which would never occur to a perfon really interefted.   In Corneille there are few inftances of a juft expreffion
of paffion.   The generality of readers, being little interefted in
fuch reprefentations, are not apt to attend to the impropriety;
but every perfon, upon reflection, would be fenfible that no perfon, really agitated with paffion, would exprefs himfelf as Vol-
taire hath made Titus do.

O de ma paffion fureur defefperée.   Act III. Scene 6.

Even our Shakefpeare himfelf, though no writer whatever hath
fucceeded fo well in the language of the paffions, is fometimes
deferving of cenfure in this refpect; as when Conftance, in King
John, fays to the meffenger that brought her a piece of difagreeable news,

Fellow, be gone, I cannot brook thy fight:
This news hath made thee a moft ugly man.

The fentiment and expreffion in the former line is perfectly
natural, but that in the latter refembles too much the comment of
of a cool obferver.   Of the fame kind, but much more extravagant, is the following paffage, which is part of the fpeech of
Conftance, giving her reafons why fhe indulged her grief for the
lofs of her fon.

Grief fills the room up of my abfent child,
Lies in his bed, walks up and down with me,
Puts on his pretty looks, repeats his words,

Remembers

> Remembers me of all his gracious parts,
> Stuffs out his vacant garment with his form:
> Then I have reason to be fond of grief.
>
> KING JOHN, Act IV. Scene 1.

Shakefpeare's talent for wit and humour, and the genius of the times in which he wrote, have, upon many occafions, betrayed him into the fecond impropriety, which is, to make perfons under ftrong emotions fpeak, as if their minds were not fufficiently engroffed with the principal object of their concern. Would even a child, apprehenfive of having his eyes inftantly burned out, fpeak as he hath reprefented young Arthur to have fpoken, in order to perfuade his executioner to defift from his purpofe?

> In good footh the fire is dead with grief.
> Being create for comfort, to be ufed
> In undeferved extremes. See elfe yourfelf,
> There is no malice in this burning coal.
> The breath of heav'n hath blown its fpirit out,
> And ftrew'd repentant afhes on its head.
>
> KING JOHN, Act IV. Scene 1.

More improbable ftill is it that King John, in the agonies of death, and with his ftomach and bowels inflamed with intenfe heat, would pun and quibble in the manner that Shakefpeare reprefents him to have done; and that, when he was not able to procure any thing to cool his inward heat, he fhould fay,

> I beg *cold comfort*, and you are fo ftrait,
> And fo ungrateful, you deny me that.
>
> Act V. Scene 9.

If we cenfure thofe writers who reprefent perfons as fpeaking in a manner unfuitable to their fituation, with much more rea-

P   fon

son may we censure those who represent persons as thinking and speaking in a manner unsuitable to *any character*, or any circumstances whatever? Among these unnatural sentiments we may rank the avowing, or open undisguised proposal, of wicked purposes: because human nature is so constituted, that direct vice and wickedness is universally shocking. For this reason men seldom entertain the thought of it in their own minds, much less propose it to others, but either under the appearance of virtue, or of some great advantage, and with some *salvo* for the immorality of it.

With admirable propriety doth King John hint to Hubert how much he would oblige him if he would remove prince Arthur out of his way. But the following soliloquy of the Bastard Falconbridge, in the same play, is certainly unnatural.

> Well, while I am a beggar I will rail,
> And say there is no sin but to be rich:
> And being rich, my virtue then shall be
> To say there is no vice but beggary.
> Since kings break faith upon commodity,
> Gain be my lord, for I will worship thee.
>
> KING JOHN, Act II. Scene 6.

In a much more unnatural and extravagant manner is Lady Macbeth represented talking to herself when she is projecting the death of the king. *Macbeth*, Act I. Scene 7.

Instances of the most absurd rant, and such extravagance as is incompatible with every character, and with every passion, abound in Dryden's plays, particularly in the part of Almanzor in the Conquest of Granada.

It is impossible not to smile when Moliere makes Harpagus (when he is about to examine upon the rack all his family, ser-

vants,

vants, fons, and daughters) fay he would apply the torture himfelf, " et a moi auffi."

Very extravagant likewife is the following fpeech, which Shakefpeare puts into the mouth of Ligarius:

> ———— Now bid me run,
> And I will ftrive with things impoffible,
> And get the better of them.
>
> JULIUS CÆSAR, Act II. Scene 3.

LECTURE

LECTURE XV.

Of Forms of Address adapted to gain BELIEF; *and, first, of those that imply* PRESENT THOUGHT, *and an* UNPREMEDITATED EXPRESSION.

HAVING obferved what I think moſt important relating to the *paſſions*, I proceed to conſider what relates to the *judgment*, in aſſenting to what is propoſed to it.

Independent of the power of *arguments*, there are ſeveral *forms of addreſs adapted to engage belief*, which abound in the works of orators. Theſe it is in the power of every ſpeaker to adopt at pleaſure, as they are, each of them, nothing more than a different manner in which arguments may be introduced and expreſſed. Since, however, they do contribute greatly to the ſucceſs of an orator, I ſhall enumerate the principal and moſt ſtriking of them, and endeavour to ſhew the cauſe of the influence which they have upon our minds.

Every art of perſuaſion founded upon nature, and really tending to engage belief, muſt conſiſt of ſuch forms of addreſs as are natural to a perſon who is himſelf ſtrongly convinced of the truth and importance of what he contends for; who is conſcious that he is perfectly maſter of his ſubject, and acquainted with every thing that can be advanced for or againſt the queſtion in debate;

debate; who is poffeffed even of a redundancy of proof for what he advances; and who is, moreover, perfectly candid and unprejudiced, willing to allow all the weight he can to the pleas of his adverfaries.

From the principle of *fympathy*, which is natural to the human mind, we univerfally feel ourfelves difpofed to conform to the feelings, the fentiments, and every thing belonging to the fituation of thofe we converfe with, and particularly of all thofe perfons who engage much of our attention. If, therefore, no prejudice intervene, we always feel ourfelves more or lefs difpofed to adopt the opinions of thofe perfons with whom we have frequent intercourfe. Confequently, we are, in all cafes, more difpofed to give our affent to any propofition, if we perceive that the perfon who contends for it is really in earneft, and believes it himfelf. Indeed, prior to our hearing any arguments, we are naturally inclined to fuppofe, that a ftrong conviction and perfuafion in other perfons could not be produced without a *fufficient caufe*; from being fenfible that a like ftrong perfuafion is founded upon fufficient reafons in ourfelves. The ideas of *ftrong perfuafion* and of *truth* being, on this account, intimately affociated together, the one will introduce the other, fo that whatever manner of addrefs tends to demonftrate that the advocate for any opinion is really convinced of it himfelf, tends to propagate that conviction.

A perfon fhews that he is fully perfuaded of the truth of what he contends for, and his confidence in the goodnefs of his caufe, when he is willing to appeal to the judgment and confcience of other perfons, and particularly when he dare appeal to his adverfary himfelf. For no perfon would ferioufly make fuch an appeal, who did not believe his caufe to be fo clear that all the

world,

world, if they confidered it, would concur with him in it. This formal appeal, therefore, to a perfon's judges, his hearers, and his adverfary, is a figure of the firft rank in oratory, and greatly conducive to the purpofe of perfuafion.

It hath ftill a ftronger effect of the fame kind when an orator breaks out into an *exclamation*, expreffing his wonder, aftonifhment, and indignation, that his opinion fhould be controverted, or his caufe oppofed; and a ftronger ftill, when not only vifible but invifible powers, when not only rational beings, but things inanimate are invoked, to atteft the truth of what is advanced. All paffions are communicative, and are univerfally propagated by the genuine expreffions of them.

Many happy inftances of thefe forms of addrefs are found in the orations of Cicero, particularly in his invectives againft Verres, Catiline, and Antony. The very firft words of his firft oration againft Catiline, which was delivered in the fenate, when Catiline himfelf was prefent, confift of a very vehement exclamation and expoftulation. " How long, O Catiline, will you " abufe our patience? &c." In a fpeech afcribed to Furius Capitolinus, in which he expoftulates with the plebeians upon the encroachments they were perpetually making upon the privileges of the patricians, is the following noble and fpirited appeal: " In the name of the immortal gods, what is it, Romans, " you would have? You defired tribunes; for the fake of peace " we granted them. You were eager to have decemvirs; we " confented to their creation: you grew weary of thefe decem- " virs, we obliged them to abdicate, &c."

In Cicero's oration for Milo, he exclaims, " O that happy " country which fhall receive this man! Ungrateful this if it " banifh him! miferable if it lofe him!" Declaiming in praife

of

of Pompey, he invokes countries, feas, havens, and iflands, as witneffes of his courage, humanity, and wifdom.

There is fomething peculiarly folemn and awful in the following apoftrophes in the fcriptures : " Hear, oh heavens, and give " ear, oh earth, for the Lord hath fpoken, Ifaiah l. 2. Be afto- " nifhed, oh ye heavens, at this; Jer. ii. 12."

Whatever, likewife, hath the appearance of *prefent thought*, and *extempore* unprepared addrefs, contributes not a little to make a perfon feem to be in earneft. He then feems to fpeak from his *real feelings*, without having recourfe to artificial helps. In this view it hath often a good effect to check one's felf, and retract what we were faying, or even to reject a fecond, and recur to a firft fuppofition; to ftop fuddenly, and make an imperfect fenfe, as if fomething juft then conceived had checked the courfe of the fentence, which was intended to have been delivered without interruption. Objections which the orator thinks proper to reply to, he may make to appear as if they occurred to his mind only the moment he mentions them; in which cafe the anfwer, not appearing to be premeditated, will be heard with the utmoft advantage. It hath, likewife, the appearance of purfuing a fudden ftart of thought, and hath fometimes a very good effect, when opportunity is taken, as if undefignedly, to make *parenthefes* in fentences, and to *digrefs* from the principal fubject or argument, and return to it again.

I think it needlefs to give examples of all thefe varieties of addrefs which derive their power from the refemblance they bear to *unpremeditated difcourfe*, in which the fentiments are fuppofed to be natural and fincere, proceeding directly from the heart; and fhall only mention one from Tillotfon, in which, with a very

" good

good effect, he retracts a single word. "What is it then can "give men the heart and courage (but I recall that word, be- "cause it is not true courage, but fool-hardiness) to out-brave "the judgments of God."

Such forms as these are most natural in great agitation of mind, when the succession of ideas is uncommonly rapid, and when, consequently, it may be expected that some thoughts should interfere with others, and occasion frequent breaks in sentences, and interruptions in a chain of reasoning. St. Paul's epistles abound with these abruptnesses; and as they have not the least appearance of *design* in them, they show that he wrote from his heart, and dictated his real thoughts and sentiments at the time of their composition. They likewise throw considerable light upon the *natural temper* of that great apostle. We see that he was a warm man, of a quick apprehension, of great ardour and vehemence in whatever he engaged in, and that he was in-clined to be hasty.

The perfection of speaking is, certainly, to speak extempore. All men must, in a greater or less degree, have tried their talent this way, and have found the difficulty of succeeding in it. Hence people listen with a continued *wonder* while a person is de-livering himself fluently without notes, and their admiration con-curs with the forementioned causes to attach them to the speaker, to his sentiments and views. Can we imagine it possible that the primitive christians, the first reformers, and, I may add, the founders of our modern sects, such as the Independants, Quakers, and Methodists, could ever have attained to so great a degree of popularity, without the talent of haranguing extem-pore? Can we then wonder at the success of a judicious and happy imitation of those extempore forms of address?

As

As a caution againſt making too free with theſe very bold forms of addreſs, which are adapted to ſhow that a man is in earneſt, and confident of the goodneſs of his cauſe, I would adviſe that no one appeal to another, unleſs it be morally certain that the perſon he appeals to, and boldly expoſtulates with, will really take his part, or, at leaſt, that it will be generally allowed that he *ought* to do it. Otherwiſe he expoſes his own vain confidence, and betrays the cauſe he eſpouſes.

Let no perſon venture to exclaim and apoſtrophize, unleſs the *importance*, as well as the goodneſs of his cauſe will juſtify it. Theſe ſtrong natural emotions are not to be counterfeited. To theſe *arcana of nature* it is hardly poſſible that *artifice* ſhould have acceſs : and if the circumſtances and occaſions of the addreſs will not juſtify ſuch vehemence of ſtyle, a man makes himſelf ridiculous by attempting the impoſition. Beſides, direct exclamations and apoſtrophes to perſons not preſent, or to things inanimate, though ever ſo juſt, ought to be uſed very ſparingly ; ſince, if they produce their natural and full effect, they raiſe the attention to ſuch a degree as cannot be kept up long.

It is, likewiſe, proper that all Engliſhmen in particular ſhould be informed, that a perſon of a liberal education in this country can hardly ever be in ſuch a ſituation, as will not render the imitation of ſome of the boldeſt, the moſt ſucceſsful, and admired ſtrokes of Roman, not to ſay Grecian eloquence, extremely improper and ridiculous. The Engliſh pulpit, the Engliſh bar, and the Engliſh ſenate, require an eloquence more addreſſed to the reaſon, and leſs directly to the paſſions, than the harangues of a Roman pleader, or the ſpeech of a Roman ſenator. Our hearers have generally more good ſenſe and juſt diſ-

Q   cernment,

cernment, at leaft they are naturally more *cool* and phlegmatic; both which qualities check a propenfity to ftrong emotions : and marks of great vehemence muft appear abfurd in a fpeaker, when the audience is unmoved, and fees nothing to occafion fuch emotion.

An audience, indeed, that is wholly *illiterate*, may have all their paffions actuated by means of admiration, or aftonifhment, and *mechanical communication*; but then there are few Englifh audiences compofed wholly of perfons of fo little reading and reflection as makes that practicable. And it is hardly poffible that a perfon whofe reading has lain among modern Englifh books, or has converfed with perfons of a liberal education, fhould not have acquired more *delicacy of tafte*, than to be taken with that grofs and direct addrefs to the paffions, which Cicero adopted with applaufe. The refinement of modern times requires that we fpeak, upon all occafions, with more temper, and ufe more addrefs in raifing the paffions.

If a perfon adopt any of the forms of addrefs which derive their beauty, force, and efficacy, from their feeming to be extemporary, as well as thofe which exprefs great earneftnefs and vehemence; all his geftures, the air of his countenance, and his whole manner, fhould correfpond to them; becaufe certain geftures and motions of the countenance univerfally accompany natural vehemence, and genuine extemporary expreffion. When thefe things, which have fo ftrong a connection in nature, are not united, the whole muft appear extremely unnatural, the *imperfect artifice* will be eafily feen through, and the impoftor be defervedly expofed.

If a perfon never attempt thefe forms of fpeech but when his temper really correfponds to and dictates them, he will feldom

fail

fail in point of propriety; becaufe the ftate of mind being ftrongly affociated with thofe correfpondent motions, they are excited mechanically and juftly. No *attention* can fupply the place of this. The external expreffions of paffion, with all their variations, correfponding to the different degrees of their emotions, are too complex for any perfon in the circumftances of a public fpeaker to be able to attend to them. Or, were it poffible, the difference between a *genuine automatic* and a *voluntary* motion, is fufficiently apparent. All motions that are automatic have a quicknefs and vigour which are loft when they become voluntary; witnefs *fighing, laughing,* the geftures peculiar to *anger,* &c. and the fame when imitated. The difference is too apparent to efcape any perfon's obfervation.

If thefe obfervations be fufficiently attended to, they will deter any prudent and confiderate perfon from attempting phrafes and modes of addrefs, expreffive of *earneftnefs,* when they do not really feel thofe emotions, which will of themfelves fuggeft the proper attitudes and geftures correfponding to them.

Thefe cautions are given in this place, becaufe they peculiarly relate to thofe forms of addrefs which exprefs earneftnefs, extreme confidence in the goodnefs of one's caufe, and that quick conception and animated delivery natural to *extemporary* fpeaking, which have now been explained. They are, indeed, applicable, but not in the fame degree, to the remaining forms of addrefs which are adapted to gain belief.

Q 2   LECTURE

LECTURE XVI.

Of OBJECTIONS, SUPPRESSION *of what might be said, and Marks of* CANDOUR.

WE more eafily give our affent to any propofition when the perfon who contends for it appears, by his manner of delivering himfelf, to have a perfect knowledge of the fubject of it, fo as to be apprized beforehand of every thing that can be objected to it, and efpecially if he feem to be mafter of more arguments than he chufes to produce. For we naturally prefume that a perfon thus furnifhed hath *ftudied* the queftion in debate, that he cannot but have weighed the arguments that appear to be fo familiar to him; and therefore that he hath determined juftly concerning it. Thefe forms of addrefs, as well as thofe which are natural to a perfon who is greatly in earneft, have been obferved, and the advantage attending them may be had by thofe perfons who adopt, or imitate them, with judgment.

Thus an able orator will fometimes difarm his antagonifts, and gain his hearers, by *anticipating* all they can alledge for themfelves, and by obviating their cavils before they have had any opportunity to ftart them; by which means his argument proceeds without interruption.

The

The chief art of an orator in anfwering objections confifts in introducing them at a proper time, juft when it may be fuppofed they may have occurred to his hearers; before they could have had time to influence their minds, and leffen the weight of his arguments. By this means an orator feems to read the very thoughts of his audience; and a proof of fuch a perfect acquaintance with his fubject, and even with the fentiments of his hearers, and of his adverfaries, about it, cannot fail to operate powerfully in his favour.

In an oration afcribed to Junius Brutus, exhorting the Romans to throw off the yoke of the Tarquins, we have an example of an objection anticipated in a very happy, mafterly, and fpirited manner. After demonftrating to the people the power they were poffeffed of to redrefs their grievances, the urgent neceffity, and peculiarly-favourable opportunity for exerting it; he makes a fudden paufe, as if he had juft perceived fome figns of diffidence in the countenances of his audience, and had difcerned the very thoughts which occafioned them; and fays, " Some of you are, " perhaps, intimidated by the *army* which Tarquin now com- " mands. The foldiers, you imagine, will take the part of " their general. Banifh fo groundlefs a fear. The love of li- " berty is natural to all men. Your fellow-citizens in the camp " feel the weight of oppreffion with as quick a fenfe as you " that are in Rome. They will as eafily feize the occafion of " throwing off the yoke. But let us grant there may be fome " among them who, through bafenefs of fpirit, or a bad educa- " tion, will be difpofed to favour the tyrant. The number of " thefe can be but fmall, and we have means fufficient in our " hands to reduce them to reafon. They have left us hoftages " more dear to them than life. Their wives, their children,

" their

" their fathers, their mothers, are here in the city. Courage,
" Romans, the gods are for us," &c.

An example of the fame nature we have in St. Paul, difcourfing about the refurrection.   " But fome will fay, How are the
" dead raifed ? and with what body do they come ? Thou fool,
" that which thou foweft is not quickened except it die," &c.
1 Cor. xv. 35, 36.

If it be not convenient to fpeak at large to an objection juft at
the time when it may moft probably be fuppofed to occur to the
audience, when yet it might be attended with fome inconvenience, and it would not be prudent, wholly to overlook it; it
may, in fome meafure, take off the force of it, if, at that time,
the orator only hint his being aware of it, and promife to difcufs
it more particularly afterwards.   In this cafe the hearer is engaged to drop his attention to it, and to defer the confideration
of it till the fpeaker himfelf take notice of it.

Sometimes there may be an appearance of impropriety in
the very *circumftances* of the oration, which muft be taken notice
of before any argument can be entered upon.   As when Demofthenes rofe up to fpeak firft in the affembly, when he was not of
a fufficient age to affume that privilege, and when Cicero engaged
in the accufation of Verres, when he had never appeared at the
bar before, but in the defence of his clients.   In both thefe cafes
thofe accomplifhed orators endeavoured to fatisfy their audiences
with refpect to thefe unexpected circumftances, before they entered upon any article of the fubject in debate.

It is a capital ftroke of eloquence, when an orator is able to re-
tort the objection of his adverfary upon himfelf; and, allowing
the truth of what is objected againft him, to fhow that, in reality, it is fo far from making againft him, that it makes greatly for

3   him,

him, and, in fact, helps to confute his opponent. Thus St. Paul frankly acknowledges the *herefy* with which his adverfaries charged him; but at the fame time intimates that his was fuch a herefy as was perfectly confiftent with, and even required by the law which they were then endeavouring to prove he had violated, infulted, and apoftatized from. " But this I confefs unto " thee, that after the way which they call herefy, fo worfhip I the " God of my fathers, believing all things which are written in the " law, and the prophets; and have hope towards God, which " they themfelves alfo allow, that there fhall be a refurrection of " the dead, both of the juft and unjuft." Acts xxiv. 14, 15.

Cicero, though not with the ftricteft regard to truth, endeavours to give a favourable turn of this kind to the objection which was made to his conduct in leaving Rome, during the prevalence of the Clodian faction. " My departure," he fays, " is object " ed to me; which charge I cannot anfwer without commending " myfelf. For what muft I fay? That I fled from a confciouf " nefs of guilt? But what is charged upon me as a crime was fo " far from being a fault, that it is the moft glorious action fince " the memory of man. That I feared to be called to account by " the people? That was never talked of; and if it had been done, " I fhould have come off with double honour. That I wanted " the fupport of good and honeft men? That is falfe. That I " was afraid of death? That is a calumny. I muft therefore " fay, what I would not unlefs compelled to it, that I withdrew " to preferve the city."

In fuch cafes as thefe, the pleafing furprize of the audience, from feeing a thing in a light fo different from what they expected, and in which it had been reprefented, and the conviction of the extreme weaknefs of the adverfary, in laying

hold

hold of arguments which really made againſt him, operate greatly in the orator's favour.

Any thing in an oration which is introduced in this form of
objection and *anſwer*, or any thing ſimilar to it, falls properly
under the conſideration of *artificial addreſs* ; ſince nothing of that
kind is abſolutely neceſſary in argumentation. In ſtrict ſynthetical demonſtration there is no part of the whole proceſs which
bears that name, or any thing equivalent to it. Every demonſtration is built upon ſelf-evident truths. If a perſon thoroughly
underſtand the proceſs as he goes along, no objection will ever
occur. If any do occur, it ſhows that he hath not ſufficiently
attended to ſomething or other that went before, and he hath
nothing to do but reviſe the ſteps he hath gone over, for his
complete ſatisfaction.

Facts and circumſtances, on which the orator doth not intend
to lay the chief ſtreſs of his argument, are often employed to good
advantage, when they are mentioned only in a ſlight and incidental manner. By this artifice an orator inſinuates, that it was
in his power to have ſaid a great deal more upon a ſubject than he
hath done ; and while he ſeems, out of a redundancy of proof,
to ſelect only a few of the moſt important arguments, the imagination of the hearer is apt to give more than their juſt weight to
thoſe which he affects to paſs over in ſilence. Beſides, it often happens that there is one point of light in which a fact, or a circumſtance, may for a moment be ſhewn to advantage ; whereas, if the
ſpeaker dwelt longer upon it, a cloſer attention would exhibit
views of it unfavourable to his purpoſe.

By this art, circumſtances which would have made no figure in
a detail, and have even given an idea of the poorneſs of a cauſe

I   in in which they were minutely infifted on, may contribute very confiderably to the fuccefs of an oration. They are hereby feen in their moft favourable light, and expofed to view no longer than they will bear it.

Thus Demofthenes, in recounting the victories of Philip, fays, " I fay nothing of his expeditions againft the Illyrians, and " Pannonians, againft Arymbas, and others, with which every " body is acquainted." Thus alfo Cicero, in one of his invectives, " I do not mention my adverfary's fcandalous gluttony and " drunkennefs, I take no notice of his brutal lufts, I fay not a " fyllable of his treachery, malice, and cruelty." And, in his defence of Sextius, " I might fay many things of his liberality, " kindnefs to his domeftics, his command in the army, and mo- " deration during his office in the province; but the honour of " the ftate prefents itfelf to my view, and, calling me to it, ad- " vifes me to omit thefe leffer matters."

When an orator fpeaks of himfelf, this flight mention or pretended omiffion of many particulars hath another advantage, that it carries the appearance of *modefty*, and on that account contributes not a little to recommend the fpeaker to the favourable opinion of his audience.

This flight mention of circumftances hath an uncommonly-fine effect when, out of a delicacy of fentiment, and a tendernefs to thofe he is addreffing, a perfon declines infifting upon what are, in reality, his ftrongeft arguments. Was it poffible for Philemon to infift upon Onefimus's paying what he owed him, after reading the following delicate and moving paffage in Saint Paul's letter to him. " If he hath wronged thee, or oweth thee ought, " put that to mine account. I Paul have written it with mine " own hand, I will repay it. Albeit I do not fay to thee, how

R   " thou

" thou oweſt unto me, even thine own ſelf beſides." Phil.
xviii. 19.

The ſame Saint Paul, ſpeaking of himſelf and the churches
of his planting, hath the following exquiſite paſſage, in his
epiſtle to the Corinthians, who had liſtened to ſome unfavourable
accounts of him. " In nothing am I behind the very chiefeſt
" apoſtles, though I be nothing. Truly the ſigns of an apoſtle
" were wrought among you, in all patience, in ſigns and won-
" ders, and mighty deeds. For what is it wherein ye were in-
" ferior to other churches, except it be that I myſelf was not
" burdenſome to you? Forgive me this wrong." 1 Cor. xii. 11,
12, 13.

It is eaſy to conceive how, upon many occaſions, it may be of
advantage not to ſay, or at leaſt to ſeem not to ſay, all we might
upon a ſubject, but leave part to be ſupplied by the hearer or
reader. This employs his faculties, and ſets his imagination
ſtrongly and effectually at work. When an orator expreſſes himſelf in ſuch a manner as to make his hearers believe he could ſay
more, and when his known ſituation makes it probable that he
might have ſufficient reaſon for puſhing his argument no farther
than he doth (as when a perſon ſpeaks or writes in defence of
new and obnoxious opinions) in this caſe, the imagination of
the hearer will never ſuggeſt too little. That ſuppreſſion, joined
with our concern to ſee a perſon, of whom we have conceived a
favourable opinion, in a ſituation which obliges him to conceal
the truth, inflames the paſſions more than any thing that could
have been ſaid, though ever ſo convincing and ſatisfactory, upon
the ſubject.

The circumſtances in which Marc Antony delivered Cæſar's
funeral oration, were peculiarly favourable to his views of excit-

ing

ing compaſſion and reſentment. Broken hints and ſilence would have a greater effect in his ſituation, than ſpeaking openly could have had in any other. For the ſame reaſon it would, no doubt, be for the advantage of chriſtianity, if unbelievers had nothing to fear from propoſing all their objections to it in the moſt open and public manner. In our preſent circumſtances, infidelity is often ſuccesfully propagated by inſinuations, obſcure hints, and affected ſneers; whereas, if all pretence for theſe artifices were cut off, by an unreſtrained indulgence of free inquiry and debate, no other method could be found by which it could be ſo conveniently propagated. In common life, is it not well known that ſcandal is always moſt effectually propagated by hints and whiſpers?

Let it, however, be remembered, as a caution againſt the improper uſe of this method of promoting any cauſe, that ſilence is ridiculous when no reaſon can be imagined, either from fear, modeſty, tenderneſs, or any other cauſe, why a perſon ſhould not ſpeak out.

Laſtly, nothing more effectually conduces to gain belief, than the appearance of *candour* and *impartiality* in the orator, and his willingneſs to be convinced if he have fallen into an error. An opinion maintained with ſo much modeſty, by a perſon ſo diffident of his own judgment, and who appears to have no motive to bias him in favour of falſehood, is ſure to be attended to without prejudice. We cannot help ſympathizing with ſuch a ſpeaker, and aſſuming his impartiality and candid diſpoſition.

We ſhow our candour when we appear to be in *doubt*, and diſcuſs our own doubts; when we freely allow as much weight as poſſible to the objections of our adverſaries; and particularly when we frankly retract what we acknowledge we had too haſtily

R 2   advanced;

advanced; alfo when, feeming to forget our own particular fituation, as advocates for one fide of a queftion, we confult with
our hearers, our judge, or our adverfaries, as if perfons on all
fides were equally impartial, and intent upon finding out the
truth. This is paying a compliment to our audience, and to our
adverfaries, which is generally returned with advantage. A decifion of a queftion, after fuch a candid and impartial difcuffion,
hath the appearance of being the unanimous determination of all
parties. It is no longer one party only that we are attending to,
but we almoft fancy fuch a candid opinion to be the refult of the
confultation of all perfons concerned.

In this cafe, the determination fhould be indeed impartial, and
what every perfon, who hears it, will think it right that all parties fhould adopt.

We have a fine picture of doubt in Cicero's defence of Cluen-
tius. " I know not which way to turn myfelf," &c.; and a
good example of an impartial and fair appeal to an adverfary, in
his accufation of Verres, " Now I defire your opinion," &c.; and
again, in his defence of Rabirius, " What could you have done
" in fuch a cafe ?" &c.

L E C T U R E XVII.

Of the PLEASURES OF IMAGINATION *in general, and of the*
Standard of GOOD TASTE.

HAVING confidered a variety of the moft important circumftances relating to the ftronger *paſſions* and emotions,
the knowledge of which more eminently contributes to form a
critic in works of tafte and genius, and alfo thofe *forms of ad-*
dreſs which are peculiarly adapted to gain *aſſent*; I come in the
third place, according to the method I propofed, to enumerate
thofe finer feelings which conftitute the *pleaſures of the imagina-*
tion, in order to afcertain the nature and kind of thofe refined
pleafures : but, previous to this, I fhall make a few general obfervations relating to the whole of this part of our fubject.

The firft circumftance I fhall take notice of with regard to thofe
exquifite feelings is, that the only inlets to them are, as Lord
Kaims obferves, the *eye* and the *ear*, and that the other fenfes
have nothing to do with them.   Colours and founds, it is remarkable, are tranfmitted to the mind, or fenforium, without any fenfible intervention of the corporeal organs by which they are
tranfmitted.   The eye and the ear, when they are in a found and
healthy ftate, are fo little affected by the impreffion of light, and
the vibrations of the air, that were it not for internal evidence,
we fhould not know that we had any fuch organs.

We

We find that when our eye-lids are clofed, we cannot fee at all, and that we are obliged to turn our eyes towards any object before we can perceive it, or we fhould not readily difcover what it is on which vifion depends. In like manner, it is eafy to conceive that a rational being, coming into the world with the perfect ufe of the fenfe of hearing, would not be able, without fome experiment of the fame nature, to find out what part of his corporeal fyftem was the medium of thofe fenfations : whereas we cannot feel, tafte, or even fmell, without being at the fame time fenfible that fome part of the furface of our bodies is affected in the firft of thefe cafes, and the tongue and nofe in the two laft.

For thefe reafons, feeling, tafting, and fmelling are confidered as fenfations of a groffer kind, and feeing and hearing as fomething of a much more refined and fpiritual nature. The former we cannot perceive without having at the fame time an idea of the corporeal inftruments by which they are conveyed to us ; whereas we contemplate ideas of the latter kind, as if we were wholly abftracted from the body. Hence, among other reafons, there is a kind of fhame annexed to the gratification of the groffer fenfes. Perfons of a refined tafte affect an indifference to their pleafures, and diffemble the fatisfaction they receive from them ; as in eating, drinking, and the like : whereas we are very differently affected towards the pleafures of harmony, which we perceive by the ear, and the beauty of colours and proportion, which we perceive by the eye.

Another obfervation which may throw confiderable light upon various affections of the mind, in the perception of thofe pleafures which we refer to the imagination, is, that fince the mind perceives, and is confcious of nothing, but the ideas that are

2

prefent to it, it muft, as it were, *conform* itfelf to them; and even the idea it hath of its own extent, (if we may ufe that ex-preffion) muft enlarge or contract with its field of view. By this means alfo, a perfon, for the time, enters into, adopts, and is actuated by, the fentiments that are prefented to his mind.

This takes place fo inftantaneoufly and mechanically, that no perfon whatever hath reflection, and prefence of mind enough, to be upon his guard againft fome of the moft ufelefs and ridiculous effects of it. What perfon, if he faw another upon a precipice and in danger of falling, could help ftarting back, and throwing himfelf into the fame pofture as he would do if he himfelf were going to fall? At leaft he would have a ftrong propenfity to do it. And what is more common than to fee perfons in playing at bowls, lean their own bodies, and writhe them into every pof-fible attitude, according to the courfe they would have their bowl to take? It is true, that all men are not equally affected by this remarkable propenfity. The more vivid are a man's ideas, and the greater is his general fenfibility, the more intirely, and with the greater facility, doth he adapt himfelf to the fituations he is viewing.

From this principle, converfing with mean and low objects gives the mind an idea of the meannefs and narrownefs of its own powers; and ideas of our own greatnefs, dignity, and im-portance, are the refult of our contemplating large and grand objects. This will be confpicuous when we confider the fub-lime in compofition.

Hence the paffions, fentiments, and views of thofe perfons whofe hiftory is written fo as to engage our attention, become for a time (if they be not extremely oppofite to our own general ftate of mind) our own paffions, fentiments, and views; and

particu-

particularly, the accounts of the magnanimity, generofity, courage, clemency, &c. in our heroes, are read with a fecret complacency and felf-applaufe, arifing from our indulging the fame temper and difpofition.

Hence, in part, arifes the difficulty of reading the hiftory of any two rival ftates, or perfonages, with abfolute indifference and impartiality. Before we were aware, we find we have entered into the fentiments, paffions, and interefts of the one or the other of them; and afterwards find it difficult to *change fides*, as it were; notwithftanding, in the progrefs of the hiftory, we may fee reafon enough to be difgufted with the party we at firft adopted. We abfurdly continue to wifh fuccefs to thofe we firft attached ourfelves to, though the reafons which attached us to them no longer exift. The failings on one fide are regarded with tendernefs and compaffion, as the failings of a friend; and the excellencies which difcover themfelves on the oppofite fide, are apt to be looked upon with envy and diflike, as an advantage in the poffeffion of an enemy.

What reader, who has once been interefted in the fortune of Athens, by reading the firft book of the Peloponnefian war, written by Thucydides, is not diftreffed to the laft degree with the mifcarriage of the flagrantly ambitious and unjuft invafion of Sicily, and the fiege of Syracufe? If any ftriking inftance of generofity, or mere courage, once intereft us in favour of a buccaneer, a highwayman, or even a dextrous cheat, how apt are we to read with pleafure of the fuccefs of the defperate adventures of the former, and of the ingenious but bafe artifices of the latter? It is poffible that perfons of age, experience, and reflection, may, in a great meafure, have corrected this mechanical propenfity; but it will ever retain a fenfible influence over the ge-

I

nerality of mankind; and thefe are almoft the only people we have to do with in the bufinefs of the paffions and imagination.

This obfervation fhows us how cautious all writers fhould be not to engage the attention of their readers too much to vicious characters; fince, when once they have, by this means, engaged our intereft in their favour, we are very backward to withdraw our good wifhes; and the intereft we take in the character and fchemes of a bad man, cannot but leave upon the mind an impreffion unfavourable to virtue. A natural love for virtue is a very infufficient fecurity againft this influence, efpecially in young minds. No writer, who hath at heart the intereft of virtue, and the happinefs of his fellow-creatures, ought to truft to it. Even the prudent and virtuous Mr. Richardfon hath interefted his reader fo much in the character of *Lovelace*, in Clariffa, that, I believe, there are few of his readers who would be difpleafed with the fuccefs of his bafe defigns upon any other woman than Clariffa herfelf, in whofe favour we have been beforehand more ftrongly interefted.

In the third place, let it be noted, that when each of the pleafures of the imagination are referred to fome *one fource*, I only mean, that ideas and fenfations of that kind are the *principal* ones that enter into its compofition. For, in fact, none of our intellectual pleafures are fo fimple as to be derived from one fingle fource only. They are all of fo complex a nature, and are fo connected with one another, that, it is probable, there is not one fentiment of pleafure or pain that can be called *intellectual* (not being a direct impreffion upon fome of the external fenfes) but what is more or lefs compounded of almoft all the other intellectual pleafures and pains too. The principle of affociation is predominant in every thing relating to our intellectual faculties:

S

and,

and, in a fituation fo expofed as ours is to *joint impreffions,* from a variety of independent objects, our fenfations cannot fail to be fo commixed and combined together, that it muft be extremely difficult, if not impoffible, completely to refolve any one of them into all their feparate, component parts. All that can be done, is, to place each pleafing object, that occurs in works of tafte and genius, under that fpecies of pleafure which originally, or moft eminently, entered into the compofition of it; and, at the fame time, not wholly to omit taking notice of other fources from which it borrows any thing confiderable.

Montefquieu, in his *Effay on Tafte,* very ingenioufly enumerates a variety of caufes which contribute to excite the fingle feeling or fenfation which the mind perceives upon the view of a regular garden. And Dr. Gerard, in his treatife upon the fame fubject, has illuftrated the fame obfervation by analizing the complex fenfation of pleafure we perceive from a view of a fine human face.

It will anfwer my purpofe better, and more eminently contribute to throw light upon feveral other important particulars relating to Tafte, to confider the pleafures we receive from the profpect of a fine *country landfcape,* and confequently from the defcription of *rural fcenes* in paftorals, and books of romance. This will, likewife, illuftrate the doctrine of ASSOCIATION, and the very probable opinion of Dr. Hartley, who fuppofed that it is the only mental principle employed in the formation, growth, and declenfion of all our intellectual pleafures and pains.

There is no perfon, who hath paffed much of his time in the country, but muft have connected with the idea of it a variety of
distinct

distinct pleasures, which are now separately indistinguishable; though the traces of them, still remaining in the mind, contribute to swell the complex sensation of pleasure which he feels upon the view of it. Among the principal ingredients in this complex sensation, we may mention the pleasures with which our external senses have a thousand times been affected in the country; the sweet smells and the fine colours of flowers, the agreeable taste of fruits, the melody of birds, and the pleasure we have received from rural sports and pastimes. These, if we be advanced in life, we may have no great relish for; yet the ideas of the pleasure we may formerly have received from these objects, still adhere to the idea of the scenes in which they were enjoyed, and recur, in a confused sensation of pleasure, whenever those scenes are presented to the mind.

To these we may add the ideas of the healthfulness, and of the comparative innocence of a country life, the apparent usefulness of husbandry; a view of the plenty of the necessaries and conveniencies of life which the earth affords; the ideas of novelty, beauty, and grandeur, with which we have, upon innumerable occasions, been struck in viewing the scenes of nature; together with the ideas of the jocundity and happiness which our fellow-creatures must frequently have shared with us in a country life.

All these sources have contributed, in a greater or less degree, to the complex sense of pleasure which a fine country prospect affords; and to these a philosophical and devout observer adds lively ideas of the power, wisdom, and goodness of God, the marks of which are so conspicuous in the vegetable and animal world. By him the Deity is seen in all his works; and though, upon the first view of a rural scene, the ideas of the Divine Be-

ing,

ing and his providence be not diftinctly perceived, they cannot fail greatly to heighten every complex fenfation into which they really enter.

From the principle of affociation we may, likewife, account for the tumultuous pleafurable fenfation we feel upon the view of the place where we paffed our infancy, the fchool where we were educated, or any other place, or perfon, with whom a great number of our ideas and fenfations have formerly been affociated, though they now form one complex fenfation, and are feparately indiftinguifhable. Even painful fenfations, as they give no pain upon reflection, unlefs they have been extremely violent indeed, only contribute to heighten the complex pleafing emotion.

Sometimes it is obfervable, that, immediately upon feeling a tumultuous fenfation of this kind, the idea of fome particular affecting circumftance will occur diftinctly, it not having perfectly *coalefced* with the general complex fenfation; whereas, by degrees, it intirely vanifhes into, and makes a part of it, and in its feparate ftate is quite forgotten. Facts of this nature are circumftances extremely favourable to this hypothefis of the mechanical generation of our intellectual pleafures and pains by the principle of affociation; and there are few perfons who attend to their feelings but muft have obferved them.

It is eafy to conceive that complex fenfations of this kind are capable of being transferred to objects which are *fimilar* to thofe with which they were originally affociated, by means of any common property. Thus the complex fenfation, connected at firft with one particular country fcene, will be excited, though in a fainter degree, by the view of any other country fcene: and thofe feelings, which were originally affociated with one particular fchool, will be revived by the fight of any other fchool, or even of any

3   thing

thing belonging to education. And, univerfally, objects poffeffed of properties common to thofe objects with which any fenfations have been firmly affociated, acquire, by their analogy to
them, a power of exciting the fame fenfations, and confequently
of affecting us in a fimilar manner with the objects whofe properties they poffefs, in proportion to their refemblance.

For example; the properties of *uniformity*, *variety*, and *proportion*, or a *fitnefs to fome ufeful end* having been perceived in
moft of the objects with which pleafurable ideas and fenfations
have been affociated, a complex pleafurable fenfation will univerfally be annexed to the marks of uniformity, variety, and proportion, wherever they are perceived; fo that by noting the
properties which are common to thofe objects which affect our
imaginations in an agreeable manner, we may be enabled to give
an enumeration of all the fpecies of the pleafures of imagination that we are capable of; or of pointing out the different
properties, and qualities, in objects which are adapted to give us
pleafure, and contribute to our entertainment in works of tafte
and genius.

Whether it will be allowed that the principle of affociation is
the fource of *all* the pleafures which are fuggefted by objects of
tafte, or not, it is manifeft that it muft have a very confiderable influence in this affair, and will help us to account for much, if not
all, of the variety that is obfervable in the taftes of different perfons.

Had all minds the very fame degree of fenfibility, that is, were
they equally affected by the fame impreffions, and were we all
expofed to the fame influences, through the whole courfe of our
lives, there would be no room for the leaft diverfity of tafte among
mankind. For, in thofe circumftances, we fhould all have affociated precifely the fame ideas and fenfations with the fame objects,

jects, and the same properties of those objects; and we should feel those sentiments in the same degree. But since our situations in life, and the occurrences of our lives, are so very various, it cannot but have happened, that different persons will have associated different ideas and sensations with the same objects; and, consequently, they will be differently affected upon the perception of them. Moreover, since mens minds are endued with very different degrees of sensibility, some persons will be affected in a stronger, and some in a weaker manner, when their sensations are of the same kind. For the same reasons, likewise, the same person is liable to be affected in a very different manner by the same objects, in different parts of his life, and in different situations and dispositions.

There seems, however, to be so great a similarity in our situations, as is sufficient to afford a foundation for a considerable *similarity in taste*; particularly in persons whose education and manner of life have been nearly the same. But a *standard of taste*, founded upon the similar influences which persons so situated have been subject to, cannot be applied to those persons whose education and manner of life have been very different. It is no wonder that a person accustomed to the refined sentiments of modern times cannot relish some of the compositions of the ancients; that what is deemed a fine taste in the East, should not be deemed equally good in Europe; or even that what is admired in France, should not always meet with the same approbation in England.

This diversity of taste would certainly be much more considerable at present, were it not for the easy intercourse there is between different nations, and different universities, particularly by means of the art of printing; by which they communicate

I   their

their feveral feelings, and thereby bring their taftes nearer to a perfect fimilarity. It confirms this obfervation, that it is generally thought that fomething of the ftrength of the Englifh writers is perceived in fome of the later French compofitions; and that our modern polite authors in England have acquired the delicacy and correctnefs of the French. The confequence of a freer intercourfe between the eaftern and weftern parts of the world would, certainly, be their profiting by our tafte, and our manner of compofition, if not our acquiring alfo fomething more of theirs. And, from this principle, we may expect that, in confequence of the growing intercourfe between all the nations of earth, and all the *literati* of them, an uniform and perfect ftandard of tafte will at length be eftablifhed over the whole world.

In the mean time, juftnefs of tafte will be determined by appealing to the general fenfe of thofe who have been the moft converfant with the fubjects of it. A deviation from this general tafte will be reckoned a fault, and a coincidence with it an excellence; and the difficulty there is in afcertaining what is this *medium of opinion* in connoiffeurs makes the bufinefs of criticifm, or the ftandard of judging in works of genius, fo vague and undetermined as it is. Perfons who have not been converfant with the fubjects of tafte are excluded from having any vote in this cafe, becaufe their minds have not been in a proper fituation for receiving the ideas and fenfations which are requifite to form a juft tafte.

LECTURE

LECTURE XVIII.

A general Account of the Pleasure we receive from Objects that oc-casion a moderate Exertion of our Faculties.

ALL beauties, and admired strokes in composition, derive their
excellence and fine effect, either from drawing out and ex-
ercising our faculties, by the views they present to our minds;
or else transferring from foreign objects, by the principle of af-
sociation, ideas which tend to improve the sense of a passage.
In what cases the effect of composition is heightened by each of
these means, and in what manner it is done, will be the subject
of the following Lectures to explain.

One property essential to every thing that gives us pleasure is,
that it occasions a *moderate exercise of our faculties.* Pleasure
consists of sensations moderately vigorous. It is, therefore, capable of existing in any degree between the two extremes of
perfect languor and tranquillity of mind on the one hand, and
actual pain and uneasiness on the other. It is observable,
likewise, that the more moderate any pleasure is, the longer
continuance it is capable of; and that the more intense any pleasurable sensation is, or the more nearly it approaches to a state of
pain, the less capable it is of a long duration.   Immoderate pleasure, as it were, oppresses, fatigues, and exhausts the mind.

Nothing

Nothing can be more evident than the truth of these principles, when applied to our external or corporeal senses. Warmth, for instance, is a sensation increasing in pleasure in all its gradations, from the torpid and benumbed state of the body, till it become actually hot and painful. Likewise a moderate and barely sensible degree of warmth is agreeable through the whole course of our lives; but we soon grow impatient of greater degrees of warmth, though for a time they may produce a more grateful sensation. In like manner, the limits of the pleasures of taste are, the insipid on the one hand, and the acrid and pungent on the other. Also the moderate pleasure which we receive from our common aliments, is always grateful; whereas viands of a high flavour, abounding with salts, which act forcibly upon the nerves appropriated to the sense of taste, though they yield a more exquisite relish for the time, soon cloy and disgust the palate. The same things may be observed concerning the remaining senses of smelling, seeing, and hearing.

To these affections of the external and corporeal senses, those of the internal and intellectual are strictly analogous. Indeed, it is impossible they should not be so, if the former be the only sources of the latter; that is, if, as was hinted before, all our intellectual pleasures and pains consist of nothing but the simple pleasures and pains of sense, commixed and combined together in infinitely-various degrees and proportions, so as to be separately indistinguishable, and transferred upon foreign objects, by the principle of association.

It is observable, likewise, that a moderate exertion of our active powers is attended with a continued perception of moderate pleasure, both as it quickens the perceptive powers, and exposes us to the influence of objects that are adapted to affect our senses;

T   but

but that a violent exertion is, for similar reasons, attended with pain and uneasiness. That this is equally true with respect both to the powers of our bodies and the faculties of our minds, is too obvious to require illustration. Indeed, it is wisely provided by Divine Providence, that both our minds and bodies are equally impatient of a state of rest and inactivity. Hence we are constantly impelled to exert ourselves with vigour in the station in which we are placed; and we can never be happy, and enjoy our being, unless we fulfil the great ends of it.

All persons, indeed, have not an equal relish for the same exercises, but in all minds there is an appetite for some or other species of it; and when once, by addicting ourselves to any kind of exercise, we have acquired a habit of it, from that time it becomes, in a manner, necessary to our happiness.

That the preceding account of the general affections of the mind with respect to pleasure, and the various degrees and gradations of it, are applicable to those which we receive from the polite arts, cannot but be obvious to all persons of reading, study, and reflection. No mind can long bear a very rapid succession of those scenes which, singly, give it the most exquisite pleasure. A judicious composer, therefore, is sensible that the most exquisite beauties in composition may be thrown away and lost, as it were, when they are placed too near together.

Besides, in a very quick succession of objects, the mind hath not leisure to perceive and attend to all their powers and relations. They lose therefore, of course, a great part of their full effect. Perhaps the finest circumstances belonging to some of the thoughts and expressions in a work of genius, may not be those which present themselves to view at the first hearing or reading. If,

there-

therefore, the mind be immediately, and without any refpite, hurried to other objects equally ftriking, it can only be affected with the groffer fenfations they convey. There could have been no leifure or opportunity for its perceiving thofe more delicate beauties, which conftitute the chief merit of works of tafte and imagination. In like manner, the grand and exquifite ftrokes of expreffion in mufic are always preceded by fuch ftrains as only prepare the mind for them, and are alfo followed by fuch as do not wholly take off the attention from them.

Moreover, all compofitions which are intended to engage our attention a confiderable time, fhould correfpond pretty nearly to the general and natural courfe of our own ideas and fenfations. A writer may be as witty, or as fublime, as he can, and he may crowd thefe graces of compofition as clofe as he pleafes; his readers cannot follow him but at a certain pace. There is a degree beyond which no perfon can accelerate the fucceffion of his ideas. If, therefore, a writer wifh to take his reader along with him, he muft, of neceffity, as we may fay, flacken his pace.

On thefe accounts, the more exquifite ftrokes of genius fhould either be confined to fhort compofitions, be fparingly introduced into works of length, or be crowded in places where the mind may take an attentive furvey of them, without drawing off its attention from objects of more importance. An *epigram* may contain as much wit as the writer can crowd into it, and the *ode* may be as full of the fublime as his imagination is capable of making it, and without any inconvenience; becaufe the whole compofition having very moderate bounds, and the attention not being folicited farther, we may attend to any part of it as long as we pleafe, and enjoy it at our leifure: but a great number of what are called the graces and mafterly ftrokes of compofition

are

are loft in a hiftory, in a heroic poem, or an interefting fcene in
a tragedy.

If thefe works be compofed in a good tafte, the attention of
the reader is fixed upon the incidents; he is *haftening* to the cata-
ftrophe, and will not ftop to examine all the beauties of the
compofition : that were an object quite foreign to the views of
a perfon whofe mind was properly engroffed by the *fubject* of the
work.   It is abfolutely impoffible to be properly impreffed with,
and to keep in view, the greater fentiments with which the mind
is infpired by fuch works as the Iliad, the Odyffee, and the
Æneid, and at the fame time give any attention to fuch minute
criticifms as fome commentators have defcended to, and taken the
pains to make upon them.   It is a fundamental rule in all kinds
of compofition, that they ought to be more or lefs elaborate, according as they are longer or fhorter; or, rather, according to
the opportunity they give the mind to attend to all the beauties
of them.

In thefe cafes, however, regard muft be had, if poffible, to the
perfons for whofe ufe any kind of compofition is made, and even to
the temper of mind in which it is moft likely to be perufed.   For
it is certain that the fucceffion of ideas, to which the tenor of a
compofition fhould correfpond, is very different in different perfons, and in different fituations of mind.   A ftyle adapted to the
vulgar, whofe minds are wholly uncultivated, whofe apprehenfions are confequently flow, and whofe feelings are ftrong, would
by no means fuit perfons whofe apprehenfions have been quickened, and whofe fenfations have been refined, by education and
reflection : nor would that ftyle, which was proper to be perufed by perfons in a tranquil and compofed ftate of mind, fuit the
                                                            fame.

fame perfon as well when the fucceffion of his ideas was accelerated by paffion, or a ftate of anxious fufpenfe.

An harangue to a multitude fhould confift of exceedingly ftrong and bold images, expreffed with great plainnefs and perfpicuity, and with confiderable intervals of intermediate ideas; whereas the ftrokes fhould be both more delicate and more frequently repeated, which are intended to make an impreffion upon an audience of cultivated underftandings and improved tafte. And it requires a ftyle extremely animated and concife to fuit a perfon whofe mind is in a kind of ferment, when the apprehenfion is more than ufually quick, and the fucceffion of ideas accelerated greatly beyond their ufual courfe.

An attention to this fame object, viz. the exercife of our faculties, will direct us to the proper medium between the *concife* and *diffufe* in ftyle. By the concife or diffufe in ftyle, I do not mean one that confifts of fhort or long periods; but by concife I mean that which leaves more, and by diffufe that which leaves lefs to be fupplied by the reader, whether the fentences be long or fhort. Thefe two kinds of ftyle have each their proper place where they may be ufed with propriety and advantage.

We cannot go on with a work of length, if every fentence require a confiderable exercife of our own faculties. It is too fatiguing, at leaft to the generality of readers. But all compofitions, and particularly thofe of fmall length, are infupportably infipid, if the writer have been fo unfeafonably officious, as to have left nothing to the exercife of the active faculties of his readers, and the whole excite nothing but a train of *paffive perceptions*.

For this reafon, the ftyle of Livy will be thought, by the generality of readers of hiftory, preferable to that of Tacitus.

whereas

whereas the concife ftyle of Marcus Antoninus, and even of Seneca, feems to be happily adapted to philofophical meditations, which are fuppofed to be read with great deliberation, and with frequent paufes for reflection.

It is no paradox to fay, that the fame ftyle will fuit a perfon when he is in a fituation which renders his apprehenfion uncommonly quick, and the fucceffion of his ideas rapid, and one which gives him leifure for reflection; though his mind be quite cool in the one cafe, and violently agitated in the other; becaufe, in both fituations, the mind will eafily fupply what the writer omits. Neither doth this encomium upon the ftyle of Antoninus imply any cenfure on the very different ftyle of Cicero: for his philofophical writings are *declamations*, and not *meditations*.

There is another method in which a writer may employ the faculties of his readers, but it is giving them a more difagreeable kind of exercife than that which was referred to above, and which is productive of a much lower kind of pleafure: I mean the trouble a writer may give his reader to underftand his meaning. If the meaning of a writer be intelligible, the exercife he gives our faculties is employed upon his fubject, in taking thofe views of things and of their relations which were indiftinctly pointed out by himfelf: and, provided thefe difcoveries be not very difficult to make, they yield a very high kind of entertainment. But if all the difficulty of a compofition be owing to frequent ellipfes, and a difordered conftruction, and, confequently, terminate when the writer's meaning is perfectly underftood; it is a bufinefs of *words* only, and can yield but little fatisfaction. Is not this the cafe fometimes with Thucydides, and Lord Clarendon?

Not

Not that a writer is,. in all cafes, to be condemned when he gives his reader fome trouble to underſtand him. Provided it be not the *chief* exercife he gives our faculties, it may, upon the whole, have a good effect. To this purpofe the tranfpofition of words and claufes from their natural order, and occafional parenthefes, are fometimes well employed. Thefe, when they are ufed moderately, occafion no greater pain from fufpenfe, than what is more than counterbalanced by the pleafure we receive, the moment it terminates, in our feeing the fenfe complete. It is certainly an advantage peculiar to ancient languages, that the words of them may be tranfpofed, for this and other purpofes, at pleafure. However, in the generality of compofitions, it is indifputable, that the proper medium of excellence is much nearer the extreme of perfpicuity than of obfcurity.

Perfons who have much leifure for reading and fpeculation may derive great advantage from thefe obfervations, concerning the moderate exercife of our faculties, in the conduct of their ſtudies. Intenfe application to the abſtract fciences, to the mathematics, and philofophy, the reading of languages that are rather difficult to us, or the bufinefs of compofition, is, undoubtedly at firſt, very fatiguing to all minds. Many perfons are foon difcouraged from fo fevere an exercife of their faculties; and it is ouly habit that can make it eafy, and reconcile the mind to it. But then the confequence of a fuccefsful application to thefe fevere ſtudies, being attended with a continued confcioufnefs of the *ſtrength of our faculties*, is a very high fenfe of pleafure, which remains very fenfibly a confiderable time after the exercife is over; whereas the pleasure we receive from the reading of history, romance, familiar essays, and poetry, though it may be very exquisite for a time, yet, if it engross all our leisure hours, it is attended with great languor and indifference; and there is scarce the least trace of pleasure left after our attention to them is over: nay, very often, though we read with pleasure, we give over with disgust, and a secret dissatisfaction with ourselves. The reason is, that, in mere reading of this kind, we are little more than passive. Trains of ideas pass before our minds, but no active powers of the soul are exerted. Life passed in that manner is mere indolence and inaction, to which, whether it be of the body or of the mind, no genuine and lasting happiness was ever annexed.

To have a full enjoyment of a studious life, the severer studies should be intermixed with the perusal of entertaining authors. In this succession, books of entertainment are read with tenfold more avidity and satisfaction. Poetry and works of fiction make a high *entertainment*, when they are made nothing more of; but they make a very poor and insipid *employment*. Infinitely preferable were it to be confined to the study of geometry, algebra, or law, without even having a glimpse of any thing more amusing, than be condemned to pass one's life sleeping over history, romances, poetry, and plays.

Application to true history seems to be the most rational of all these; but unless history be read either with a view to gain a knowledge of mankind, in order to form our own conduct; or with some scientific view, in order to determine some important subject of rational inquiry, it is nothing better than reading romance. By reading history with some farther view, as a *means* to a farther end, we

3

we make it a *fcience*.   It then engages our active powers.   It is a ferious bufinefs, and is capable of being purfued with continued and increafing ardour.   Otherwife, hiftory is no more than an amufement; and, confidering what hath ever been the ftate of the political world, and the general objects of hiftorians, it muft exhibit many fcenes extremely difagreeable to a reader of humanity and delicacy.

U   LECTURE

LECTURE XIX.

Of NOVELTY.

TO the general account of the pleafures we receive from the exercife of our perceptive and active powers, I fhall fubjoin a particular account of thofe properties of objects which derive their power of pleafing from the fame fource.

To this, in the firft place, we muft have recourfe for the charms of NOVELTY. For the firft perception of an object makes a much ftronger impreffion than any fubfequent perception of it. This muft neceffarily be the cafe if perception depend upon any mechanical laws affecting the brain. Upon whatever principle we account for it, the oftener any fenfations are repeated, the lefs we are affected by them. But the chief fource of the charms of novelty is the exercife of our active powers. Both previous to the perception of any new object, if we have any intimation of it, and immediately upon the perception of it, whether it be a new fcene in nature, a new train of adventures, or a new fyftem of principles, the mind is full of expectation, and is eagerly employed in furveying it; which keeps the attention ftrongly awake, and gives the object an opportunity of making a deep impreffion. Whereas when this firft curiofity is gratified, and the object is become familiar, we view it in a more

curfory

curfory and fuperficial manner; there being then no reafon for fo clofe an attention to it, as we expect no new knowledge or information.

This conftant appetite, as we may call it, for novelty, feems to be infeparable from beings indued with the faculty of reafon and reflection, and whofe happinefs depends upon the ufe they make of the advantages attending their fituation. Being habitually in queft of happinefs, we naturally examine every new object with peculiar attention; but when once we are acquainted with all the properties and powers of it, and know how much it is capable of contributing to our main purpofe, our examination is finifhed, and the motive for our curiofity is at an end. Moreover, to apply a general obfervation made in a preceding lecture, as the mind conforms itfelf to the ideas which engage its attention, and it hath no other method of judging of itfelf but from its fituation, the perception of a new train of ideas is like its entering upon a new world, and enjoying a new being, and a new mode of exiftence.

So loud and inceffant is the call for novelty in the pleafures of the imagination, that the generality of readers feel little or no defire to re-perufe a performance which is calculated rather to pleafe than to inftruct. If a fecond perufal do give pleafure, it is either by the difcovery of new beauties, or a confiderable time after the firft perufal, when the fubject, or the method of treating it, hath been almoft forgotten, and when, confequently, it is in a manner new: for no perfon, I believe, would throw away his time upon a performance which he was beforehand fatisfied could prefent him with no new ideas, or new views of things.

If the reafon why we firft engage in any new ftudy, or undertake to read any work of genius, be not explicitly the profpect

of

of being entertained with new objects, and new reflections, as is often the cafe, we, notwithstanding, never cease to be under the influence of that principle during the whole time that we are employed about it. The prospect of advantage in general, or the expectation of receiving instruction and improvement, may have been our first and leading motive to those pursuits; but the ultimate ends of our conduct are not of a nature to be attended to constantly, and to influence particular actions. Whatever motive it was that first put our faculties in motion, it is generally, in these cafes, the charms of novelty that keep up the vigour of their exertion. And a happy provision it is in our constitution, that when great and important motives, from the necessary nature of things, intermit their influence, there are a variety of other *subsidiary springs of action* at hand, which are sufficient to carry on the work with vigour, by the help of only occasional reinforcements from the original and first-moving power. Thus a person undertakes a journey with a view to some advantage he expects to derive from it, yet he may soon lose sight of this, and, notwithstanding, continue to travel with pleasure; not propelled by his original impulse, but entertained with a variety of scenes which his change of place continually presents him with.

This craving appetite for novelty hath produced many very whimsical and extravagant effects in works of taste and genius. To this many new schemes of philosophy, new species of composition, and new peculiarities of style, owe their birth. Novelty is the surest and the readiest road to fame, for all the numerous competitors for that exquisite species of satisfaction; the first inquiry concerning any performance in literature always being, Is there any thing *new* in it?

Nor

Nor is the defire of novelty lefs confpicuous in other objects of tafte. What other recommendation have the *Chinefe tafte*, and the revival of the *Gothic*, in architecture, the pantomime entertainments, with all their varieties, on the theatre, and the new forms in which mufical entertainments are daily exhibited? Doth not a regard to novelty influence our choice of the furniture of our houfes, interfere in the difpofition of a garden, and fuggeft alterations in the fafhion of our cloaths? Why elfe doth a lady of tafte in drefs, difcover more confcious fatisfaction the firft time fhe makes her appearance at an affembly, among the firft in a fafhionable drefs, than fhe would have done if fhe had not been feen in the fame drefs till a month afterwards, when the *convenience*, and other properties of the habit, remain the fame?

Even the mere *unexpectednefs* of objects is often had recourfe to, as a fubftitute for abfolute novelty. A well-known object, occuring in a fituation in which it was wholly unlooked for, makes a ftronger impreffion upon the mind than it would have done if it had been expected. In the latter cafe, the mind is occupied with the idea, at leaft, of the object, before the actual perception of it; and therefore the difference in the previous and fubfequent ftate of mind, is only the difference between an *idea* and a *fenfation*, a difference in degree only. In the former cafe, the fenfation is made at once, without any previous idea, which makes a difference more than in degree only. Befides, in this cafe, the relations and circumftances, if not the object itfelf, are new to us. Alfo the fenfible contraft which hence arifes between the two ftates of mind, before and after the perception of an unexpected object, contributes to heighten the fenfation.

I

By means of this contraſt, familiar ideas, occurring in unexpected ſituations, may occaſion a greater agitation of mind,
than new ideas of a ſimilar nature. The reaſon is, that every
idea which is become familiar to us, muſt have acquired a variety
of aſſociations. Theſe aſſociated circumſtances, occurring to the
mind at the ſame inſtant with the ideas to which they are connected, immediately ſtrike the mind with the ſenſe of any ſeeming inconſiſtency there may be, between them and the new and
unexpected ſituations in which we meet with them. Thus the
ſudden appearance of a friend, whom we thought to have been
in a diſtant place, affects us more ſenſibly, than ſeeing any
face that is quite new to us, in the ſame place and circumſtances.
With the latter we have connected no ideas of any circumſtances
which have the leaſt ſeeming inconſiſtency with the circumſtances
in which we find them: with the other, we have connected ſuch
ideas.

The ſenſation which we feel upon the unexpected appearance
of a well-known object, is termed *ſurprize*; whereas an object
perfectly new is ſaid to excite our *wonder*.

The gratification which the mind is ſure to receive from ſurprize, may add ſomething to the influence of thoſe other motives
which carry ſome people with ſo much eagerneſs to the gaming-
table. There the continual expectation of events, on which a
great deal is depending, and of which we can; with no degree of
certainty, form the leaſt conjecture, keeps the attention awake to
an extreme degree; which always prepares the mind for receiving a ſtrong impreſſion. If we be intereſted in the event, our
paſſions of hope and fear, being gratified in their turn, greatly
augment the internal agitation, ſo as often to carry it beyond the
limits of pleaſure, and make it terminate in the moſt painful and
tormenting anxiety.   LECTURE

L E C T U R E XX.

Of the S U B L I M E.

GREAT objects pleafe us for the fame reafon that *new* objects do, viz. by the exercife they give to our faculties. The mind, as was obferved before, conforming and adapting itfelf to the objects to which its attention is engaged, muft, as it were, enlarge itfelf, to conceive a great object. This requires a confiderable *effort of the imagination*, which is alfo attended with a pleafing, though perhaps not a diftinct and explicit confcioufnefs of the ftrength and extent of our own powers.

As the ideas of *great* and *little* are confeffedly relative, and have no exiftence but what they derive from a comparifon with other ideas; hence, in all fublime conceptions, there is a kind of fecret retrofpect to preceding ideas and ftates of mind. The fublime, therefore, of all the fpecies of excellence in compofition, requires the moft to be intermixed with ideas of an intermediate nature; as thefe contribute not a little, by their contraft, to raife and aggrandize ideas which are of a rank fuperior to themfelves. Whenever any object, how great foever, becomes familiar to the mind, and its relations to other objects is no longer attended to, the fublime vanifhes. Milton's battle of the angels, after the prelude to the engagement, would have been read with no greater

emotions

emotions than are excited by the hiſtory of a common battle, had not the poet perpetually reinforced his ſublime, as it were, by introducing frequent compariſons of thoſe ſuperior beings, and their actions, with human combatants and human efforts. It is plainly by means of compariſon that Horace gives us ſo ſublime an idea of the unconquerable firmneſs of Cato :

> Et cuncta terrarum ſubacta,
> Preter atrocem animum Catonis.

For the ſame reaſon a well-conducted *climax* is extremely favourable to the ſublime. In this form of a ſentence, each ſubſequent idea is compared with the preceding; ſo that if the former have been repreſented as large, the latter, which exceeds it, muſt appear exceedingly large. The effect of this we ſee in that ſublime paſſage of Shakeſpeare, inſcribed upon his monument in Weſtminſter Abbey :

> The cloud-capt towers, the gorgeous palaces,
> The ſolemn temples, the great globe itſelf,
> And all which it inherit, ſhall diſſolve,
> And, like the baſeleſs fabric of a viſion,
> Shall leave no wreck behind.

The intermediate ideas which are introduced to increaſe the ſublime, by means of compariſon with the object whoſe grandeur is to be inhanced by them, ought to be of a *ſimilar* nature; becauſe there is no compariſon of things diſſimilar. The difference between them ſhould be nothing more than that of greater and leſs : and even in this caſe, it often happens that the contraſt of things between which there is a very great diſparity (as will be explained hereafter) produces the *burleſque*, a ſentiment of a quite

oppo-

oppofite nature to the fublime.   It is not improbable but that many of Mr. Pope's readers may affix ludicrous ideas to the following lines, which, in his own conception, and that of his more philofophical readers, were very fublime.

> Who fees with equal eye, as God of all,
> A hero perifh, or a fparrow fall;
> Atoms, or fyftems, into ruin hurl'd;
> And now a bubble burft, and now a world.
>
> ESSAY ON MAN. Ep. I.

Sparrows, *atoms*, and *bubbles*, do not make the fame figure in the eye of the generality of mankind, that they do in that of a philofopher.

It follows from thefe principles, that no conception can be fublime which is not *fimple*.   If any fcene prefent a crowd of feparate objects, the mind views them in *fucceffion*, though in a very quick and rapid one, and exerts no extraordinary effort to conceive and comprehend any of them.   However, an idea that doth confift of parts may appear fublime, if the parts of which it confifts be not attended to, but the aggregate of them all be perceived as one idea.   This is eafily illuftrated by the ideas of *numbers*.   Very large numbers, as a *thoufand*, *ten thoufand*, and a *hundred thoufand*, prefent great and fublime ideas upon the firft naming of them, which continue fo long as we endeavour to furvey the whole of them at once, without attempting to refolve them into their component parts; but the arithmetician, who is ufed to compofe and decompofe the largeft numbers, is confcious of no fublime idea, even when he is performing the operations of *addition* and *multiplication* upon them.

X

Objects

Objects of the firſt rank in point of magnitude, and which chiefly conſtitute the ſublime of deſcription, are large rivers, high mountains, and extenſive plains; the ocean, the clouds, the heavens, and infinite ſpace; alſo ſtorms, thunder, lightning, volcanos, and earthquakes, in nature; and palaces, temples, pyramids, cities, &c. in the works of men. See a fine enume-ration of thoſe ſcenes of nature, which contribute the moſt to the ſublime, in Akenſide upon this ſubject:

——————— Who but rather turns
To heaven's broad fire his unconſtrained view,
Than to the glimmering of a waxen flame?
Who that, from Alpine heights, his lab'ring eye
Shoots round the wide horizon, to ſurvey
The Nile or Ganges roll his waſteful tide,
Thro' mountains, plains, thro' empires black with ſhade,
And continents of ſand, will turn his gaze
To mark the windings of a ſcanty rill
That murmurs at his feet? &c.

PLEASURES OF THE IMAGINATION, Lib. I.

But the account here given of the ſublime, by no means con-fines it to the ideas of objects which have ſenſible and *corporeal* magnitude. *Sentiments* and *paſſions* are equally capable of it, if they relate to great objects, ſuppoſe extenſive views of things, require a great effort of the mind to conceive them, and produce great effects. Fortitude, magnanimity, generoſity, patriotiſm, and univerſal benevolence, ſtrike the mind with the idea of the ſublime. We are conſcious that it requires a great effort to exert them; and in all caſes when the mind is conſcious of a ſimilar exertion of its faculties, it refers its ſenſations to the ſame claſs.

If

If the virtues above mentioned were more common, the idea of them would not be so sublime.

Who that considers the sentiments of Diomedes, when he prays to Jupiter to *give him day, and then destroy him*; the answer of Alexander to Parmenio (who had told him that he would accept the offers of Darius, if he were Alexander) *And so would I, if I were Parmenio*; and much more the prayer of our Saviour upon the cross, in behalf of his persecutors, *Father, forgive them, for they know not what they do*: who, I say, that attends to these sentiments, can entertain a doubt that they produce feelings similar to those which we receive from the view of grand and elevated objects? Or a person need only to read the following passage from Dr. Akenside, to be convinced that there is a true sublime in sentiment:

> Say why was man so eminently raised
> Above the vast creation? Why advanced
> Thro' life and death to dart his piercing eye,
> With thoughts beyond the limits of his frame;
> But that th' Omnipotent might send him forth,
> In sight of mortal and immortal powers,
> As on a boundless theatre, to run
> The great career of justice, to exalt
> His gen'rous aim to all diviner deeds? &c.

There is no surer method of discovering those sensations and ideas, which are apprehended to be analogous by mankind in general, than by observing the analogies of *words* in various languages; for the one will correspond to the other. As mankind, when the bulk of any language was invented, were not in a situation to invent superfluous terms, we may naturally conclude they would content themselves with the same term when there was a

great

great refemblance in the ideas they reprefented; but in no other cafe, if they could avoid fo great an inconvenience. If this clue be allowed to be of any ufe to us, in claffing our ideas and fenfations, there will remain no doubt but that there are a variety of things, not material, which raife fenfations fimilar to thofe which are excited by objects which have corporeal magnitude and elevation.

How elfe came a man of diftinguifhed abilities to be called a *great man?* Why do we fay that a benevolent man is of an *open* as well as generous temper? and that a covetous man hath a *narrow* foul? How came the epithets *proud, haughty*, and *lofty,* to be fynonymous? and how came the terms *fuperior tafte, advancement in honour, head of the table, high note* in mufic, *afcending feries* in numbers, and *high* and *low, near* or *diftant,* with refpect to *time,* to prevail fo generally, and to become fo familiar, that the figure is perfectly evanefcent? Moreover, how came robes of ftate to be made large and full, and thrones to be lofty, &c.? Whence comes it that largenefs of fize contributes to make a perfon look majeftic? And how came the Scythian ambaffadors to be furprized to find *Alexander the Great* to be a *little man?*

I might mention a great many more terms borrowed from corporeal magnitude, extenfion and elevation, applied to things which have none of thofe qualities; but thefe are fufficient to fhow that the perception of the fentiments, difpofitions, and circumftances, to which they are applied, are attended with a confcioufnefs of a feeling, fimilar to that which is excited by the view of objects which have the qualities of corporeal magnitude, extenfion, and elevation; that is, with the fublime.

The

The fublime of fcience confifts in general and comprehenfive theorems, which, by means of very great and extenfive confequences, prefent the idea of *vaftnefs* to the mind. A perfon of true tafte may perceive many inftances of genuine fublime in geometry, and even in algebra; and the fciences of natural philofophy and aftronomy, exhibit the nobleft fields of the fublime that the mind of man was ever introduced to. Theorems may alfo be fublime by their relating to great objects.

For many things which, confidered in themfelves, and abftracted from every thing that is foreign to them, are incapable of the fublime, infpire that fentiment by their affociation with others that are capable of it. From this fource it is that the ideas of wealth, honour, and power, borrow their fublime. It is the *caufes*, the *adjuncts*, or the *effects* of thefe things, that are contemplated, when they fill and charm the foul. *Wealth* carries with it the idea of a large eftate, and abundance of every thing that can contribute to the enjoyment of life. From *honour* we never feparate the idea of the ftrength of body, the capacity of the mind, or the great atchievements by which it was procured. With thefe alfo we join the number of people among whom a perfon is renowned, the extent of country through which his fame fpreads, and the length of time to which it extends. To the idea of *power* we join ideas of the good or evil it may produce, and of the multitudes which are fubject to its controul. In the idea of a *conqueror*, we may clearly diftinguifh the idea of a great extent of country fubdued; and in the idea of *nobility*, that of a long train of illuftrious anceftors. A fimilar analyfis would fhow us the fublime of *friendfhip*, *patriotifm*, and many other abftract ideas.

The

The grandeur of a *palace*, befides what it derives from its exceeding other houfes in bulk, is derived from the ideas of the labour, expence, length of time, and number of perfons neceffary to the erection of it; and from ideas of the wealth, honour, and power of him who inhabits it. Celebrated buildings and cities *in ruins*, along with thefe ideas, prefent that of the length of time that hath elapfed fince they flourifhed; and the whole fenfation is greatly magnified by a comparifon of their former magnificence with their prefent defolation. The grandeur and peculiar awfulnefs with which we are ftruck upon the view of a *temple* is, in a great meafure, derived from the ideas we have annexed to it of the power of the Deity to whom it is facred; as all that is fublime in the idea of a *fenate-houfe*, or other public building, arifes from the idea of the *ufe* to which it is appropriated.

The *contempt* of power, wealth, and grandeur, is more fublime than the *poffeffion* of them; becaufe, after a view of thofe great objects, it prefents us with the view of a *mind* above them. So that it is not true, that " nothing is great the contempt of " which is great."

Though, in fome cafes of this fpecies of *transferred fublimity*, the analyfis of a complex idea fhould prefent no one idea which, fingly taken, could be called fublime; yet, fo long as thofe ideas continue feparately indiftinguifhable, the mind perceives not a number of fmall objects, but one great one; as in the cafe before explained of the fublime of numbers.

As moft of our emotions are of a complex nature, we are in great danger, unlefs we be extremely attentive, of making miftakes in the diftribution and analyfis of them. Hence emotions of *terror* have been often claffed with the fublime. But terror

is

is a mixed fenfation, compofed of the very different fenfations of *fear* and *grandeur*, to the latter of which it owes all its fublimity. For, when we are in a fituation in which we have nothing to fear, the fight of a monftrous beaft, of a giant, or of the fea in a ftorm, &c. prefents little more than the pure fublime, heightened by the fecret pleafure we take in the idea of our own fecurity. The pure fublime partakes nothing of fear, or of any other painful emotion.

Moreover, the pure fublime, by ftrongly engaging, tends to fix the attention, and to keep the mind in a kind of *awful ftillnefs*; whereas it is of the nature of every fpecies of the pathetic to throw it into an *agitation*. Hence the fenfations we feel from *darknefs* and *profound filence*, refembling the ftillnefs the mind is thrown into when the attention is ftrongly fixed by a fublime object, partake of the nature of the fublime; as we may perceive in the following excellent paffage of Dr. Young.

> Night, fable goddefs, from her ebon throne,
> In raylefs majefty, now ftretches forth
> Her leaden fceptre o'er a flumb'ring world.
> Silence how dead! and darknefs how profound!
> Nor eye nor lift'ning ear an object finds.
> Creation fleeps. 'Tis as the general pulfe
> Of life ftood ftill, and Nature made a paufe—
> An awful paufe, prophetic of her end.
> And let her prophecy be foon fulfill'd:
> Fate, drop the curtain. I can lofe no more.
>
> NIGHT-THOUGHTS, I.

Hence alfo deep and flow notes in mufic bear a nearer relation to the fublime than fhrill and quick founds.

It

It may be obferved, that the account here given of the Sublime confines it to the *fentiment*. However, as the term (which
hath been ufed in a more vague fenfe than almoft any other
term in criticifm) is frequently applied to *language*, I fhall briefly
explain how the fublime is affected by language.

Ideas in themfelves fublime may intirely lofe that quality by
being expreffed in terms which have connexions with trivial and
mean objects, or in metaphors borrowed from fuch objects. In
this cafe the *fecondary affociations* which accompany thofe words
are transferred upon the object defcribed by them, and deftroy the
fublime they would otherwife have. Though, therefore, in general,
the *plaineft terms* are the moft favourable to the fublime, as they exhibit the moft juft and the ftrongeft idea of the object; yet every
term, however plain and intelligible, that hath ever had the leaft
connexion with *mean fubjects*, or even which hath been chiefly
ufed by perfons of a low and illiberal clafs of life, fhould be carefully avoided. What can be more fublime than the following
paffage in the Pfalms? " He looketh on the earth, and it trem-
" bleth. He toucheth the hills, and they fmoke," But it is
greatly lowered by fome ludicrous images in the following pa-
raphrafe.

> The hills forget they're fix'd, and in their fright
> Caft off their weight, and eafe themfelves for flight.
> The woods, with terror wing'd, outfly the wind,
> And leave the heavy, panting hills behind.

On the other hand, the *mock-heroic* is introduced when words
which have generally been annexed to great and important fubjects, are ufed to exprefs mean or trivial things. The oppofition
of ideas fo contrary to one another makes a high burlefque.

Some-

Sometimes a *periphrasis* comes seasonably in aid of the sublime, by giving the mind an opportunity to dwell upon the idea, and see the whole extent of it. Thus the phrase, *Nine times the space that measures day and night to mortal men*, in Milton, suits the following sublime passage in which it is introduced, much better than if he had barely said so many *days*. The former mode of expression, as it were, detains the idea of the *angels rolling in the fiery gulph*, longer in the mind; during which time our wonder and astonishment are continually rising higher and higher.

> ———— Him th' Almighty Power
> Hurl'd headlong flaming from th' ethereal sky,
> With hideous ruin, and combustion, down
> To bottomless perdition, there to dwell
> In adamantine chains and penal fire,
> Who durst defy th' Omnipotent to arms.
> Nine times the space that measures day and night
> To mortal men, he with his horrid crew
> Lay vanquish'd, rolling in the fiery gulph,
> Confounded, though immortal.
>
> PARADISE LOST, Book I.

Proper names of great objects are often preferable to general terms, as they realize the ideas, and fix the attention to them. Thus, to mention the *Alps*, the *Andes*, or *Teneriffe*, presents a greater idea than saying, *very high mountains*; and to say, the *Nile*, the *Ganges*, or the *La Plata*, is to speak more magnificently than to say, *great rivers* only. Thus, the simple and sublime Ossian affects the imagination of his reader much more strongly by the hill of *Cromla*, the *waves of Inistore*, the reeds of the *lake of Lego*, than he could have done by the use of any more general and abstract terms. This effect would be more sen-

sible

fible, if we were acquainted with the objects introduced in this manner.

Next to the *pathetic*, of all the excellencies of good compofition, the *fublime* promifes the moft lafting reputation to an author. Compofitions which are calculated only to *pleafe* and to *divert*, are beings of a day. Few of them, even by the favour of a very extraordinary coincidence of circumftances, reach pofterity, in comparifon of thofe which *fhake* and which *elevate* our fouls. Let us only look into our own breafts, and we fhall find that we are very differently affected to the writer who pleafes the imagination, and to the poet or orator who either raifes and enlarges our conceptions, or who thoroughly interefts our paffions. The former we may *admire*, but we may alfo foon *forget*. Our efteem for the latter rifes to *reverence*; and when the pathetic and the fublime are joined (as they are capable of the moft intimate union, and are perhaps never found in a very high degree intirely feparate) they produce the ftrongeft and the moft lafting attachment.

A genius formed for the fublime is a mind which is naturally difpofed to take the moft extenfive views of things, whofe attention is turned to view every thing in the grandeft and nobleft point of light ; whereas other minds are more inclined to attend to what is *little* and *beautiful* in the objects they view. And as every thing we are converfant with hath various, and very different properties, every mind hath an opportunity of indulging its own tafte, by contemplating thofe forms of things which afford it the moft pleafing gratification.

I cannot conclude this article without obferving, that inftances of the true fublime abound no where more than in the Scriptures.

3

Never

Never were grander ideas prefented to the human mind, than we find in the reprefentations of the Divine Being in Ifaiah, particularly chapter XL. in the book of Job, in feveral places in the Pfalms, and in the writings of Mofes.

The falfe fublime, or the *bombaft*, will be confidered when I treat of the Hyperbole.

LECTURE XXI.

Of the Pleasure we receive from Uniformity, *and* Variety; *and
first of* Comparisons.

THE pleasure we receive from the view of objects in which
there is a visible mixture of *uniformity and variety*, hath,
no doubt, more sources than one : however, as one of its
sources is the moderate exercise which such objects give to our
faculties, I shall treat of it in this place.

To comprehend an object, the parts of which have no sort
of analogy to one another, we must of necessity go over the
whole of it ; and after this survey, which (from the uniform
manner in which our minds are employed when we attend to
it) must be very tedious, nothing but the *memory* is exercised,
to connect and retain the idea of the whole : whereas the moment
we perceive that the parts of any object are analogous to one another, and find, or are informed, what that analogy is, the sight
of a part, without any farther investigation, suggests the idea of
the whole ; and the *judgment* is most agreeably and successfully
employed in completing the image.

This is very evident upon the view of a part of any thing
the proportions of which are known, as of an animal body,
of a regular curve, or polygon, a regular building, a re-

gular

gular garden, or of a confiftent fet of political, philofophical, or theological principles. With what fatisfaction may we often hear perfons fay, upon feeing part of fuch an object, or fuch a fcheme, " You need fhew me no more: I fee the whole." When being fhewn fo little of an object fuffices to comprehend it, it fhews confiderable experience, and an extenfive acquaintance with the forms and properties of things.

To difcern the analogy of the things we are converfant with, is to become poffeffed of the clue of knowledge, by which we are led, with unfpeakable eafe and fatisfaction, through the feeming labyrinths of nature. In this manner, by the help of a few general principles, we become mafters of a great extent of valuable fcience : whereas, without fuch general principles, which are derived from the knowledge of the analogy or uniformity of things, our fpeculations prefent nothing but a fcene of confufion and embarraffment.

Moreover, wherever we fee analogy in objects, we fee the marks of *intelligence* and *defign* ; which will be mentioned hereafter as another fource of pleafure in works of genius and imagination : and the more complex is the object we view, or the greater the variety we perceive, confiftent with ftrict analogy, the more doth it employ our faculties to comprehend it, and the higher idea do we conceive of the intelligence of the being who formed it. Befides, the *contraft* there is between two properties fo different as *uniformity* and *variety* in the fame object, contributes not a little to increafe the pleafure refulting from a view of the whole.

But perhaps it is to *affociation* that we are indebted for the greateft part of the pleafure we receive from the view of uniformity and variety. In fact, almoft every pleafing object in

nature

nature or art is poſſeſſed of it.   The human body, all animal bodies, and all vegetable nature, infinitely various as thoſe objects
are, have their parts formed with perfect analogy to one another.
Theſe properties are, likewiſe, for reaſons of convenience, imitated in our houſes, in our gardens, in our furniture, utenſils,
and, in ſhort, in every thing in which the ingenuity or induſtry
of men are employed.   Can it be any wonder then, when every
thing around us, that is adapted to give us pleaſure, hath theſe
properties, that even the firſt appearance of them in objects,
the uſes of which we are wholly unacquainted with, ſhould be
pleaſing ?

The pleaſure we receive from what is called the *juſt pro-*
portions of objects, is borrowed, by aſſociation, from the idea
of the *uſes* to which ſuch proportions are ſubſervient.   What is a
well-proportioned plough, a well-proportioned houſe, or a well-
proportioned ſhip, but things, or inſtruments, of ſuch a form as
is found by experience to be the moſt proper and convenient for
the purpoſes to which they are applied ?   If proportion be any
thing different from this, it muſt coincide with the idea of uniformity and variety.

From this ſource of uniformity and variety, is derived the pleaſure which *compariſons, metaphors,* and *allegories,* in works of genius and imagination, give us.   This is a conſideration diſtinct
from that of the light they throw upon a ſubject.   Compariſons
give us clear ideas of things, by means of the reſemblance between the ideas they exhibit and thoſe which a writer hath occaſion to introduce ; in which it is evident that the property of
ſimilarity or uniformity alone is concerned ; though we may conſider it as heightened by its contraſt with thoſe properties in the objects which are not ſimilar.   But uniformity alone, however heightened

ened, doth not affect the imagination with any sense of pleasure. In order to produce this effect, it is necessary that variety be joined to it.

Let us take for an example the following celebrated simile in Addison's Campaign.

> So when an angel, by divine command,
> With rising tempests shakes a guilty land,
> (Such as of late o'er pale Britannia past)
> Calm and serene he guides the furious blast;
> And, pleased th' Almighty's orders to perform,
> Rides in the whirlwind, and directs the storm.

The light which this simile throws upon the principal object in the poem, can only arise from the *resemblance* there is between the situation of the hero and that of the angel, dispensing death an ' destruction, at the command of a sovereign, with perfect calm- .is. These are the only points in which we perceive any considerable resemblance in the two objects. But if there had been no circumstances in which they had *differed*, the simile would never have met with that applause with which it hath almost universally been received. For where would have been the advantage of comparing Marlborough to any other hero in exactly similar circumstances? In this case, there would have been a much nearer resemblance, but no poetical beauty, because no variety. Nay, in reality, in the most striking circumstance in the situation of Marlborough, we perceive no sort of resemblance in that of the angel, viz. in his intrepidity in braving danger; yet, perhaps, this capital difference contributes more to the pleasure which these two views jointly give to the imagination, than any other circumstance

cumftance belonging to either of them. For what could give us a higher idea of the courage of Marlborough, in danger, than to reprefent him to be as calm as an angel in no danger at all? yet this circumftance would have appeared quite foreign to the purpofe, and have given no pleafure at all, if the angel had not been employed in a fimilar manner, viz. *directing the courfe of death.*

It is evident, therefore, that it is to the joint influence of thofe circumftances in which two objects agree, and of thofe in which they differ, that we muft afcribe the power of comparifons to raife pleafing ideas in our minds. In other words, the pleafure we receive from them is of the fame nature with that which we receive from a view of thofe objects in which there is a due mixture of uniformity and variety. Confequently, the chief excellence of a comparifon (and, for the fame reafon, of a metaphor and allegory) muft depend upon the proportion there is between the degrees of uniformity and variety, or the points of refemblance and difference, in the principal object, and that to which it is compared.

The following fimile of Homer neither illuftrates the object he is defcribing, by exhibiting the fame idea in greater ftrength, nor are the circumftances of the two cafes fufficiently different to give any pleafure to the imagination.

> This juft rebuke inflamed the Lycian crew,
> They join, they thicken, and th' affault renew.
> Unmoved th' embodied Greeks their fury dare,
> And fix'd, fupport the weight of all the war.
> Nor could the Greeks repel the Lycian powers,
> Nor the bold Lycians force the Grecian towers.

As,

As, on the confines of adjoining grounds,
Two stubborn swains with blows dispute their bounds;
They tug, they sweat, but neither gain nor yield
One foot, one inch of the contended field :
Thus obstinate to death, they fight, they fall,
Nor these can keep, nor those can win the wall.
ILIAD XII. 505.

That there can be no merit in a simile in which there is little or no resemblance between the objects compared, is too obvious to require an example. For it is manifest that the primary, the proper, and direct use of a simile, is to give clearer and stronger ideas of a thing than the plain description of it would suggest; and this end is not answered, unless the objects, or the circumstances in which they are placed, be similar. Indeed, if we consider only this primary use of comparisons, separate from the pleasure they give to the imagination (which is all along supposed to be only a secondary and subordinate consideration) in no case whatever would there be any real use of variety in a simile, if uniformity alone would suggest the ideas we want to illuminate (as we may say) more distinct and vivid. For, considering similes as serving the purpose of *illustration*, the use of those circumstances of diversity, which are exhibited in two objects that are compared together, is to heighten, by their contrast, the ideas of those circumstances in which they resemble one another.

Hence, perhaps, it is, that when the object introduced in a comparison presents the idea we want to illustrate in a very full and clear light, writers (perhaps without attending to the reason of it) content themselves with mentioning those circumstances of resemblance; and that they do not distinctly point out the circumstances of diversity, but in cases where the ideas of resemblance

Z   would

would not be fufficiently vivid without a contraft. Nay, if the
refemblance be very ftrong, it is reckoned fuperfluous, and often
abfurd, to proceed beyond a fimple *metaphor*, which is a fimile
contracted to its fmalleft dimenfions.

If we only confider that the primary ufe of a fimile is to give
clearer and ftronger ideas than we could convey without it, and
that an explicit and direct fimile fuppofes an excurfion of the
mind from the object it is intended to illuftrate, we may eafily
determine both the cirumftances in which the ufe of fimiles is
juft and natural, and fix proper bounds for the length of them.

Let a perfon be in whatever fituation he will, if he be in a condition to make ufe of language at all, he will endeavour to give
as clear an idea as he can of every thing that he would prefent to
the mind of another. Though, therefore, a man be in the greateft
agitation of mind poffible, and wholly occupied with any train of
ideas, he will feize upon any circumftance in nature that will help
him to give a clear idea of whatever he would wifh to communicate
to another perfon. The difference between a perfon whofe mind
is wholly ingroffed with any train of ideas, and another whofe
attention may be eafily diverted from it, is, that the former
will dwell no longer upon foreign objects than is neceffary, in
order to their fupplying him with proper terms by which to exprefs his own ideas : whereas, in the mind of another perfon,
when once a foreign object is brought into view, fome of its attributes, and other circumftances affociated with it, may not be
prevented from following it (as they naturally tend to do) by the
fudden recurrence of the former train of ideas.

For example, a perfon in extreme pain will naturally cry out
to his friend, *Oh, I burn, I am torn to pieces, I am upon the
rack*, &c. but then his mind is fo wholly and intenfely ingroffed

with

with the sensations of pain, that though the foreign circumstances of *burning*, *tearing to pieces*, and *being upon the rack*, do,
from their resemblance to his situation, occur to his mind, and
suggest to him the strongest language by which to express his
own feelings, they have no power of introducing any other circumstances connected with them ; and therefore the previous
train of ideas and sensations returns instantly. A person in such
a situation would never think of the *flame*, *smoke*, and *ashes* that
attend burning, or think of the *coup de grace* when he mentioned
the rack. But a person who is merely describing an interesting
scene, or a person who, after his first transports of grief are sub-
sided, is at leisure to contemplate his calamitous situation, when
he knows the whole extent of it, can hardly be supposed to have
his mind so wholly engrossed with the subject, as not to admit
and give some attention to a few circumstances the most closely
connected with those images which were introduced to illustrate
his ideas.

From the preceding account of similes, viz. that they are used
in order to give clearer ideas of things than any terms arising
from the subject itself would convey, it follows, that they are superfluous and ridiculous upon trifling occasions, as in common
discourse, where the plainest language is quite sufficient ; and
since direct similes suppose a considerable excursion of the mind
from the principal subject of its thoughts, it is manifest, as was
hinted before, that they must be very unnatural in the mouth of
a person in great *distress*, or any kind of *agitation of mind*. Shakespeare, through the luxuriance of his imagination, frequently
errs in the former case ; and Dryden, Lee, and most of our other
tragedians, in the latter : for which they are finely ridiculed in
the *Rehearsal*. This is owing to their not entering sufficiently

Z 2   into

into the paffions they defcribe. A perfon who reprefents another as under the influence of any paffion, fhould almoft forget that he is only defcribing, and fhould feel himfelf : otherwife his mind will be in fo different a fituation from that of the perfon he is defcribing, that it will be abfolutely impoffible that the fame thoughts fhould occur to him ; at leaft that they fhould occur in the fame order, or engage the attention equally. And, particularly, he will be in danger of giving part of that attention to *foreign* and *incidèntal circumflances*, which a perfon really interefted gives wholly to his own feelings.

The following paffage from Shakefpeare may ferve for an example of the improper ufe of fimiles upon trivial occafions. A gardener fays to his fervant,

> Go, bind thou up yon dangling apricocks,
> Which, like unruly children, make their fire
> Stoop with oppreffion of their prodigal weight.
> Give fome fupportance to the bending twigs.
> Go thou, and, like an executioner,
> Cut off the heads of too-faft-growing fprays,
> That look too lofty in our commonwealth.
> All muft be even in our government.
>
> RICHARD II. Act III. Scene 7.

And in the following paffage from the Mourning Bride, we fee the unfeafonablenefs of direct fimiles in great agitation of mind :

> *Zara.* The mute not yet return'd. Ha, 'twas the king.
> The king that parted hence, frowning he went.
> His eyes like meteors roll'd, then darted down
> Their red and angry beams ; as if his fight

Would,

Would, like the raging Dog-ſtar, ſcorch the earth,
And kindle ruin in its courſe.

Act V. Scene 3.

On the other hand, who doth not readily excuſe, in Oſſian, the eaſy extenſion of the following ſimile to a cloſely-connected circumſtance, though it be foreign to his immediate purpoſe, and in the midſt of a very intereſting ſcene?

" Where are the mighty kings? Nor by the ſtream nor wood
" are they. I hear the clanging of arms. Their ſtrife is in the
" boſom of that miſt. Such is the contention of ſpirits in a
" nightly cloud, when they ſtrive for the wintry wings of the
" winds, and the rolling of foam-covered waves."

TEMORA, Book VIII.

Or who, that conſidered the ſituation of Cardinal Wolſey, was ever offended at the following mixture of compariſon and metaphor which he uſeth?

Farewel, a long farewel to all my greatneſs!
This is the ſtate of man. To-day he puts forth
The tender leaves of hope, to-morrow bloſſoms,
And bears his bluſhing honours thick upon him:
The third day comes a froſt, a killing froſt,
And when he thinks, good eaſy man! full ſurely
His greatneſs is a ripening, nips his root;
And then he falls as I do. I have ventured,
Like little wanton boys that ſwim on bladders,
Theſe many ſummers on a ſea of glory,
But far beyond my depth. My high-blown pride
At length broke under me, and now hath left me,

I

Weary

Weary and old with fervice, to the mercy
Of a rude ftream that muft for ever hide me.

SHAKESPEARE's HENRY VIII.

And if, in any circumftances, there be nothing forced and unnatural in a perfon's making a fmall excurfion from the ideas of
his own calamitous fituation, or in another perfon's turning his
eye for a moment from the view of an interefting fcene, much
more natural is it to make thofe digreffions in the defcription of
ftill fcenes. And thefe principles fhow us the reafon why extended
fimiles give univerfally more fatisfaction in the defcription of a ftill
fcene, than in the reprefentation of a very active and bufy one.
In the former cafe, the mind is in no hafte, as we may fay, to
return to the principal fubject; in the latter, it is often impatient
of the leaft diverfion from it. Hence it is, with pleafure, that
we hear the following extended fimile of Milton, in the defcription of Paradife:

———— ———— ———— Now gentle gales,
Fanning their odoriferous wings, difpenfe
Native perfumes, and whifper whence they ftole
Thofe balmy fpoils. As when to them who fail
Beyond the cape of Hope, and now are paft
Mozambic, off at fea, north-eaft winds blow
Sabean odours from the fpicy fhore
Of Araby the bleft; with fuch delay
Well pleafed they flack their courfe, and many a league
Chear'd with the grateful fmell, old ocean fmiles.

PARADISE LOST, Book IV.

To

To this I fhall add another, of a parallel nature, from Virgil, becaufe the propriety of it hath been difputed.

> Regina ad templum forma pulcherrima Dido
> Inceffit, magna juvenum ftipante caterva.
> Talis in Eurotæ ripis, aut per juga Cynthe,
> Exercet Diana choros, quam mille fecutæ
> Hinc atque hinc glomerantur Oreades.　Illa pharetram
> Fert humero, gradienfque deas fupereminet omnes.
> Latonæ tacitum pertentant gaudia pectus.
> Talis erat Dido, talem fe, læta ferebat
> Per medios. ———
>
> ÆNEID, Lib. I. 496.

In this example the comparifon is certainly quite completed before the laft circumftance refpecting Latona; but it is a circumftance fo clofely connected with the fcene in which it is introduced, and the mind of the reader is, from the nature of the fcene, fo much at liberty, as to admit it with great eafe. The fcene in which it is introduced doth not return with fo much violence as to make us impatient of that unneceffary circumftance. And when this is the cafe, thefe little excurfions from the principal fubject make an agreeable kind of epifodes. The mind, as it was naturally led into them by their connection with the fcene introduced in the comparifon, can feel no want of connection or propriety in the circumftance, and it returns to the principal fubject agreeably refrefhed, and with renewed ardour.

Provided the reader feel no impatience at the mentioning of thofe foreign circumftances, the digreffion to take notice of them can hardly be pronounced faulty, till the laft-mentioned circumftance be fo remote from the principal object, that the mind can-

not,

not, at one eafy glance, fee the connection; for then, indeed, the *unity of the whole* is loft. They are two quite different and diftinct fcenes that we are prefented with. It is a ftill greater fault to make fo much of a fimile, that the attention of the reader fhall be more engroffed by it than by the principal and original figure.

However, to take but little notice of any circumftances that are foreign to the principal defign of the compofition, though pretty clofely connected with objects which are introduced for the fake of giving clearer ideas of it, fhows that the mind of the writer was very much intent upon his fubject. We may add, that it generally fhows more of *nature*; whereas a writer, who frequently purfues trains of fuch foreign ideas, difcovers more attention to *art*, and a fondnefs for *ornament*.

But this remark is by no means to be extended to thofe fimiles in which, though they be long, there is no excurfion from the points of refemblance; as the following of Homer:

> Fierce they drove on, impatient to deftroy,
> Troy charged the firft, and Hector firft of Troy.
> As from fome mountain's craggy forehead torn,
> A rock's round fragment flies, with fury borne,
> (Which from the ftubborn ftone a torrent rends)
> Precipitate the pond'rous mafs defcends:
> From fteep to fteep the rolling ruin bounds,
> At every fhock the crackling wood refounds.
> Still gathering force, it fmokes, and, urged amain,
> Whirls, leaps, and thunders down impetuou to the plain,
> There ftops.—So Hector, their whole force he proved,
> Refiftlefs when he raged, and when he ftop'd unmoved.
>   Iliad, Book XIII. 187.

Neither

Neither can Offian, in the two following fimiles, be faid to be carried away by his imagination beyond the points of refemblance in the objects with which he prefents us Speaking of a general engagement, to which the armies defcended from two oppofite hills, he adds;

" At once they plunge in battle. Steel pours its gleam on
" fteel. Like the fall of ftreams fhone the field, when they mix
" their foam together from two dark-browed rocks." TEMORA,
Book V.

Defcribing a hero in the fame field of battle, he fays;

" Through the hoft are the ftrides of Foldath ; like fome dark
" fhip on the wintry waves, when it iffues from between two
" hills, to fport on the echoing feas." *Ibidem.*

Perhaps it may be the moft advifeable, that writers fhould en-deavour to exprefs nothing more than the points of refemblance in fimiles. If the objects be confiderably different, points of difference enow, for any ufeful purpofe, will neceffarily force themfelves into the defcription.

In confidering where fimiles may be ufed with propriety, it may, perhaps, be laid down as a maxim, that they are the moft complete, and give the moft pleafure to the imagination, when the two objects compared have a ftrict refemblance in thofe points in which the fenfe of the paffage, in which they are introduced, requires that they fhould refemble, and are as different as poffible in every other. In this cafe, there will be the ftrongeft contraft produced, and the fenfe of uniformity will be heightened by the contiguity of the points of diverfity.

A a

Hence

Hence the peculiar ftrength of the fimiles of *Offian*, who almoft always illuftrates human actions by the appearances of inanimate nature. His *woods*, his *headlong torrents*, his *mifts*, his *clouds*, and his *tempefts*, make a greater figure, and imprefs the mind much more ftrongly than any fimilar allufions to any thing in the brute creation. In what fituations can we imagine any thing approaching nearer to human life, could, with advantage, take the place of the *fun* and the *clouds*, in the following paffage, by which he illuftrates the manner in which Cathmor filences the anger and contention of two of his chiefs?

" They funk from the king on either fide, like two columns
" of morning-mift, when the fun rifeth between them on his
" glittering rock. Dark is their rolling on either fide, each
" towards its reedy pool." TEMORA, Book IV.

I am aware of but one exception to this maxim, which is, that an object may be compared to another, which, by the principle of affociation, will transfer upon it ideas that ought by no means to be connected with it. Thus, when a very great object is compared to a very trifling and mean one, though they may refemble in the circumftances in which the purport of the paffage, in which the fimile is introduced, requires them to refemble; yet, befides that the defcent, as it were, of the mind from a great to a mean object, is difagreeable; thofe ideas of meannefs and littlenefs in the object to which the great object is compared, will adhere, in fome meafure, to the great object itfelf. Whofe ideas of the Greeks are not leffened by the following comparifon, though very juft, if we confider the principal defign of it?

Mean

Mean while the troops, beneath Patroclus' care,
Invade the Trojans, and commence the war.
As wafps, provok'd by children in their play,
Pour from their manfions by the broad high-way,
In fwarms the guiltlefs traveller engage,
Whet all their ftings, and call forth all their rage:
All rife in arms, and with a gen'ral cry
Affert their waxen domes, and buzzing progeny.
Thus from the tents the fervent legion fwarms,
So loud their clamours, and fo keen their arms.

ILIAD, Book XVI. 312.

For the fame reafon, if we intend to give an agreeable reprefentation of any object, we fhould carefully avoid comparing it to any thing difagreeable or difgufting.

It is, therefore, an ufeful general rule, that no object fhould be compared to any thing but what is, in point of greatnefs or dignity, of nearly equal rank with itfelf; and that, in grave and ferious compofition, all comparifons fhould be rather *above* than *below* the rank of the object to be illuftrated. To compare a grand object to a low one, as will be obferved hereafter, makes the *burlefque*; and to compare a low object to a grand one, makes the *mock-heroic*.

It hardly needs be mentioned, in this place, that in no fimile fhould any object be introduced that is not *well known :* for if the allufion be obfcure, how is the fubject illuftrated by it?

As the ufe of comparifons is to give ftrength and colour to ideas, comparifons that are merely *verbal* are certainly abfurd in all ferious compofitions. To try whether any be fo, change the terms for others that are fynonymous to them. By this means we difcover the following comparifon in Shakefpeare to be merely ver-

A a 2

bal.

bal. " In breaking oaths he is ftronger than Hercules:" becaufe, if we read, In *forfwearing* himfelf he is ftronger than
Hercules, there is not the leaft appearance of fimilitude in the
two ideas left.

But the fame reafon will not lead us to condemn thofe comparifons which are termed *figurative:* for, if ideas have obtained the
fame name on account of their *fimilarity*, the one may really illuftrate the other.   Of this nature are many comparifons in Virgil,
Ovid, and all the ancient claffics; as alfo in Pope, and others
the moft correct of our modern poets.   Thus Galatea, in Virgil,
is faid to be *fweeter than the honey of Hybla*.   In this cafe, fince
the object of the paffion of love hath obtained the name of *fweet*,
from its raifing in us fenfations fimilar to thofe excited by things
which affect the external tafte with the fenfe of fweetnefs, we are
certainly affifted to conceive more ftrongly of the pleafure the
fpeaker took in the object of his love, by his comparing it to the
fweetnefs of honey.

Indeed, comparifons of this kind occur fo frequently in the
moft ferious writers, of all nations, and all ages, that from this
circumftance only I think we may reafonably conclude there is a
foundation for them in nature.   The Pfalmift David fays, that
" the law of God was fweeter to him than honey and the honey-
" comb;" and that " the poifon of afps was under the tongue
" of his enemies."

However, as we probably catch the firft hint of thefe comparifons from the *words*, they may lead an incautious writer into
thofe comparifons which are merely verbal.

LECTURE

L E C T U R E XXII.

Of the Nature *of* METAPHORS.

A Metaphor hath already been defined, to be a simile contracted to its smallest dimensions. Hence, in using metaphors, the mind makes the least sensible excursion from the
ideas that engage its attention. So short is the excursion, that
when a metaphor is used, the moment the mind hath catched
the idea of any resemblance to the thing which it is about to express, it immediately transfers the terms belonging to the foreign
object to it, as if they were one and the same thing. So that, in
fact, using metaphors is nothing more than giving new names
to things.

The advantage of using metaphors is, that we can borrow a
name from a thing which contains the quality we mean to express in a greater degree than the subject to which we ascribe it;
and by this means can often suggest a stronger idea of a quality
than any terms orginally appropriated to our subject could convey. Besides, along with the name, other ideas, as of dignity
or meanness, agreeableness or disagreeableness, and the like, will
be transferred to the object to which it is applied. So that, by
means of the complex ideas which accompany the names of

I   things,

things, we can give juft what fize and colour we pleafe to any thing we are defcribing.

Moreover, as metaphors are moft naturally taken from fenfible things, and particularly from vifible objects, in perufing a difcourfe abounding with well-chofen metaphors, the mind is entertained with a fucceffion of agreeably-varied *views* and *landfchapes*. And though thefe profpects be extremely tranfient, they cannot fail to contribute confiderably to a reader's entertainment.

I may add that, though, in fome of thefe refpects, a comparifon hath the advantage of a metaphor; yet, in one refpect, a metaphor gives a more fenfible pleafure than a comparifon. This arifes from the harfhnefs and impropriety there, for a moment, appears to be in the ufe of a metaphorical inftead of a proper term; which increafes the fatisfaction we inftantly receive from approving of the new application of the word. That this contraft between the ufual and unufual fenfe of words is a neceffary ingredient in the pleafure we receive from metaphors, is evident; becaufe, when metaphors have, by frequent ufe, become evanefcent, they have no more pleafing effect than the proper names of things; and becaufe, in order to become fully fenfible of all the beauty of metaphorical expreffions, we muft diftinctly attend to the original meaning of fuch terms, at the fame time that we perceive their figurative application in the paffage before us.

I fhall exemplify thefe obfervations by that ftrong and happy metaphor of Virgil, I have mentioned once before, by which he calls the two Scipios *the thunderbolts of war*. This image might have been extended to a long fimile; but the fituation of the hero did not admit of fo great an excurfion from his principal

3   fubject.

subject. The poet, therefore, having first laid hold of the idea of resemblance as it occurred to his mind, without multiplying the objects of his attention, by expressly comparing his heroes to thunderbolts, calls the heroes themselves the thunderbolts. This was evidently only giving a new name to his heroes, but with this great advantage, that the ideas we conceive of the *rapidity* and *destructive power* belonging to thunderbolts are hereby transferred upon them. At the same time, likewise, the ideas of grandeur accompanying a scene of thunder and lightning, throw a considerable degree of the *sublime* into their characters, and the mind of the reader is entertained with a momentary *prospect* of so solemn and grand a scene in nature. Moreover, along with this, the *opposition* between the two very different senses of the word (which, however harsh it may appear for a moment, we presently see the propriety of) heightens the pleasureable sensation.

Highly ornamental as metaphors are in discourse, it is to *necessity* that we are indebted for the first use of them. It was neither possible, nor convenient, that every different object should have a distinct name. That would have been to multiply words, both to the overburthening of the memory, and the prejudice of science. For it greatly favours the propagation of knowledge to call things that are similar to one another by the same name. Without this there could have been no such thing as general principles, or general knowledge. Now it is one and the same process by which we make general or abstract terms, and by which figurative expressions are invented. The difference is only in degree, not in kind.

Suppose, for instance, we had never seen but one *horse*; unless we give the same name to things that are similar, and even

to

to things that are not in all refpects fimilar, we muft have given another name than *horfe* to every other animal we fhould afterwards have met with of the fame fpecies : becaufe, not only is it abfurd to fuppofe that any two things are the fame, but that any two individuals of the fame fpecies fhould be exactly alike.

If objects differ but little, we give them the fame name in what we call a *literal fenfe*; as, to the *heads*, the *mouths*, the *eyes*, the *hearts*, &c. of men and other animals. To thefe the fame names are fo conftantly applied, that it is impoffible to fay to which they originally and properly belonged. In calling thefe, therefore, by the fame names, we fay we ufe no figure ; whereas the term *figure* begins to be applied when, however commonly a name may be applied to any thing, it is well known to have been applied to fomething elfe originally. For example ; it is equally proper and literal to fay the *foot of a man*, or the *foot of a beaft*, though they differ confiderably in form ; but the moment we attend to it, we perceive that the *foot of a chair*, or the *foot of a mountain*, is a figurative expreffion, though it be as common as the other ; and we ufe it a thoufand times without being fenfible of the figure. In this cafe the figure is faid to be *evanefcent*.

When any term is conftantly applied to a variety of objects, and it is impoffible to fay to which of them it belonged originally, though they be confiderably different, the definition of that term muft be framed fo as to comprehend all thofe ideas. Thus if we define the terms *head*, *mouth*, *eye*, or *foot*, we muft exprefs our definition in fuch a manner, as to be equally applicable to the heads, the mouths, the eyes, or the feet of brute or other animals, as well as to thofe of men ; for the literal meaning of thofe terms extends to both. But the definition of the

words

words muſt not be extended to take in their figurative applications. Thus, it is not neceſſary that the term *foot* ſhould be defined ſo as to be applicable to the lower part of a mountain, though the lower part of a mountain be univerſally called the *foot* of it.

In many caſes, however, it will not be eaſy to determine where the literal ſenſe of a word ends, and where the figurative ſenſe begins; as in the terms *face*, *voice*, *cheeks*, and many others, which have been applied to men and brute animals ſo promiſcuouſly, that ſome perſons may be inclined to call the application of them to brute animals figurative, while others will contend that it is literal: whereas, in other caſes, the analogy is ſo faint, that the ſame term cannot, without a ſenſible harſhneſs, be applied to the different objects; as when trees are called the *hair of mountains*, or the walls of cities their *cheeks*.

This harſh metaphor is by philoſophers called *catachreſis*. Of this kind we may term that expreſſion of Milton's denoting the paſſage of Satan from hell to this world, *ſails between world and world*.

From this it appears that there is a gradation in metaphors, proceeding from thoſe in which the analogy between two objects is ſo great, that the figure is evaneſcent, through all the different degrees of reſemblance, till we come to thoſe in which the analogy is ſcarce perceptible, and conſequently the metaphor is harſh and unnatural: and all the rules concerning the uſe of metaphors muſt have reſpect to this gradation.

It is worth while, however, to take notice, how much it is in the power of cuſtom to ſoften the harſhneſs of metaphors. And in nothing, perhaps, is the authority of cuſtom more arbitrary and capricious. In ſome caſes the application of the ſame name

B b   to

to things is quite familiar, where the refemblance is very obfcure; and, in other cafes, where there is the ftrongeft refemblance between the two things, it would give the greateft offence to an ear formed by cuftom to hear them called by the fame name. Who would not make himfelf ridiculous by confounding the terms appropriated by ufe to the voices of different animals; as the *lowing of the ox*, the *bleating of fheep*, and the *barking of the dog?* And yet who ever calls a part of the fea running up into the land by any other name than that of *an arm of the fea*, though the refemblance it bears in fhape, or ufe, to the human arm is extremely faint? In like manner, have we any other name for the two extremities of an army than the figurative one of *wings*, though they refemble wings no more than they do *horns*, by which, indeed, the Greeks and Romans moft frequently expreffed them?

In arranging figures, therefore, according to their feveral degrees, between the extremes of what hath been termed evanefcence on the one hand, and what is called bold and harfh on the other, we muft by no means be governed by a regard to the *analogy of things* only; but muft, along with this, confider the arbitrary decifions of *cuftom*, in the idioms of particular languages. Thus we muft fay, that fuch expreffions as *an arm of the fea*, and the *wings of an army*, are nearly literal, and fcarce deferve the name of figures, though the refemblance be very fmall; as well as the *wings of the flying fifh*, and the *horns of an altar*, where the refemblance is very great; but that fuch phrafes as the *wings of the wind*, and the *bofom of the fea*, are highly figurative, though they have a much better foundation in the analogy of nature. The cafe is, that the former are ufed fo frequently, that, whether the refemblance be greater or lefs, they

are

are little more than common names of things, and when we use
them, we never think whence they were borrowed; whereas the
latter are seldom used, and never without our perceiving whence
they were borrowed. And it was observed before, that it is essential to the pleasure we receive from a metaphor, that we, at
the same time, perceive distinctly the two different applications
of the same term.

L E C T U R E   XXIII.

Rules for the Use of METAPHORS; *and of* ALLEGORIES.

HAVING explained the nature of metaphors, and traced the sources of the pleasure we receive from them, I proceed to lay down rules for the proper *use* of them. These will be easily deduced from the preceding account of their nature and end.

Since metaphors are used to give strength and colour, as it were, to ideas, we naturally use them when our own ideas are peculiarly *vivid*, and when, consequently, we wish to communicate the same ideas, in the same strength, to the minds of others. They are, therefore, very properly put into the mouth of a person under any emotion of mind; and the stronger are his emotions, the bolder figures he naturally uses. The truth of this observation may be verified every day: for, if we take notice, we shall find that we never hear any man either speak with vehemence, or converse when his mind is in a gay and lively humour, without using frequent metaphors. When our own ideas are very vivid, they naturally, by association, suggest ideas of objects in which they exist in greater strength; and these we instantly transfer upon the objects we are describing, in order to give ideas of them to others more similar and adequate to our own. Thus some kinds of *pain* will often suggest the similar idea of *burning*,

and

and we inſtantly cry out, *we burn*.   In ſuch a ſituation of mind, terms appropriated to the objeĉts we are deſcribing, would not ſuggeſt our ideas of them to another perſon in ſufficient ſtrength. Without looking abroad, it is curious to obſerve in what different manners we feel ourſelves diſpoſed to ſay things according to the humour we are in ; in what plain terms we ſpeak when our minds are languid, and how metaphorically when we have a flow of ſpirits.

Metaphors muſt, for this reaſon, be abſurd, when a man's ideas and ſenſations are not peculiarly vivid.   For a man to uſe figures then, would be to endeavour to convey ſtronger (which is, in faĉt, *other)* ideas to the minds of the perſons he is ſpeaking to, than he conceives himſelf.   Of this we have ſome diverting examples in the *Treatiſe on the Bathos*.   It will, likewiſe, be found exemplified in the paſſage which was quoted to ſhow a like improper uſe of compariſons.

The moſt important rule reſpeĉting the choice of metaphors, where they are proper, is, that different metaphors ſhould not be confounded together in the ſame ſentence : becauſe, in this caſe, the ſenſe, if it be realized in the imagination, will appear to imply an *abſurdity*.   And, ſince every new application of a word that hath the effeĉt of a metaphor, doth raiſe an idea of the objeĉt to which it was primarily affixed, for the ſame reaſon that every ſcene preſented to the mind of the reader ſhould be, at leaſt, *poſſible*, and conſiſtent, theſe pieces of ſcenery, though ever ſo tranſient, ſhould be ſo too ; and when there is a manifeſt inconſiſtency in ſuch little piĉtures, a reader of taſte is juſtly offended.   Out of the numberleſs examples I might produce of this fault in writers, I ſhall ſeleĉt the following from Shakeſpeare, in which the marriage of King John with Conſtance is referred to.

For

For by this knot thou fhalt fo furely tie
Thy now unfured affurance to the crown,
That yon green boy fhall have no fun to ripe
The bloom that promifes a mighty fruit.

KING JOHN.

Here it may juftly be afked, how can the *tying a knot* prevent
the fun's *ripening fruit?* The King's marriage with Conftance is
certainly very properly expreffed by tying a knot; and, as that
event would cut off the reafonable hopes that Arthur might otherwife entertain of fucceeding to the throne, this is likewife beautifully defcribed by faying he would then have *no fun to ripen the
bloom which promifed a mighty fruit.* But though thefe metaphors,
when viewed afunder, appear proper and beautiful, when they
are joined, the refult is a manifeft abfurdity.

Not only fhould writers avoid the near union of different terms
which are highly metaphorical, they fhould alfo favour the ima-
gery which metaphors raife in the mind, by intermixing no plain
and natural expreffions with them. Thus, in the paffage quoted
above, the *boy* fhould have been kept out of fight, and the *tree*
or *plant* have been fubftituted in its place for the *fun* to act upon.
In this view, likewife, the author of the Bathos juftly cenfures
the following lines of Blackmore:

A waving fea of heads around them fpread,
And ftill frefh ftreams the gazing deluge fed.

For when *a croud of people* are, by the power of figure, meta-
morphofed into a *deluge*, it is deftroying the agreeable illufion too
foon, and raifes an inconfiftency in our ideas, to give *eyes* to it;
though the objects that compofed this metaphorical deluge really
had eyes.

I

And

And yet, to fhow how delicate this affair is, and what extreme attention it requires wholly to avoid this fault, we may obferve, that this fame hypercritical writer, even while he is upon the fubject, falls into it himfelf.

" Thus an ingenious artift, painting the fpring, talks of a " fnow of bloffoms, and thereby raifes an unexpected picture of " winter."——But how can a *picture be raifed* by a perfon's *talking* of any thing while he is painting?

Indeed, the frequency of inaccuracies of this kind, where the figure is not ftrong, and the little notice that is, notwithftanding, taken of them by the generality of readers, fhow that they are of very little confequence. The cafe is, that the images which fuch metaphors prefent, are feen but for a moment, and then very obfcurely; fo that, though there may be fome little inconfiftency in them, in fuch a tranfient view they eafily pafs unnoticed. It is only when we exprefsly *attend* to thefe faint metaphors, and by a direct effort of the mind draw out the fcene at large, and thereby, as we may fay, raife and heighten all the colours of it, that the impropriety is obferved. But how few do this? and, are critics fo minutely employed worthy the notice of a writer?

When a figure is become abfolutely evanefcent, and long ufe hath made the metaphorical term more familiar than the proper name of the thing, or circumftance denoted by it, it is pains employed to very little purpofe to trace out the long-forgotten allufion, in order to fhow its *latent inconfiftency* with any thing it is connected with. Who can expect that fuch phrafes as thefe, *fallen into an error*, to *fpend time* upon a thing, to be *incenfed at* a perfon, &c. fhould be ufed with any regard to the latent figure they contain.

contain. It is impossible however for any person to construct many sentences without exposing himself to the same censure; terms which are ultimately figurative abound so much in all languages. All our intellectual ideas are expressed in terms borrowed from sensible things; but who, in using them, attends to the sensible images they may suggest? Or, whoever attends to ideas of *local position*, which every *preposition* implies?

I may add, that the persons who are the most liable to these inaccuracies, are those who are the most perfectly acquainted with a language, and to whom the terms and idioms of it are the most familiar. For, by frequent use, the latent figurative sense of a word is wholly overlooked, and such a figurative expression suggests nothing but the idea of the object intended to be illustrated by it. However, nothing in criticism requires less judgment and ability than to discover these little inaccuracies, if a man will look so low. Such minute critics are finely exposed in a paper of the Tatler.

So remote are the two extremes in the vividness of metaphors, that the evanescent require no attention at all to their connection with other ideas; whereas the boldest and strongest require so much, that not only do they introduce confusion when they are *intermixed*, but they even give pain and disgust when they *succeed* one another at very short intervals. When metaphors raise very vivid and distinct ideas of foreign scenes, to change them very fast, is like hurrying us from one part of the creation to another, with a rapidity that gives us pain.

An easy and good test, in most cases, of the propriety of strong metaphors, is to imagine them reduced to *painting*, and consider how the images would look in that mode of expression. A person of a
lively

lively imagination naturally doth this, and confequently to him improprieties in metaphors appear much more difgufting than they do to other perfons, to whom they fuggeft the idea of the fcene, from which they were borrowed, very faintly.   To a perfon of this lively turn of mind, who eafily recurs to the original fcenes from which metaphors are drawn, the following ftring of metaphors, in an exquifite poem of Pope's (though, fingly taken, they be uncommonly happy) as they fucceed one another without any interval, may poffibly have a difagreeable effect :

> What is this *abforbs* me quite,
> *Steals* my fenfes, *fhuts* my fight ?
> *Drinks* my fpirits, *draws* my breath ?
> Tell me, my foul, can this be death ?

Though there fhould be no inconfiftency in imagining the fame thing to have the different properties of *abforbing*, *ftealing*, *fhutting*, *drinking*, and *drawing* ; yet the ideas of thefe feveral actions can hardly be brought fo near one another without confufion, if the images be a little raifed by an attention to them.

As metaphors are contracted fimiles, they muft neceffarily have many excellencies and defects in common with them. Of this kind are the following. The moft ftriking metaphors, or thofe which give the moft fenfible pleafure, are thofe in which there is perceived at firft the greateft difference between the two ideas that are fignified by the fame word, and afterwards the greateft refemblance. From this fource, chiefly, is derived the charm of the following metaphors, a *gay thought*, a *bright expreffion*, the *wings of the wind*, the *impervious ocean :* though the two firft have the additional advantage of being allufions to *objects of fight*, which are always peculiarly diftinct and pleafing ; and the laft gives us, likewife, the idea of

C c   *human*

human sentiments, which will be mentioned hereafter as a distinct pleasing object. This rule is to be understood with the same exception, as the rule similar to it respecting comparisons.

Shakespeare uses a low and degrading metaphor when he makes King John exhort the people of Angiers to *save unscratched their city's threatened cheeks*; meaning that they should save their walls from being battered.

The allusion is merely verbal, when, in the same play, Constance, lying on the ground, is made to say,

> ———— For my grief's so great,
> That no support but the huge firm earth
> Can bear it up.

Figures of this sort are nothing more than *puns*; for the sense of the passage depends upon the double-meaning of the word. Grief is said to be supported in a figurative sense, but the earth supports things in a literal sense.

ALLEGORIES are continued metaphors; that is, they are descriptions of certain objects in terms borrowed from others : so that though one set of objects only be named, whenever allegories be used, there must be a constant attention to the similar properties of them both. The following account of the sons of Edward in Shakespeare's Richard the Second is allegorical :

> Edward's seven sons, whereof thyself art one,
> Were seven fair branches springing from one root.
> Some of these branches by the destinies cut :
> But Thomas, my dear lord, my life, my Glo'ster,
> One flourishing branch of his most royal root,
> Is hacked down, and his summer leaves all faded,
> By Envy's hand, and Murder's bloody axe.

All

All the rules refpecting propriety and confiftency that are neceffary to be obferved in metaphors, are equally requifite in allegories! They differ only in this; that allegories, in common with comparifons, imply a confiderable excurfion of the mind
from the principal object of its thoughts ; and therefore, though
a man in the greateft agitation of mind would not refufe a metaphor, he may eafily be fuppofed to have his thoughts fo much
engaged as not to be at liberty to attend fo particularly to a foreign object, as is neceffary in order to note *many points of refemblance*, and make an allegory. Allegories, therefore, as well
as comparifons, are the language of men tolerably compofed, or
only moderately elevated. The following allegorical fpeech of
Califta, in the Fair Penitent, is unnatural:

> Is it the voice of thunder, or my father ?
> Madnefs! confufion ! Let the ftorm come on ;
> Let the tumultuous roar drive all upon me ;
> Dafh my devoted bark. Ye furges, break it.
> 'Tis for my ruin that the tempeft rifes.
> When I am loft, funk to the bottom low,
> Peace fhall return, and all be calm again,
>
>   FAIR PENITENT, Act IV.

It requires uncommon fkill and caution to conduct a long allegory with propriety ; becaufe few things are analogous in many
refpects, at the fame time that they are fufficiently different to
make the analogy pleafing. Moreover, it is very difficult to
make an allufion intelligible, and at the fame time never name
the thing we mean in direct terms, which we muft by all means
avoid ; as it would introduce the greateft confufion into the metaphor.

Bunyan,

Bunyan, whofe invention was certainly very fertile, has often forgotten himfelf, and helped out his wire-drawn allegories by the thing allegorized. Thus, defcribing the paffage of Chriftian and Hopeful through the river which reprefents death, he introduces fome perfons telling them they would find it deeper or fhallower " according to their faith in the Lord of the place to " which they were going."

Dryden's Hind and Panther contains much of the fame abfurd mixture of allegory and the thing allegorized. " What rela-" tion" (fays Lord Halifax in his remarks upon it) " has the " Hind to our Saviour? or what notion have we of a Panther's " title? If you fay he means the Church, how doth the Church " feed on lawns, or range in the foreft? Let it be always a " Church, or always a cloven-footed beaft; for we cannot bear " this fhifting the fcene every line."

LECTURE

LECTURE XXIV.

Of CONTRAST *in general, and particularly of* WIT, *the* rifible, *and the* ridiculous.

HAVING confidered the pleafure we receive from the *exer-cife of our faculties,* and all thofe pleafures of tafte in which it is a principal ingredient, we pafs to another medium of pleafure in works of genius and imagination, viz. CONTRAST. And it the more naturally folicits our attention in this place, as we have feen that it hath a confiderable fhare in the pleafure arif-ing from comparifons and metaphors, which were laft treated of.

Indeed, I fhall have no objection to any perfon's confidering contraft as one particular manner in which our minds are ftrongly affected.

If two objects, in any refpect fimilar, prefent themfelves to our view at the fame time, we naturally expect, and, as it were, wifh to find a *complete refemblance* in them; and we are, in fome meafure, furprized and difappointed to find them different. This difpofition to make every thing perfect and *complete in its kind,* will be taken notice of, and farther illuftrated, in its proper place hereafter. Here then, as in all other cafes of *furprize* and *difap-pointment,* our attention is ftrongly engaged to the circumftances in which the two objects differ, as ftrongly as it was at firft engaged

gaged to thofe in which they agreed ; fo that the fame principle, by which we are led to make every thing *complete*, now leads us to enlarge and extend the circumftances in which they differ. Thefe, in their turn, will make the circumftances of refemblance appear furprizing. And thus the mind will naturally turn its attention alternately to the circumftances of *refemblance* and thofe of *difference* with great celerity, and both will have the advantage of being confiderably augmented. In all this time, the *furprize*, the quick *fucceffion of thought*, and the *enlargement of our ideas*, cannot fail to introduce a pleafureable ftate of mind. I may add, that the greater is the refemblance in fome things, and the greater the difference in others, the more fenfible will the effect be, and the greater the pleafure refulting from it. Thefe obfervations any perfon may exemplify to himfelf, by viewing at the fame time even two houfes, two gardens, or two trees of the fame kind, that are very different in fize. In this pofition they both affect us more fenfibly and more pleafurably than if they had been viewed feparately, when their refemblance and their difference had not been fo apparent, or fo perfectly afcertained.

A familiar example will ferve to make us fenfible how neceffary ftrong circumftances of refemblance are to make us feel the greateft effect of the circumftances of difference. A *dog* is not confidered as diminutive with refpect to an *elephant* ; though, therefore, they be placed ever fo near together, our ideas of the elephant are not raifed, nor our ideas of the dog diminifhed. We did not expect they fhould be equal. But upon introducing another dog confiderably larger than the former, we immediately cry out, What a prodigious large dog ! while the other appears to our imagination lefs than he did before. Our furprize, and,

confeconsequently, the imagined disproportion between the two dogs becomes greater, if we be told, or perceive, that they are of the same kind, as both mastiffs, both greyhounds, &c.; and both these effects are sensibly greater still, if we be told they are of the same litter. The same use may be made of our observation of the differences in the persons, the abilities, the fortunes, and tempers of men of the same nation, the same family, the same parents, the same education, and the same external advantages.

In all these cases, any extraordinary quality of an object is, in a great measure, lost upon us, unless it be perceived in conjunction with a very different degree of the same quality. Indeed, if we only consider that the ideas of *great* and *little* are only relative, and the terms comparative, we might conclude, that they must have their most sensible effect, whatever it is, when they are viewed in circumstances the most favourable for that comparison, and where the relation of which they consist may be perceived with the most advantage.

We see, likewise, that the effects of all kinds of contrasts are the strongest in persons of a lively imagination, and to the same person when his apprehension is the quickest; because, by a lively and vigorous imagination, two different objects are comprehended with the most ease: consequently the ideas of their relation are peculiarly strong, and make the greatest figure.

I shall add another observation or two. Our relish for *novelty* and *surprize* contributes not a little to the pleasure we feel upon perceiving strong resemblances in things that differ, and differences in things that resemble one another. For it is very observable, that every species of contrast affects us much more sensibly the first time we perceive it, than ever it doth afterwards. We are sensible, likewise, that it requires considerable *sagacity*

and

and *ingenuity* to difcern many of thofe unexpected *refemblances* and differences, which, in a manner that will be explained hereafter, is another confiderable ingredient in the pleafure we receive from thofe contrafts.

One remarkable confequence of perceiving fome fpecies of contrafts, particularly in perfons of an irritable conftitution, is *laughter*; of which it will be proper, therefore, to give fome account in this place. Laughter, when it firft appears in children (according to that profound obferver of human nature, Dr. Hartley) is a *nafcent cry*, raifed by pain, or the apprehenfion of pain, fuddenly checked, and repeated at very fhort intervals. Thefe alternate momentary fears and momentary joys are very obfervable in the laughter of young children when they are tickled. Afterwards, the fame automatic motions and geftures of which laughter confifts become affociated with lefs and lefs *fimilar caufes* perpetually. Then almoft any brifk emotion or furprize, fuddenly checked, and recurring alternately, will produce it; and at laft any ftrong oppofition, or contraft, in things, whether they be perfonally interefted in them or not. When we are advanced in life, a variety of paffions, and a regard to decorum, check the propenfity to laughter; whereas many idiots continue to laugh upon the flighteft occafions imaginable.

This progrefs is exactly fimilar to many other proceffes in human nature, whereby a variety of the fame motions and geftures become affociated with caufes that are flighter and flighter continually, till at laft any thing bearing the fainteft refemblance to the original caufe will be fufficient to excite them. In this cafe, the extreme celerity with which the attention is reflected from the circumftances of refemblance to thofe of difference, al-

l   ternately,

ternately, upon the perception of a contraſt, coincides remarkably with the quick ſucceſſive pulſes in a fit of laughter.

The laughter, and all the pleaſure ariſing from the contraſt,
ceaſes, when the mind, after vibrating, as it were, between the
points of reſemblance and difference, at length reſts in the medium ; and then the inconſiſtency, which was ſo ſtriking at the
firſt view, no longer affects us. Theſe effects may, however,
be revived after ſome interval, eſpecially if, by an expreſs effort
of our minds, we endeavour to magnify the circumſtances of reſemblance and difference. But when the bounds of the reſemblance and of difference are perfectly known, and every idea
belonging to the ſubject is anticipated by the mind, the moment
they are mentioned, the repetition of them produces very languid effects, in compariſon of the firſt ſenſation. The *ſurprize*
is then over. Hence, books of jeſts, apophthegms, or any ſpecies of mere *wit*, are ſeldom read a ſecond time. They will only
bear to be repeated in *company*, and in freſh company, for a reaſon that will be mentioned preſently.

This *contraſt*, the nature and general effects of which have
now been explained, human genius hath diverſified, and
branched out, into a great variety of pleaſing ſcenes, by varying
the *ſubjects* and the *degrees* of it. To this we muſt not only allow the conſiderable ſhare that hath been aſcribed to it in *meta-*
phors, and other ſources of pleaſure in works of genius, that
have been or will be mentioned, but muſt acknowledge that we
are principally indebted to it for the pleaſure we receive from
antitheſis, from objects that are *riſible*, or *ridiculous*, from the
mock-heroic, *burleſque*, *parody*, *irony*, *repartee*, *wit*, *humour*, *rid-*
dles, and *puns* ; with many other entertainments of the ſame
kind, for which we have no diſtinct name.

D d

Indeed,

Indeed, the terms of criticifm do ſo little correſpond to all the varieties of the diviſions and ſubdiviſions of this copious ſubject, and have been uſed with ſo little uniformity and preciſion by critics; that, in order to avoid confuſion, I ſhall generally deſcribe the ſeveral feelings and occaſions of them, in the firſt place, and afterwards mention terms by which I apprehend they may be moſt conveniently denoted. In this caſe, the terms may be applied differently at pleaſure, without controverting the principles advanced in theſe lectures; which will be laid down, independent of the uſe of any *words* whatever. And as a great part of what has been written upon this ſubject has been to fix the uſe of words, this method will reduce the ſubject, thus ſeparated from the diſputes about words, into a ſmall compaſs, and we ſhall have a much clearer and more beautiful view of all the degrees and variations of it.

To make the eaſier tranſition to this ſubject of oppoſition or contraſt, from that of metaphors, which derive a conſiderable part of their beauty from this ſource, I ſhall try the effect of contraſt in a ſingle epithet, in which a word is uſed in a meaning ſeemingly quite contrary to its uſual ſenſe, and yet with ſufficient analogy to make it extremely pleaſing.

Mr. Spence, in his excellent eſſay upon the Odyſſee, ſpeaking of the candour and generoſity of the ancient critics, and of the envy, ill-nature, and captiouſneſs of thoſe among the moderns who bear that name, ſays, *Zoïlus was the only modern critic among the ancients.* That the beauty of this expreſſion depends upon the ſeeming oppoſition between the uſual ſenſe of the word *modern*, and that which muſt be given to it here, is very evident; for only change the words, and ſay, " Zoïlus was the only cri-
" tic

" tic among the ancients whofe temper refembled that of the
" moderns;" and though the fenfe remains the fame, the fpirit and poignancy of the expreffion is gone.

If it will affift us to analize our thoughts and feelings upon
this fubject, I fhall cite a few more thoughts and expreffions
which have a fimilar effect.   Pliny, in his panegyric addreffed to
Trajan, fays, *Solus omnium pater patriæ effes antequam fieres*.   The
fame author, fpeaking concerning Trajan's entry into Rome, fays,
that *fome* proclaimed aloud that *they had feen enough after they had
feen you*; and others, again, *that they muft live longer*.   The pe-
culiarly-fine effect of this paffage arifes from fuch different fentiments being formed, with equal appearance of reafon, from the
fame event.   It is as if the fame caufe produced oppofite effects.
To mention only one example more; Cicero fays to Cæfar, *You
forget nothing but injuries*.   We fee where the beauty of this
thought lies, the moment we reflect that other men forget every
thing elfe fooner than injuries.

In the two former of thefe examples, there is an oppofition
both in the *fenfe* and in the *words*; in the two latter there is nothing verbal.   Such oppofitions of ideas, or of the different fenfes of words, may tend to produce a *fmile*, but I think not fenfibly enough to make them be termed *rifible*.   If the ingenuity
capable of difcovering fuch oppofitions as appear in thefe expreffions, will not be termed *wit*, it is becaufe the fubject of
them is too *ferious*, and not diverting enough to entitle them
to it.

It is certain, that if the fubject be very *ferious*, notwithftanding there be the happieft mixture of refemblance and diverfity,
and the moft unexpected in the world, we never *fmile* or think

D d 2   of

of applying the term *wit* to it. Of this we may make experiment in the following admirable lines of Mr. Pope:

> All nature is but art unknown to thee;
> All chance, direction which thou can'ft not fee.
> All difcord, harmony not underftood;
> All partial evil, univerfal good.

In this paffage, the fame objects prefent us, in one view, with the idea of *nature*, in another of *art*; in one of *chance*, in another of *defign*; in one of *difcord*, in another of *harmony*; in one of *evil*, and in another of *good*. This paffage, therefore, by the ftrong oppofition which it exhibits of the properties, not only of fimilar, but of the fame objects, as viewed by different minds, and in different lights, bears a confiderable refemblance to the paffages quoted above, in which the fame things are called by different names; but the extreme ferioufnefs of the fubject checks every tendency to fmile, and with this, I think, the paffage will lofe the name of *wit*, in the modern ufe of the word. For it muft be noted, that formerly the ufe of this term was much more extenfive, and was applied, without fcruple, to every obfervation which fhewed ingenuity, whether diverting or ferious.

I fhall readily allow the following paffage, quoted before from Mr. Pope, to be truly fublime:

> Who fees with equal eye, as God of all,
> A hero perifh, or a fparrow fall;
> Atoms, or fyftems, into ruin hurl'd;
> And now a bubble burft, and now a world.

3   I quote

I quote it again, in order to fhow, by comparing it with the following paffage, the very different effects of contrafts, fimilar in
every refpect, except the *dignity of their fubject.*

> This day black omens threat the brighteft fair,
> That e'er deferved a watchful fpirit's care.
> Some dire difafter, or by force or flight;
> But what, or where, the Fates have wrapt in night.
> Whether the nymph fhall break Diana's law,
> Or fome frail chma jar receive a flaw;
> Or ftain her honour, or her new brocade;
> Forget her prayers, or mifs a mafquerade;
> Or lofe her heart, or necklace at a ball;
> Or whether heav'n has doom'd that Shock muft fall?
>
> RAPE OF THE LOCK, Canto II.

The *oppofition of ideas* is equally ftrong and pointed in both
thefe paffages. But, in the former, the tendency to *fmile*, which
the oppofition of ideas fimply confidered would raife, is over-
ruled by the *fublime*, which the grandeur of the fubject excites;
in the latter, which, if I miftake not, will be univerfally acknowledged to be a fpecimen of refined *wit* and *humour*, it is not.
Moreover, is not the term *humour* applied to it, on account of its
being *diverting under the appearance of gravity*, feeming to
reprefent trifles as of the fame importance with things of infinitely greater confequence? as it is termed *wit*, becaufe the fubject
is *gay*, and eafily admits a *fmile*.

An object that is purely and fimply *rifible*, is any thing in
which there is perceived a great *incongruity* or *difproportion*, provided the object, at the fame time that it is of fome confequence,
be not capable of exciting a more ferious emotion. As a man
with

with an immoderate long nose, or a very short one (no nose at all would raise our horror) a rich dress with a dirty rag tied to it, and a group of risible objects, may be seen in the following passages from Hudibras, Canto I.

> When of his hose we come to treat,
> The cupboard where he kept his meat.
> His puissant sword unto his side
> Near his undaunted heart was tied;
> With basket-hilt that would hold broth,
> And serve for fight and dinner both.
> When it had stabb'd or broke a head,
> It would scrape trenchers, or chip bread,
> Toast cheese or bacon ; though it were
> To bait a mouse-trap, 'twould not care :
> 'Twould make clean shoes, and in the earth
> Set leeks and onions, and so forth.

It is needless to point out the opposition between the proper uses of the things here mentioned, and those they are supposed to be put to, which makes a scene so highly diverting. It is said above, that the circumstances which occasion laughter must be of *some consequence:* for we frequently see the greatest inconsistencies in things that are wholly *indifferent* to us, without feeling the least provocation to laugh.

But the most frequent, and the most abundant scenes of mirth and laughter, are incongruities relating to *human sentiments,* which some distinguish by the name of *improprieties.* Such are the blunders and mistakes, the false taste, the absurd speeches and actions of some of our own species. Whenever *design* enters into
any

any thing that occasions mirth, the person that laughs seems to entertain a slight degree of *contempt* for the object of his mirth, and in that respect feels an agreeable consciousness of his own superiority over him. This circumstance of a degree of contempt consistent with laughter, added to a risible object, seems to intitle it to the character of *ridiculous*.

That a consciousness of *self-esteem* really enters into the feeling of *ridicule*, I think is manifest, from the peculiar pleasure that is universally taken in repeating diverting incidents *in company*. Very often the same person will hardly ever be weary of entertaining different companies with the same diverting stories ; and such stories seem to be told with the same kind of satisfaction with which persons obliquely hint their own praises. This supposition is, likewise, favoured by the observation, that persons, who are remarkable for their vanity and love of praise, take the most sensible pleasure in every thing into which ridicule enters ; and that men of very great humility, candour, and benevolence, are not easily provoked to laugh at the foibles of their fellow-creatures. And since all valuable *politeness* is founded upon humility and benevolence ; hence, directly to ridicule any body is now thought, by persons of the best taste, to be inconsistent with true politeness.

Objects truly ridiculous are such as *pride in rags, conceit in ignorance*, and *hypocrisy in gravity, a violent passion raised by a trifling cause*, and *great disproportion between the means and the ends* of human actions. Hence we laugh at the schemes of the Laputans, to extract sun-beams from cucumbers, to make books by a machine, and to soften marble for pillows and pincushions. Also it is the opposition between words and sense, that raises the laugh at those blunders in speech which are known by the name

I

of

of *bulls*; and it is the oppofition between the fubject and the language, that makes us confider a fublime fubject treated in a low ftyle, and a mean fubject in a lofty ftyle, as equally ridiculous.

In reality, *men* can hardly be the object of a laugh, that is not more or lefs a laugh of *derifion*, and is excited by the ridiculous ftrictly fo called; becaufe we connect the idea of *defign* with every thing belonging to men. Thus a little man wearing a long fword, or a rich coat covering dirty linen, are objects that are rather ridiculous, than merely rifible.

Even in a mere *perfonification*, if but a diftant refemblance of the fentiments, actions, and characters of human beings, be perceived in brute creatures, we may have feelings very fimilar to thofe excited by *the ridiculous* among our own fpecies. This we may have been fenfible of in our obfervation of the *pride of a turkey-cock*, the *gravity of the owl*, and the *tricks of a monkey*, and of a variety of animals trained up for diverfion. To a lively imagination, prone as we are to perfonification, there may occur objects really ridiculous, even in the inanimate creation. It is, perhaps, owing to our imagination being fo prone to perfonification, that objects rifible and ridiculous have been fo generally confounded. Or perhaps, rather, we never do laugh (except we be provoked to it mechanically) but when we, fecretly at leaft, perfonify the object of our laughter, and fo the rifible and ridiculous may differ only in degree, and not in kind.

It feems to favour this hypothefis, that we view many objects and fcenes in which are great incongruities, and which are neither adapted to excite any great or ferious emotion, nor can be faid to be abfolutely of no confequence to us, at which we, notwithftanding, perceive no inclination to laugh; as when a botanift

nift finds a well-known plant in an unexpected place. And, in general, though the attention of the curious be ftrongly drawn to fuch objects as we call *lufus naturæ*, and they feem to excite no fentiment capable of ftifling a laugh, if it were ftrongly prompted ; yet, though in the eye of a virtuofo, a *lufus naturæ* bears every characteriftic that is ufually given of a rifible object, no inclination to laugh is felt; unlefs, in a gay humour, we fecretly perfonify fuch objects, and wonder how the *ftrangers came there*, and what is their *bufinefs*.

If this obfervation be juft, we fhall be able to determine what particular kind and degree of confequence an object, in other refpects rifible, muft be of, in order to move laughter ; viz. it muft produce a *perfonification*. Then, if any incongruity attend it, and it be not capable of exciting a ferious emotion, the tendency to laugh will be inevitable. However, left this obfervation fhould not be found to be univerfally juft, the definition in the former part of the lecture is left to ftand in more general terms.

To fhew that any ferious emotion will deftroy the property we call either rifible or ridiculous in objects, we may confider the cafe of *Sancho Panca* fallen into a hole, which he took to be a deep pit, in the dark, and clinging to the fides with his hands and feet, in the utmoft dread of being dafhed to pieces, and all the while within a foot of the bottom. This, efpecially confidering the character of the man, is certainly an object highly *rifible*. Perhaps no perfon could have refrained from laughing, if he had found him in that fituation ; yet, if we had feen him in the fame pofture, and his danger had been real ; or, perhaps, if we had found any perfon for whom we entertained a higher kind of refpect, in the fame fituation, and without danger, we fhould not

E e   have

have been difposed to laugh at all. Our *anxiety* and *concern* in the former cafe, and our *refpect* in the latter, would have overpowered it.

We, likewife, fee that, in perfons of little ferious religion, and great levity of mind, nothing will excite more profufe laughter, than the application of paffages of Scripture to very foreign and ludicrous purpofes; whereas the fame thing will ftrike every ferious perfon, who entertains a profound veneration for the Scriptures, with the greateft horror; or if the greatnefs and unexpectednefs of the contraft fhould, in fpite of himfelf, as it were, furprize him into a laugh, he will foon recollect himfelf, and be very uneafy about it. We, likewife, fee every day, that the fame views provoke only the laughter and ridicule of fome perfons, and the ferious indignation of others.

LECTURE

L E C T U R E XXV.

Of BURLESQUE, PARODY, *the* MOCK-HEROIC, HUMOUR, *and* IRONY.

TO make a fudden tranfition from a very high to a very low object that is fimilar to it, though fuch a tranfition be in itfelf difagreeable, yet, by means of the contraft which it produces, it may affect the mind with a lively fenfe of pleafure. This we may perceive in the following lines of Butler:

> The fun had long fince in the lap
> Of Thetis taken out his nap;
> And, like a lobfter boil'd, the morn
> From black to red began to turn.
>
> HUD. Part II. Cant. II. Ver. 29.

This effect is called *burlefque*; and a great object degraded in this manner, and placed in the fame light with a mean and contemptible one, is faid to be burlefqued; the meaning of which is, that the ideas of meannefs annexed to the leffer object are, by this comparifon, transferred to the greater, and adhere to it by affociation. Thefe transferred ideas, being the reverfe of the fublime, deftroy the effect of every thing fimilar-to it in the idea

E e 2

of

of a great object; and the confequence is, that the great object is afterwards mentioned with lefs refpect and reverence than it was before.

A *Parody*, which is the application of a paffage of any author to a foreign, and generally lower purpofe, is a kind of burlefque of a grave and ferious writer : and confequently parodies have often an unfavourable effect upon the original author. For thofe foreign allufions will often occur in reading the original paffage, and prevent it from having its proper and intended effect.

For this reafon, if it be a matter of importance to preferve our reverence for any writings (as, for inftance, the fcriptures) it is advifeable not to liften to fuch ludicrous applications of them. The unhappy effect of fuch applications is never wholly loft, till the allufion be forgotten. Should the allufion even mifs of its ufual effect upon light minds, and raife horror and indignation at the firft hearing, it may not find the mind in fo favourable a difpofition every time that it occurs ; or if it do, ftill, as the fentiments of *indignation* are foreign to the defign of the paffage, it is defirable that nothing even of that kind come in view when we read it.

Neither art, fcience, profeffion, character, nor any thing elfe, however venerable or refpectable, is exempt from the power of ridicule ; becaufe there is no fetting bounds to thofe analogies in nature or art which give rife to it. We fee the greateft things analogous to the leaft, and the leaft to the greateft, without end or limit : infomuch that it is impoffible to name an object in any clafs of things (let us make the diftribution of them as we pleafe) but fome other object may be found analogous to it in any other clafs, even the moft remote we can think of. And whenever

I   thefe

thefe analogies are brought into view, the refult is an alteration
in the ideas of both the objects in which the analogy is perceived,
occafioned by the reciprocal influences of the one upon the other.
They are univerfally either increafed or diminifhed, raifed or de-
preffed, &c. and the effect is more or lefs permanent, in proportion as the analogy is more or lefs ftriking. This effect is the
fame, whether the objects be brought together in order to be *compared* or *contrafted*, becaufe *analogy* is the foundation of both,
and they differ only in this, that when things are compared, the
points of *refemblance* are chiefly attended to; whereas, when they
are contrafted, the circumftances of *difference* are principally noted.   But it is neceffary, in order to their producing their refpective effects, that the circumftances of difference be attended to in
the former cafe, and thofe of refemblance in the latter.

Confidering how far and how wide analogies extend themfelves
through all the parts of nature; how poffible is it that an object,
the moft refpectable in the world, may be difcovered to be fo
analogous, in fome refpects, to another, even the moft contemptible, that the oddnefs of the contraft fhall produce a laugh?
May not the moft ferious and fenfible paffage of any author
whatever be applied to a purpofe fo foreign, and yet fo fimilar to
its original ufe, as infallibly to produce the fame effect? But
fhould we, notwithftanding this, in our *judgments* (however our
imaginations might, for a time, be impofed upon) entertain a
lower idea either of the object, or of the paffage that was thus
burlefqued? How then is *ridicule the teft of truth?* It requires
only an attention to the nature of contraft to refute the fallacy.
Ridicule can only difcover contrafts capable of producing a laugh;
and, confidering the levity and irritability of fome perfons minds,

there

there is nothing in nature but what hath connections and analogies which produce contrasts capable of doing it.

The grave and respectable character of Socrates was so effectually turned into ridicule by Aristophanes, that it was not in the power of any of his friends to forbear laughing at his expence. It is even said that he himself could not refrain from smiling: though that might be affected in him, in order to turn off the edge of the ridicule. However, there seems to be no reason why a person, in whom pride or vanity doth not greatly predominate, may not laugh at himself; since it is only the sense of *honour* being wounded that makes us insensible of the pleasures of contrast, when we ourselves are the subject of it.

If nothing affected the sense of ridicule but inconsistencies of *opinions* with *truth*, it would bid fair to be the test of truth. It is true, that such inconsistencies *do* affect that sense, and appear ridiculous; but what makes it indeterminate, and of no use in this case, is, that a variety of analogies, contrasts, and comparisons, which imply no inconsistency with truth, do likewise affect us in a similar manner. For it requires nothing but that two objects, or two parts of the same object, seen at the same time, be very like in some things, and very unlike in others, in order to excite the sense of ridicule. The dress and customs of Asiatics appear ridiculous to Europeans, and those of Europeans to Asiatics; but doth it follow from thence that there is any *real impropriety* in either, any thing contrary to the nature, fitness, and truth of things?

Besides, we see that the same things affect different persons in in a very different manner, according to the previous state of their minds: so that, before nothing but *falsehood* could affect the mind with the sense of ridicule, it is necessary that all a person's

previous

previous notions be juſt. For it is an inconſiſtency with what we apprehend to be truth that appears ridiculous to us. Thus, no doubt, the opinion of Copernicus, that the earth had a revolution both about its own axis, and about the ſun, would be received with ridicule when it was firſt publiſhed ; and if mankind had acquieſced in that teſt, that certain truth would have been exploded, without farther examination. It is reverſing the order of nature to *judge* in conſequence of *laughing*. It is evident, we ought rather to forbear laughing till we have employed our judgment, to ſee whether we have reaſon to laugh or not.

But though ridicule be not the teſt of truth, it hath very conſiderable uſes. For as every laugh is made at the expence, and to the prejudice of the thing, or character, that is ridiculed, it makes us ſolicitous to keep ourſelves, and every thing we revere, from the edge of it, which can only be done by ſeparating from every venerable object every thing which, on account of its connections and analogies, would ſuggeſt the idea of any thing low and contemptible. The conſequence of which is, that ſuch objects are made more of a piece, and more perfect in their kind, at leaſt more agreeable to *common opinions*, and the *prevailing taſte*. What a ridiculous mixture of great and low images would every mode of religion, every ſcheme of philoſophy, every ſpecies of compoſition, and every human character preſent, if the fear of ridicule did not make men ſolicitous to avoid ſuch incongruous circumſtances ?

The reverſe of paſſing from a *high to a low* object, is to paſs from a very *low to a high* one. This tranſition, at the ſame time that (for a reaſon which will be given hereafter) it is in itſelf agreeable, lays the mind open to the ſame ſpecies of pleaſure

(ariſing

(arifing from contraft) with the pleafures of ridicule; with this difference in the effect, that, in this cafe, the low object being that to which the mind hath been attentive, and confequently that to which it will refer all the related ideas that arife in the fcene in which it is introduced, will have an air of grandeur and importance given to it, by being exhibited in the fame light with the fublime object. It is true, that, as in the cafe of ridicule, the fublime object is liable to be degraded by the fame means; but not being kept fo long in fight, the effect is more tranfient.

Mr. Pope aggrandizes an altercation between a company of gentlemen and ladies, by the following magnificent comparifon:

> So when bold Homer makes the gods engage,
> And heavenly breafts with human paffions rage;
> 'Gainft Pallas, Mars, Latona, Hermes arms,
> And all Olympus rings with loud alarms:
> Jove's thunder roars, heav'n trembles all around,
> Blue Neptune ftorms, the bellowing deeps refound;
> Earth fhakes her nodding tow'rs, the ground gives way,
> And the pale ghofts ftart at the flafh of day!
>
> RAPE OF THE LOCK, Cant. V. v. 45.

Low images, aggrandized in this manner, by pompous language and fublime comparifons, produce what is called the *mock-heroic*.

The fame air of gravity and ferioufnefs is preferved through the whole of what is called *humour*; which differs from the *mock-heroic* in nothing, but that the fubject and ftyle of it are lower, and therefore it fuits better with the tone of converfation; whereas we never apply the term *mock-heroic* but to compofitions, and generally to poetic compofitions, becaufe they are generally

nerally intended to be an imitation of, and parody upon, the true *heroic*.

There is a ftroke of genuine humour in the following anfwer of Falftaff to young Harry.

Harry.   " Ay, a good amendment of life in thee, from pray-
" ing to purfe-ftealing.
Fal: " Why, 'tis my occupation, Hal; 'tis no fin for a man
" to labour in his vocation."

                    Firft Part of HENRY IV. Act I. Scene 2.

The following paffage, from Arbuthnot's account of what paffed in the city of London when the comet was expected, is, likewife, an excellent ftroke of humour, but of that fpecies of it which is called *ironical*.

" If the reverend clergy fhowed more concern than others, I
" charitably impute it to their great charge of fouls; and what
" confirmed me in this opinion was, that the degrees of appre-
" henfion and terror could be diftinguifhed to be greater or lefs,
" according to their ranks and degrees in the church."

I cannot, however, help remarking upon this paffage, that the humour of it would be much improved if the word *charitably* were dropped; fince that word doth but too plainly point to a very different conftruction upon the conduct of the clergy, which ought by all means to have been kept out of view: fince, in every inftance of true humour, the fenfe intended to be conveyed, and which makes the contraft with that which is expreffed, is always fufficiently obvious, to occur of itfelf, without the help of any thing in the expreffion to point to it.

                    F f   A piece

A piece of perfect *irony* is the speech of Elijah to the priests of Baal, in the following passage : 1 Kings xviii. 26, 27.

" And they called on the name of Baal, from morning until
" noon, saying, Oh Baal, hear us ! But there was no voice,
" nor any that answered. And they leaped upon the altar which
" was made. And it came to pass, at noon, that Elijah mocked
" them, and said, Cry aloud; for he is a god : either he is talk-
" ing, or he is pursuing, or he is in a journey ; or peradventure
" he sleepeth, and must be awaked."

If the above instances of humour and irony be admitted, these two species of wit (at the same time that they must both be allowed to be of the nature of the mock-heroic, but lowered, as we may say, to the tone of conversation) must differ in this respect, that the term *Humour* is applied to every thing that is diverting, under the appearance of gravity ; whereas *Irony* is always meant to expose, and turn into ridicule. All irony therefore is humour, but all humour is not irony.

If there were no other signs of our ideas, and indications of states of mind, than *words*, it might justly appear surprizing, that a person should say one thing, and mean another, and yet his real meaning be perfectly understood. But the *tone of voice*, the *gesture*, and a variety of other *circumstances*, may sufficiently indicate a man's real meaning, without regard to words, and even by the help of words of a contrary meaning ; because tones, gestures, and other circumstances, have, by use, acquired as fixed associations with *states of mind* as articulate words. Some of these signs of ideas, which are independent of words, are universal ; so that any person, using them, may speak ironically,

and

and yet be fure of being underftood : but there are particular methods which particular perfons have adopted, or have fallen into,
which is the reafon why ftrangers cannot be fo certain when a perfon fpeaks ironically, as thofe who are well acquainted with him,
and know his peculiar fentiments and manner. However, if a
perfon who fpeaks ironically be mifunderftood for a time, it is
a circumftance that hath often no unfavourable effect, as it
often occafions the greater diverfion at laft. In reality, a new
contraft is hereby produced, between our firft and our latter apprehenfions of the perfon's meaning. Perhaps, the moft complete
fcene of irony and ridicule is, when a conceited coxcomb in a
company fhall interpret that to be a compliment, which every
body elfe fees was intended to expofe him ; which, in this cafe,
it moft effectually doth.

Though it appears, by the preceding account of the *burlefque*
and the *mock-heroic*, that there is a confiderable refemblance between them, the latter hath this great advantage over the former ;
that, in burlefque, there is an avowed attempt to divert and
promote laughter, by odd combinations of ideas ; whereas in the
mock-heroic, and in ftrokes of humour, we are prefented with
the fame odd combinations, but the attempt to divert, by means
of them, is concealed under an air of gravity and ferioufnefs,
which is a high additional contraft. The writer of burlefque is
to be underftood literally ; the author of the mock-heroic, or the
writer of humour, fays one thing, and means another. The
former is like a perfon who fays, " I will tell you a comical
" ftory, that will make you laugh." The latter fays, of the fame
ftory, " It is a ferious affair, and not to be laughed at." Though,
therefore, the effect of the mock-heroic and the burlefque differ

F f 2   only

only in degree, they are of so *different a character*, that it is a great offence againſt propriety to confound them.

Notwithſtanding this manifeſt impropriety, there are few writers who aim at the mock-heroic, that can help putting themſelves, now and then, in the place of their hearers, and laughing at their own ſtory; ſo that we have few pieces which are throughout in the ſtyle of the genuine mock-heroic. *Cervantes* is univerſally confeſſed to be the beſt model for this ſpecies of writing, and he hath been happily imitated by Mr. *Cambridge* in the *Scribleriad*.

Pope's Rape of the Lock, notwithſtanding its great merit, is not altogether free from the forementioned inconſiſtency. Who would imagine that the poet, who affects to be ſo ſerious as he doth in the greateſt part of his work, even when he ſpeaks in his own perſon, ſhould introduce it by telling us, almoſt in ſo many words, that he will tell us a very ridiculous and diverting ſtory?

What can have a greater appearance of gravity than the following exclamation of the poet, in his own perſon, upon Belinda's triumphing too ſoon upon a ſucceſsful throw of her cards?

> Oh thoughtleſs mortals! ever blind to fate,
> Too ſoon dejected, and too ſoon elate;
> Sudden theſe honours ſhall be ſnatch'd away,
> And curs'd for ever this victorious day.

Cant. III. Ver. 101.

The

The greater part of the poem is in the fame ferious ſtrain;
but how unſuitable to this are the very firſt verſes?

> What dire offence from am'rous cauſes ſprings,
> What mighty conteſts riſe from *trivial things*,
> I ſing.—This verſe to C——— much is due;
> This e'en Belinda might vouchſafe to view.
> *Slight* is the ſubject, but not ſo the praiſe,
> If ſhe inſpire, and he approve my lays.

How much more propriety is there in the following ferious introduction to the Scribleriad:

> The much-enduring man, whoſe curious ſoul
> Bore him with ceaſeleſs toil from pole to pole,
> Inſatiate, endleſs knowledge to obtain,
> Through woes by land, through dangers on the main,
> New woes, new dangers, deſtin'd to engage,
> By wrathful Saturn's unrelenting rage,
> I ſing.

It is hardly neceſſary to obſerve, that, both with reſpect to the
mock-heroic, and in every other caſe in which objects that are
very different are contraſted and compared, the reſemblance
ſhould be as great and as ſtriking as the difference: otherwiſe the
contraſt or compariſon will not be borne with any pleaſure. A
want of this ſeems to render Mr. Pope's attempt to parody that
ſublime paſſage of Moſes, *Let there be light, and there was light*,
weak and ineffectual.

The

The ſkilful nymph reviews her force with care,
Let Spades be trumps, ſhe ſaid; and trumps they were.
                    RAPE OF THE LOCK, Cant. III. ver. 45.

Such poor attempts at parody as this affect only the perſons who make them. The original paſſages themſelves ſuffer no injury from them, as they were obſerved to do from a happy and ſuc-ceſsful parody.

LECTURE

L E C T U R E   XXVI.

Of RIDDLES, PUNS, *and the serious* ANTITHESIS.

THE pleasure we receive from the solution of *riddles* may not improperly be mentioned under this head of Contrast. The generality of riddles are nothing more than very strong and harsh metaphors, or rather allegories, and the pleasure we receive from them is in proportion to the greatness of the analogy between two things which are very different. Of this nature is the famous riddle of the Sphynx, " What creature is " that which walks upon four legs in the morning, upon two at " noon, and upon three at night?" Every thing that strikes us in the application of this to a *man*, is to find that *hands* and a *staff* are called *legs*, when, like them, they rest upon the ground, and support a person; that *infancy* is the *morning*, *middle age* the *noon*, and *old age* the *evening* of life.

Some other riddles are of another kind, and particularly that of Samson; " Out of the eater came forth meat, and out of the " strong came forth sweetness." The figure in this riddle is not a metaphor, because *a lion* is not called *the eater*; nor *honey*, *sweetness*, on account of their resemblance to one another; but on account of another relation which will be explained when I treat of the *Metonymy*.

A con-

A contraſt of *ideas* is not always neceſſary to pleaſe and to divert : a *verbal contraſt*, ariſing from the different meanings of the ſame term, is often ſufficient. A word uſed in different ſenſes is called *a pun*, or a play upon words ; ſuch is that upon the word *grace*, in the following paſſage of Shakeſpeare, who abounds in this ſpecies of wit :

Fal. " God ſave thy grace; majeſty I ſhould have ſaid, for " grace thou wilt have none.
Henry. " What none !
Fal. " No, by my troth, not ſo much as will ſerve to be a " prologue to an egg and butter."

Firſt Part of HENRY IV. Act I. Scene 2.

The word *grace* is, in fact, uſed in three ſenſes in this paſſage ; and it is true that the three ideas ſignified by it, viz. a *title of honour*, *goodneſs of heart*, and *a grace before meat*, have no real reſemblance, as they agree in nothing but that they happen to be ſignified by the ſame term ; which is no relation founded in nature, but is merely accidental, and arbitrary. Yet, ſince the reſemblance in expreſſion appears to be, in fact, ſufficient to make the difference in ſenſe very ſtriking and diverting, it ſeems to be enough to intitle it to the name of *wit*, in common with other diverting contraſts, which the ingenuity of men hath hit upon.

Sometimes we meet with a *double contraſt*, viz. both in the ideas, and in the words; as in the following paſſage of Mr. Pope :

Here thou, great Anna, whom three realms obey,
Doſt ſometimes counſel *take*, and ſometimes tea.

RAPE OF THE LOCK, Cant. III. v. 7.

If

If the ambiguous word *take* be changed in this paſſage, the contraſt in ſenſe is ſufficiently ſtriking: but the uſe of that word,
which happens to be equally applicable to *counſel* and *tea,* though
in very different ſenſes, ſeems to give an additional beauty, of
this lower kind, to the paſſage.

There is a like double contraſt in the old inſcription,

> Beneath this ſtone my wife doth lie:
> She's now at reſt, and ſo am I.

The reaſon why puns have been ſo much condemned of late,
notwithſtanding both the *ingenuity* requiſite to diſcover them, and
their well-known *effects,* ſufficiently prove them to be a ſpecies
of *wit,* ſeems to be, that they have been generally miſapplied ;
that is, the pleaſure they give us is of a nature unſuitable to
the proper effect of the works in which they have often been introduced.   To ſay they are no ſpecies of wit, becauſe they will
not bear *tranſlating* into another language, is too weak to need
any refutation.   But when they have occurred in ſermons, in
tragedies, in a variety of ſerious compoſitions, and in conver-
ſations upon ſerious ſubjects, it is no wonder they have been
perceived to have a diſagreeable effect, and that the groſs abuſe
of them hath made the uſe of them to be univerſally condemned.
Indeed, puns accord only with the tone of compoſitions which
abound with the ſlighteſt and moſt trifling contraſts ; inſomuch
that they have an ill effect when intermixed in many ſpecies of
wit.   They can only pleaſe in a peculiarly gay humour, when
the mind is uncommonly irritable, and diſpoſed to be diverted
with any thing.

Indeed, for the ſame reaſon that we condemn the uſe of puns,
we alſo condemn the uſe of any ſpecies of wit, of any contraſts

G g

intended

intended to divert; fince thefe, with regard to their effects, differ only in degree, and not in kind. They are univerfally improper when they do not accord with the reft of the piece in
which they are introduced; that is, when the temper of mind
which is requifite to relifh them is not naturally produced by
the general ftrain of the compofition. In all ferious compofitions, therefore, of whatever kind, they ought carefully to be
avoided; as alfo the frequent ufe of the grave *antithefis*, when
we would appear to be in earneft, and more intent upon the
fubject than the manner of compofition. The ftrong and pointed
antithefis occurs fo feldom in real ferious life, and hath fo remarkable an effect whenever it doth occur, that the frequent ufe of
it never fails to fuggeft the appearance of *art*, and *ftudied introduction*. And *affectation*, of all kinds, is univerfally difgufting.
This is the reafon why the frequent and unneceffary ufe of it in
compofitions hath always been looked upon, by the beft writers,
as a fymptom of the declenfion of juft and natural tafte; as when
it appeared in the works of Lyfias among the later Greeks, and
of Seneca among the later Romans.

In times when writings were not common, as at the dawn of
genius and knowledge, no perfon would think of compofing
any thing, unlefs he had fomething of importance to communicate: confequently his attention would be engroffed by his *fubject*, and he would introduce the antithefis, and the other more
ftriking beauties of compofition, no oftener than they naturally
occurred. But later writers, obferving the uncommonly-fine effect
of thefe forms of expreffion, would naturally have their attention
divided between their *fubject* and thofe beauties which adorn *compofition*; or, rather, they would be apt to fuit their fubject to
thofe forms of expreffion. And fince the attention of the writer

4   himfelf

himself was chiefly engaged by them, the performance muft appear beautiful to himfelf, and his judgment be perverted. Whereas, to a reader whofe mind was attentive to the fubject of the treatife, the fame things would appear unnatural and difgufting. And it is certain, that no forms of expreffion, or the frequent recurrency of any, can ftand the teft of found criticifm, and the judgment of ages, which are improper with regard to the profeffed nature and purport of the work in which they are introduced. For, however they may be admired by the authors themfelves, or thofe who read with a view to obferve the particular beauties of compofition, they can never be generally and long admired.

The admirers of fuch glittering compofitions have narrow views; their attention is withdrawn from the fubject, and, confequently from the true beauties and proprieties of it. And it is only the moft *general views*, thofe which comprehend the whole of a fubject, and every thing that bears any relation to it, that can lead to a right judgment of a work. Whenever, therefore, fuch compofitions are feen in their true point of light, and the general purport of them is compared with the natural effect of their particular parts, their want of propriety muft be feen and expofed.

We fee here, then, one reafon of the great admiration in which the ancient writers of any nation are almoft univerfally held. As they had no beauties of compofition to copy after, they have more of nature and true propriety in them. This is remarkably the cafe with refpect to Homer and other very ancient Greek poets, and Offian the ancient Gallic poet.

But this obfervation is not applicable to the late revivers of learning in this weftern part of the world. They had Greek and

Roman models of compofition to copy after. In fact, we no where fee ftronger inftances of *affectation* than in their writings. Shakefpeare himfelf, notwithftanding the ftrong bent of his genius to *natural propriety*, abounds with mifplaced wit. In fome of the graveft paffages in his works, we meet with ftrokes which tend to raife a laugh, inftead of correfponding with the more ferious emotions that arife from the fcene with which he prefents us. Perhaps it is this palpably ridiculous extravagance of wit in that age, and more efpecially ftill in the fucceeding one of Charles the Second, that hath contributed more than any thing elfe to the eftablifhment of the good tafte that feems to prevail at prefent.

As there is no fault in compofition which there is fo much danger of falling into, in a pretty advanced ftate of literature, and efpecially by young writers, who are apt to be prodigioufly ftruck with every appearance of *ingenuity*, and whofe comprehenfion of mind is not fufficiently large to judge of the propriety of their introduction, I fhall felect a paragraph or two from the fermons of Dr. South, an admired writer in the age of Charles the Second, which will make the meaning of thefe obfervations, and the reafon of them, very evident.

Difcourfing concerning man in a ftate of innocence, he fays: " As it is reafonable to imagine that there is more of defign, " and confequently more of perfection, in the laft work, we " have God here giving his laft ftroke, and fumming up all into " man; the whole into a part, the univerfe into an individual.— " We might well imagine that the great artificer would be more " than ordinarily exact in drawing his own picture.—Thefe were " notions not defcending from us, but born with us; not our " offspring, but our brethren; and (as I may fo fay) fuch as
" were

" were taught without the help of a teacher.—Could any diffi-
" culty have been propofed, the refolution would have been as
" early as the propofal.   It could not have had time to fettle into
" doubt.   Like a better Archimedes, the iffue of all his enquiries
" was an ευρηκα, an ευρηκα, the offspring of his brain, without
" the fweat of his brow.   Study was not then a duty.   Night-
" watchings were needlefs.   The light of reafon wanted not the
" affiftance of a candle.   This is the doom of fallen man, to la-
" bour in the fire, to feek truth *in profundo*, to exhauft his time
" and impair his health, and perhaps to fpin out his days, and
" himfelf, into one pitiful controverted conclufion.—Certainly
" that muft needs have been very glorious, the decays of which
" are fo admirable.   He that is comely when old and decrepid,
" furely was very beautiful when he was young.   An Ariftotle
" was but the rubbifh of an Adam, and Athens but the rudi-
" ments of paradife."

It is needlefs to point out the paffages I fhould particularly object to in thefe paragraphs.   Thefe, and fuch-like ftrokes, certainly fhow ingenuity, and, fingly taken, might be thought excellent: The fault is, that they are often mifplaced and unfeafonable.

The ferious Dr. Young is by no means free from this kind of
affectation.   The pointed antithefis abounds too much in his celebrated poem *the Night-Thoughts*.   Some of his antithefes are
little more than verbal.   The tendency of the following, and a
variety of other fingle ftrokes, feem to have an effect unfavourable to the defign of the whole work, and of the particular places in which they are introduced.

> Even filent night proclaims my foul immortal,
> Even filent night proclaims eternal day :

For

For human weal heaven hufbands all events,
Dull fleep inftructs, nor fport vain dreams in vain.

Night the First.

Such ftrokes as thefe make the generality of readers admire a
writer while they are reading him; but that writer alone will fecure the lafting admiration of the judicious, who difappears,
and is loft in his fubject while we are reading, and occurs only
to our reflection afterwards. Thofe after-reflections, however,
will do him ample juftice, and more than make him amends for
our feeming to have loft fight of him for a time.

LECTURE

LECTURE XXVII.

Of METONYMY.

WE have feen the extenfive influence of *affociation* in forming all the pleafures of imagination that we have hitherto
enumerated, and we have feen the probability of that opinion,
which reprefents all our *intellectual pleafures* as derived originally
from *fenfible impreffions,* varioufly mixed, combined, and tranf-
ferred from one object to another, by that principle. Some of
thefe were remote, and perhaps, to perfons unufed to fuch fpeculations, *obfcure* effects of that great and univerfal agent in the
affections of the human mind. We fhall now take a view of
fome of the more manifeft and immediate effects of it, in tranf-
ferring ideas belonging to fome words upon others related to them.

From hence, in particular, refults the ftriking effect of the
rhetorical figures called *metonymy* and *fynecdoche.* Thefe terms
are applied when, inftead of the proper name of any thing or
attribute, a name is borrowed from another object, which ftands
in any other relation to it than that of actual *refemblance,* which
is referred to *metaphor.*

It is almoft endlefs to enumerate all the relations of things
which afford a foundation for this figure of fpeech. Some of
the principal of them are thofe of *caufe and effect,* in all its varieties,

rieties, *the subject and its attributes*, or circumstances; the *agent and the instrument*; *general and particular, abstract and concrete terms:* and *the whole and its part*, which alone is referred to *synecdoche*. For example, we put the effect for the cause when we say *day arose*, instead of saying the *sun arose*; an attribute, or circumstance, for the subject in *cedant arma togæ*; a particular for a general term, when we say *a Mæcenas* for a *patron of learning*, and *a Nero* for a *tyrant*; an abstract for a concrete term, when we say, *favours conferred upon insensibility*, rather than *upon the insensible*. Examples might easily be given of the converse of all these, and of many others.

The advantage of using such terms, borrowed from related objects, instead of proper terms, is that, at the same time that the new name sufficiently characterises the object we intend to express, so that it is impossible to mistake it, the figurative expression transfers upon it some foreign idea, which will serve to improve the sense of the passage. Moreover, it tends agreeably to engage and exercise the faculties of a reader to take him a little out of the way of common expression. This figure, likewise, greatly assists *personification*, by which a composition is greatly animated, as it exhibits living and thinking objects.

When Virgil says, *Bibet Germania Tigrim*, using the name of a *country* for that of the *inhabitants*, it is impossible the reader should hesitate a moment about the true sense of the passage (for were there the least danger of a mistake the term would have been improper) several ideas, particularly that of *immobility*, necessarily adhering to the name of the country, augment the improbability of the fact, and thereby heighten and improve the expression. A similar effect is produced, and a similar advantage is gained by Herodotus, when he says, *the whole theatre,*

theatre, inftead of the perfons in the theatre, *burft into tears*. There is alfo the fame happinefs in thofe familiar expreffions, *the eloquence of the bar, and of the pulpit*.

When a perfon is called *a Mæcenas*, ideas of honour and efteem are more readily tranferred to him, than if he were called in plainer terms *a promoter of learning*, and *a patron of learned men*. Every pleafing idea of this kind hath been fo long and fo intimately connected with the name of that favourite of Auguftus, that we thereby convey more definite and ftronger ideas than we could by any other, though longer form of expreffion.   With the fame advantage is a tyrant called *a Nero*, a poet *a fecond Homer*, and a philofopher *a fecond Sir Ifaac Newton*.   There is a kind of *accumulation of meaning* in thefe expreffions, by means of long, extenfive, and repeated affociations of ideas.   In all thefe cafes, likewife, the confcioufnefs a reader hath of his being fenfible of the force of thefe expreffions, in confequence of his being acquainted with the characters alluded to, gives no fmall pleafure.

We fee that, in many cafes, the name of a *part* of a thing will fuggeft the idea of the *whole* with greater clearnefs and ftrength than the name of the whole itfelf.   For the idea of fome principal part may have a clofer connection with the idea of the whole, than even the *name of the whole* hath with its own proper correfponding idea.   Nor will this appear to be any paradox, if we confider that the name of any thing cannot raife a diftinct idea of the whole, without raifing that of its feveral parts.   It is evident that thefe fcripture-expreffions, *Give us this day our daily bread*; and, *Having food and raiment be therewith content*, fuggeft a ftronger, and, in fact, no lefs determinate an idea of all that is intended by them, than any more general and comprehenfive terms would have done. Also when Æneas, in Virgil, says only, *Hostis habet muros*, though the *walls* were but a part of the *city*, and, in themselves considered, the least valuable part; yet, as they were that part of it in which its *strength* chiefly consisted, to say that the enemy were in possession of them, signifies their being masters of the whole town, more fully than if the whole town had been expressly mentioned.

By the help of this figure, a writer may very happily introduce, and keep in view, those peculiar properties of persons and things which his subject requires him to pay a particular attention to. To do this, he may denominate things from those particular properties or relations which he has in view. Thus Virgil, treating of *corn*, with respect to the cultivation of it, very happily, upon the mention of a shower, says, *boum labores diluit.* An author, after representing his hero in distress by the darkness of the night, might very properly say, at length *the light*, or *the day*, rather than *the sun*, *arose*; and any writer, treating of the eloquence of Cicero, would frequently use the term *orator*, and *our orator*, instead of his proper name. Or if a dialogue were made between any particular philosopher, and any particular soldier, for instance, upon the subject of their several professions, one would naturally, instead of repeating their proper names often, call them *the philosopher* and *the soldier*. With equal propriety the ancients used the term βιη ηρακληειη, *the force of Hercules*, the quality he was most remarkable for, instead of the direct proper name *Hercules*; and with equal beauty might a speech of Nestor have been introduced, by saying, Thus spake *the wisdom of Nestor*.

If it require more words than one to denominate an object from its properties or circumstances, the figure is called a *periphrasis,*

2

phrafis. Thus, *boum labores* is properly a periphrafis to exprefs *corn*. It is with great propriety that Shakefpeare makes King John fay, when he furrendered his crown, " Thus I yield up " into your hand the circle of my glory;" becaufe the *crown* was only valuable as an emblem, or badge of *glory*.

The metonymy, in common with the metaphor (though not generally in fo great a degree) may have the advantage of increafing the pleafure that any expreffion gives us, by bringing in view a fhort *fcene* or *landfchape* relating to an object. Thus, *a well-fought field* fuggefts a greater and ftronger idea than a well-fought *battle*; becaufe, the battle being fought upon the field, the idea of the field introduces the picture of a battle upon it more readily and effectually than the proper term *battle*, which hath a more remote connexion with thofe particular fcenes. The term *battle* muft firft raife the idea of a *field*, before it can exhibit any thing that paffed upon the field.

That metonymy affifts *perfonification*, is not only very evident, when the name of an author is put for his invention, &c.; as, *Ceres* for *bread*, *Bacchus* for *wine*, *Venus* for *love*, in the old adage, *Sine Cerere et Baccho Venus friget*; but it is fufficiently apparent in many other inftances, when no actual names of perfons are mentioned; as in the following expreffions, in which the properties only of thinking beings are attributed to unthinking fubftances; *jovial wine*, *giddy brink*, *drowfy night*, *mufing midnight*, *panting height*, *advent'rous fong*, or in this,

Why peep your coward-fwords half out their fhells ?

It is often with peculiar elegance that qualities are perfonified, inftead of the perfons poffeffing them; as when Milton reprefents Satan faying,

H h 2   —————Or

——————— Or have ye chose
This place, after the toils of battle, to repose
Your wearied virtue?

Paradise Lost, Book I.

There is the same happiness in the following expressions, *When youth and beauty shall be laid in dust. Favours are often conferred upon insensibility.* In these expressions the abstract terms, *youth, beauty,* and *insensibility,* have a much finer effect than the words *young, beautiful,* and *insensible,* would have had. It is exhibiting an unmixed instead of a mixed character, and that personified. If by the change of the term *insensible* for *insensibility,* for instance, the advantage of personification had been lost, amends could hardly have been made for it by any other circumstance; but as that advantage is not lost, much is gained by the change from an *insensible man* to *insensibility itself in person.* An insensible man, as he is still *a man,* might be made sensible of an obligation, but *insensibility* cannot.

It is pleasing to observe how the sense of an expression improves, by being *concentrated,* as it were, in the change of an attribute, first from the plural to the singular number, and then from the singular number to an abstract idea personified. If, for instance, instead of saying *Old men are venerable,* we say, *An old man is venerable*; our idea becomes less vague, more determinate and clear. And the advantage of personification may be preserved, while the idea is freed from every thing foreign to it, and which might spoil its effect, when we say, *Old age is venerable.*

Epithets are sometimes beautifully tranferred from one subject to another by means of this figure, as may have been observed in the examples that were given of this figure's assisting personification.

fication. It is, likewise, obfervable in the following expreſſions, *pale death*, *a ſtupid moment motionleſs they ſtood:* THOMPSON. *Cæcis erramus in undis:* VIRGIL. The connexion of ideas ought to be very ſtrict, to make this transferring of epithets eaſy and natural; the impropriety, when theſe expreſſions are literally taken, is ſo great: for nothing can be more evident, than that it is abſurd to ſay, that *death* itſelf is *pale*, or that the *waters* themſelves were *blind*.

As no other relation of ideas affords ſo eaſy and natural a foundation for giving new names to things, as that of *reſemblance*, more caution is requiſite in the uſe of the metonymy than of the mataphor. Metaphors more often improve upon reflection than metonymies. Even the name of an object for the *ſound* of it is barely tolerable in the following line of Thompſon:

The ſudden waterfall ſwells in the breeze.

WINTER, Line 738.

And, perhaps, we ſhould not bear ſo well with the expreſſion laſt quoted from Virgil, and indeed many other of his metonymies (in which he abounds more than moſt other writers) if we attended to them a little. It is often particularly harſh to uſe the name of the *effect* for that of the *cauſe*. Thus *panting height*, and *aſtoniſhed thought*, have been juſtly obſerved to be ſtrained and uncouth expreſſions.

Notwithſtanding the metonymy be, in its own nature, a harſher figure than the metaphor, it is remarkable what power cuſtom hath to reconcile us to it. Witneſs theſe common expreſſions, a *happy ſtate*, a *blind way*, to *drink a glaſs of wine*, or a *diſh of tea*; to keep a *good houſe*, or a *good table*; to *write a fine hand*,

to

to *read any author*. Thefe, and many other expreffions of the
fame nature, are fo familiar, that the figure is abfolutely evanefcent; fo that they hardly deferve to be confidered as figures,
as it is only by an exprefs attention to them that we difcover them
to be figurative. However, it can hardly be faid of any metonymy, as it may be of fome metaphors, that they are fo wholly
evanefcent, that a perfon may hefitate before he can determine
whether an expreffion contain the figure, or not. To *write a good
hand*, is as common an expreffion as any that is in ufe, and the
figure it contains approaches as near to evanefcence as any I can
now recollect; and yet no perfon can think that the *writing* can
be called the *hand*, without a figure.

The general rule for the ufe of the metonymy is plainly this;
that in all cafes, provided the fenfe be in no danger of being miftaken, a writer is at liberty to fubftitute, inftead of a proper term,
any word which, by its affociations, can bring along with it ideas
that can ferve to heighten and improve the fentiment. But it
follows from this obfervation, that when the fenfe doth not require to be heightened and improved, as in the ordinary forms of
expreffion in converfation, on which no emphafis is ever laid,
the figure is impertinent and ufelefs: as when Profpero, in the
Tempeft of Shakefpeare, fpeaking to his fifter Miranda, fays,

> The fringed curtains of thine eyes advance,
> And fay what feeft thou.

To mention the *eye-lids* at all, much more to denominate them
by fuch a figurative periphrafis, was quite fuperfluous.

This figure is worfe than impertinent and ufelefs, when the
figurative expreffion exhibits any idea that is unfavourable to the
fentiment; as when Æneas, in Virgil, fays,

Tres

Tres adeo incertos cæca caligine foles
Erramus pelagi.   Æneid.

The poet ought by all means, in this place, to have contented himfelf with faying that they wandered *three days* in darknefs. To fay that they wandered *three funs* in black darknefs, hath too much the air of a contradiction, though, in many other fituations, the term *funs* might have a happy effect when put for days.

Periphrafes and epithets, as they ferve to denominate and characterize objects, come under this general rule, that nothing ought to be put for, or enter into the name of any object, or be ufed to diftinguifh it, that hath no relation to thofe properties of it which we have principally in view. The reafon is, that, by this means, a writer would lead his reader from his own views and purpofe. Thus it is improper to add the epithet *mortal* to *man*, unlefs man be confidered in the paffage in which it is introduced with regard to his mortality, and that idea would give ftrength to the fentiment. In every epithet a regard ought to be had to the general defign or purport of the paffage in which it is introduced. For example, when Neptune is fpoken of as a *perfon*, no attribute ought to be afcribed to him which agrees to nothing but *the fea*; as in the following paffage of Pope's Odyffee :

Hear me, oh Neptune, thou whofe arms are hurl'd
From fhore to fhore, and gird the folid world.
                                ODYSSEE, B. IX. v. 617.

In like manner, in prayer, we ought not to invoke the Divine Being by the mention of any attribute, as *almighty*, *infinitely wife*, and *gracious*, promifcuoufly; but chufe thofe which there

is

is the greatest propriety in our having a view to, in the subfe-
quent petition.

There is almost a tautology in epithets when they convey
no idea that is not expreffed, or implied, in fome other words
in the fentence. This is certainly faulty, as in the following
line :

> And impious fons their *mangled* fathers *wound*.

In the following, and perhaps in the preceding, there is an
impropriety with refpect to the order of time, which is apparent
upon a little attention to them :

> Submerfas obrue puppes.   Æneid I. 73.

> And mighty ruins fall.   Iliad V. 411.

LECTURE

L E C T U R E   XXVIII.

Of the HYPERBOLE, and BOMBAST.

WHEN any thing that is afferted in a difcourfe exceeds the truth, an *hyperbole* is faid to be ufed. In fact, in every fpecies of metonymy (and the fame may be faid of all the other figures) there is a departure from *literal truth*; but, as was explained in the cafe of Irony, it is in fuch a manner as that no-body can be impofed upon, or mifled by it, and it is attended with advantages to the fenfe, which could not have been had by a rigorous adherence to truth.

The reafon why the hyperbole is, in appearance, a greater violation of truth than moft other figures, is only this, that in the hyperbole the untruth lies in the *affirmation itfelf*, whereas in moft other figures it is concealed in an *epithet*, which however (were the fentence refolved into its conftituent parts) would alfo be a direct untruth in the affirmation.

The advantage of ufing an hyperpole, is, that the idea of one object may be heightened and improved by ideas transferred from other objects, and affociated with it. Thus when the Divine Being fays to Abraham, " I will make thy feed as the duft of " the earth; fo that if a man could number the duft of the earth, " then fhall thy feed alfo be numbered," Gen. xiii. 16; the

idea

idea of a number almoſt infinite is transferred from the duſt of the earth to the children, or deſcendants, of Abraham; and by this means we are enabled to conceive a greater idea of them than we could have done by the help of any plain and literal expreſſion.

This manner of expreſſion, though not ſtrictly agreeable to truth, is extremely natural when the imagination is raiſed, and a perſon is labouring for an expreſſion adequate to his ideas. In ſuch a ſituation of mind, as no expreſſions literally true ſufficiently anſwer his purpoſe, a writer is obliged to have recourſe to objects which can ſupply him with ſuch as will do it. The expreſſions to which theſe views give riſe, are, however, ſo circumſtanced, that we inſtantly enter, as it were, into the mind of the writer, we feel the difficulty he was under, and ſee the reaſon why he made choice of ſuch hyperbolical language; and as we are led into no miſtake by ſuch terms, they are, in fact, to us who enter into his ſituation and feelings, more true and juſt expreſſions of thoſe feelings than any plainer terms could have been.

Beſides, if we conſider that, by reaſon of the narrowneſs of our faculties, terms expreſſing the greateſt magnitudes and numbers, yea terms denoting infinities themſelves, raiſe only indeterminate and finite ideas in our minds, we may eaſily conceive that the *ſtate of mind* produced by an attempt to realize hyperbolical expreſſions, may not be more than barely adequate to the ideas intended to be conveyed. Let us, for example, endeavour to form an idea of a number equal to that of the *duſt of the earth:* the conception may not, in fact, reach to a juſt idea of the vaſt numbers of the poſterity of Abraham. So that hyperboles, thus properly circumſtanced, may, by the appearance of falſehood, lead the mind nearer to the truth than any expreſſions more literally true. In this caſe it ſeems to be very evident, that if the Divine

Being

Being had only said that the seed of Abraham should be *exceedingly numerous*, or had even assigned the *precise number* of them, the idea excited in the mind of Abraham, by such an expression, would not have been so near the truth, as that which is produced by the attempt to conceive a number equal to that of the *dust of the earth*.

It may perhaps, therefore, be no great paradox, if it be laid down as a maxim, that hyperboles are then only proper where they serve to lead our conceptions nearer to the truth than any other forms of expression; and that they must be condemned, as strained and *unnatural*, when the idea they excite in our minds really exceeds the idea that ought to be excited by the object described by them. The following account of the valour of Henry the Fifth, in Shakespeare, is certainly extravagantly hyperbolical:

> England ne'er had a king until his time:
> Virtue he had deserving to command:
> His brandish'd sword did blind men with its beams:
> His arms spread wider than a dragon's wings:
> His sparkling eyes, replete with aweful fire,
> More dazzled and drove back his enemies
> Than mid-day sun fierce bent against their faces.
> What should I say, his deeds exceed all speech;
> He never lifted up his hand but conquer'd.
>
> First Part of HENRY VI. Act I. Scene 1.

In many cases the generality of readers may be apt to think an hyperbole overcharged, for want of entering into an author's sentiments and views of things. A person, for instance, who

I i 2   had

had feen a ftorm at fea might not think the following lines in
Virgil's defcription of one much overcharged :

——————— Atque imo barathri ter gurgite vaftos
Sorbet in abruptum fluctus rurfufque fub auras
Erigit alternos, et fidera verberat unda.

ÆNEID. lib. III. ver. 421.

Likewife, if we only make proper allowance for the notions
which the common people of all countries ftill entertain of *murder*, and how much they imagine a particular providence is
concerned to detect and punifh murderers, we may not, perhaps,
be very fevere upon the following fpeech of the Baftard to Haf-
tings, upon his fufpecting him to have murdered prince Arthur :

——————— If thou didft but confent
To do this moft cruel act, do but defpair,
And if thou want a cord, the fmalleft thread
That ever fpider twifted from her womb
Will ftrangle thee.   A rufh will be a beam
To hang thee on.   Or would'ft thou drown thyfelf,
Put but a little water in a bafon,
And it fhall be as all the ocean,
Enough to ftifle fuch a villain up.
I do fufpect thee very grievoufly.

KING JOHN, Act IV. Scene 7.

The extravagant hyperbole is the common fault of thofe
writers who aim at the fublime, and the ftyle that abounds with
it is generally termed the *bombaft*.   As the hyperbole is a figure
that has a very ftriking effect, and is extremely eafy in itfelf (for
what can be eafier than to exceed the truth in defcription ?) writers
whofe

whofe aim was to elevate and aftonifh their readers have often adopted it, without confidering how few circumftances there are in which it can be admitted with propriety. They have not always confidered whether every thing preceding, and accompanying that figure, would contribute to make it carry along with it a conviction, that no other form of expreffion could fo clearly convey the proper idea. For if it be the *expreffion*, and not the *idea*, that furprizes a reader, it is a fure mark that the expreffion was improper; fince, when it is proper, it only conveys the idea, and doth not draw any attention upon itfelf.

Had thefe things been confidered, we fhould not, perhaps, have feen many hyperboles at the beginning of a compofition, introduced in places where the ideas did not require to be elevated or enlarged by any foreign affiftance, or put into the mouths of perfons who were not under the influence of any ftrong paffion, or a very lively imagination. Of all our late writers of character, Dryden and Lee feem to have been the moft intemperate in the ufe of the hyperbole.

As great a departure as an hyperbole is from truth, and confequently as ftriking as this figure muft be, cuftom has perfectly reconciled our minds to many very extraordinary inftances of it; particularly when the hyperbole flows from a lively imagination, and is not uttered in the vehemence of paffion. Any perfon may amufe himfelf in feeing this verified, if he only take a turn upon a bowling-green, and obferve when a bowl is faid, by fome perfons engaged in the diverfion, to be *a mile*, or *a hundred*, or *five hundred miles*, *from the jack*. Befides, how many familiar expreffions, in common converfation, pafs without cenfure, which yet are extravagantly hyperbolical; as when we fay, *A man is nothing but fkin and bone*, &c.

Perfons

Perfons of little reading, and confequently grofs conceptions, have little feeling of, or relifh for, any thing but what is very extravagant. Nothing but the marvellous and fupernatural hath any charms for them; but as their tafte refines, in confequence of a greater attention to, and more exact knowledge of, human nature and the world, they learn to diftinguifh and relifh the more delicate beauties of compofition; they become difgufted with every thing that is extravagant, and can admire nothing that deviates far from ftrict propriety.

Accordingly, we fee that the ftyle of the generality of writers (which muft keep pace with the general improvement of tafte) approaches nearer to a medium. The books which took with the generality of readers in the laft age are little read, and are little capable of pleafing, now. Indeed, fomething fimilar to this may be obferved in every individual. Few perfons, when they are advanced in life, and their judgment ripened, can relifh the compofitions which charmed them when young. We are told that Milton would read, with the greateft avidity and rapture, all the books of chivalry and romance that he could meet with, when he was young; but we can never imagine that he would have borne with any patience thofe extravagant fictions, and the bombaft ftyle in which they were generally compofed at the time that he wrote the Paradife Loft.

LECTURE

LECTURE XXIX.

Of PERSONIFICATION.

ANOTHER fource of pleafure in works of genius and imagination, is the views which writers take frequent opportunities of prefenting to us of *human fentiments*, *human paf-fions*, and *human actions*. As the fentiments and actions of our fellow-creatures are more interefting to us than any thing belonging to inanimate nature, or the actions of brute animals, a much greater variety of fenfations and ideas muft have been excited by them, and confequently adhere to them by the principle of affociation. Hence it is of prodigious advantage, in treating of inanimate things, or merely of brute animals, to introduce frequent allufions to human actions and fentiments, where any refemblance will make it natural. This converts every thing we treat of into thinking and acting beings. We fee *life*, *fenfe*, and *intelligence*, every where. The effect of this figure is fo pleafing, that when there is no kind of deception in the cafe, if the refemblance be fufficiently ftrong, and other circumftances favour the figure, the impropriety of the perfonification gives not the leaft offence.

In fact, this figure is become fo general, that it is almoft im-poffible to difcourfe about any thing, in the calmeft manner in the

2　　　　　　　　　　　　　　　　　world,

world, without borrowing fome part of our language from the
regions of life and fenfe.   Even the moft abftrufe mathematicians
and metaphyficians cannot always fo far abftract themfelves from
human life, as not to retain many terms borrowed from the actions and paffions of mankind.   The metaphyfical terms *agent*
and *patient*, always carry along with them ideas which the definitions of them do not include.   And, provided the foreign ideas
do not affect the propofition formed out of them (as was perhaps
the cafe in the old philofophy) they give fome degree of *colour*
and *life* to thofe abftract ideas, without being attended with any
inconvenience.

The ideas of *male* and *female* are, in the Englifh language, fo
ftrictly confined to objects that have *fex*, and confequently *life*
and *fenfe*, that I queftion whether any term implying fex, to
whatever it be applied, do not excite a momentary idea of thofe
qualities.   Can the following paffage in Milton be read without
a mental perfonification ?

> Firft in his Eaft the glorious lamp was feen,
> Regent of day, and all th' horizon round
> Invefted with bright rays, jocund to run
> His longitude thro' heaven's high road : the grey
> Dawn and pleiades before him danced,
> Shedding fweet influence.   Lefs bright the moon,
> But oppofite, in levell'd Weft, was fet,
> His mirror, with full face borrowing her light
> From him, for other light fhe needed none.
>
> PARADISE LOST, Book VII. l. 370.

Perhaps it may not appear quite chimerical to fuppofe, that the
extenfion of fex in moft fouthern languages, to almoft all inanimate things, may have taken its rife from a lively imagination,
perfonifying almoft every thing.   The

The flighteft perfonification is that which proceeds no further than a fimple metaphor, or metonymy, in which a new name is borrowed from the affections of fenfible and thinking beings, and transferred upon thofe that are infenfible; as in fuch phrafes as the following, *imperious ocean, thirfty ground, furious dart*, &c. Such expreffions as thefe are ufed by perfons under no emotion of paffion, and with very little elevation of fancy. Yet, even in thefe cafes, the imagination muft, for a moment, afcribe fenfibility to thofe infenfible objects, or we could never bear the epithets while we were reading them. A perfonification is, at leaft, a metaphor derived from the idea of fenfible and thinking beings; and every metaphor is fomething more than a bare comparifon. In comparifons (as was obferved before) the difference between any two objects is preferved, whereas in metaphors they are confounded, and one of the things is changed as it were, in idea, into the other. The firft hint of a perfonification, like that for a metaphor, may be a comparifon; but, by the power of imagination, it ends in fomething more.

I fee no difficulty in the perfonification of paffions, qualities, and other things of an abftract nature, which have no real exiftence; as of *pleafure* and *revenge*, in the following paffage of Shakefpeare:

——————————— For pleafure and revenge
Have ears more deaf than adders, to the voice
Of any true decifion.——

TROILUS AND CRESSIDA, Act II. Scene 4.

Or of flander:

——————————— No, 'tis flander,
——————————— Whofe tongue

K k   Out-

Out-venoms all the worms of Nile, whofe breath
Rides on the pofting winds.——

Cymbeline, Act III. Scene 4.

Our ideas, in this cafe, it is true, are not abftract; but the ideas of *perfons* with the characters of the paffion or quality defcribed, which are not difficult to form.

Ideas of the properties and affections of thinking beings are fo familiar to our minds, and the animate and inanimate parts of nature abound fo much in mutual analogies, ftronger or weaker, that no perfon, of the leaft imagination, can help being frequently ftruck with thofe refemblances. The very circumftance of our being obliged to have recourfe to fenfible ideas, and the terms which exprefs their relations, when we fpeak of intellectual things, cannot fail greatly to extend thofe analogies. As intellectual ideas are conftantly denoted by terms originally borrowed from fenfible things, thefe terms will carry back with them their new affociations, and transfer them upon the objects to which they originally belonged; and as there are few terms which have not been thus applied, we can hardly felect a fentence but a lively imagination might find in it fome hint for perfonification.

From this flight and momentary perfonification, which doth no more than juft give a hint for an *epithet*, and will not bear to be extended beyond it, we may perceive, in different examples of this figure, the images transferred from the regions of life and fenfe growing more and more lively, till at laft inanimate things fhall be fo effectually perfonified, as to excite very ftrong *emotions* and *paffions* in the human mind; which could not be effected without our previoufly imagining them to be fo far endued with fenfe and defign, as to have become the proper authors of

I

fome

some good or harm that hath befallen us. It is neceffary, like-wife, that the inanimate object be viewed for some fenfible fpace of time in this light, if the paffion it excites be expreffed in words or actions; for thofe effects are not momentary.

As the relifh for this figure muft depend upon the livelinefs of the imagination, which is extremely various in different perfons, and indeed very variable in the fame perfon, it muft be impoffible for any one perfon to give rules whereby to judge in what cafes any precife degree of it is proper. All that can be done is to note, by a regard to the general ftate and feelings of the human mind, the circumftances in which we imagine they will be gene-rally judged proper or improper.

One obfervation, I think, is pretty obvious, that a long-con-tinued perfonification is more natural when it is fuppofed to be the work of a lively imagination, than the mechanical effect of a ftrong and ferious paffion; and that it is of importance to pre-ferve a diftinction between thefe two kinds of perfonification. To fome it may, perhaps, appear hardly probable, that a man who preferves the ufe of his fenfes fhould be really angry with a *tem-peft* fo long, as was neceffary to make the following fpeech, which Shakefpeare hath put into the mouth of King Lear upon that occafion:

> Rumble thy belly-full; fpit fire, fpout rain;
> Nor rain, wind, thunder, fire, are my daughters.
> I tax you not, you elements, with unkindnefs,
> I never gave you kingdoms, call'd you children;
> You owe me no fubfcription. Then let fall
> Your horrible pleafure.—Here I ftand your brave,
> A poor, infirm, weak, and defpifed old man.
> But yet I call you fervile miniflers,

That have with two pernicious daughters join'd
Your high-engendered battles 'gainst a head
So old and white as this.   Oh! oh! 'tis foul.

Act II. Scene 3.

It leſſens the improbability (if there be any) of a man's being
ſerious all the while, that the tempeſt, and conſequently the
provocation, was continued through the whole of it.   There is,
however, a manifeſt impropriety in Congreve's repreſenting Al-
meria, when ſhe was exceedingly exaſperated at her father's un-
kindneſs, making the following long and ſerious invocation of
the earth:

Oh earth, behold, I kneel upon thy boſom,
And bend my flowing eyes to ſtream upon
Thy face, imploring thee that thou wilt yield.
Open thy bowels of compaſſion, take
Into thy womb the laſt and moſt forlorn
Of all thy race.   Hear me, thou common parent,
— I have no parent elſe—Be thou a mother,
And ſtep between me and the curſe of him
Who was—who was, but is no more, a father,
And brands my innocence with horrid crimes;
And for the tender names of child and daughter,
Now calls me murderer and parricide.

Mourning Bride, Act IV. Scene 7.

If we conſider, beſides, that the earth was no way concerned
in her grief, this ſpeech will appear more unnatural, ſuppoſing
the ſpeaker quite ſerious; and ſhe was much too ſerious to make
it in the gaiety of her imagination.

Whereas

Whereas the following much longer perſonification of Sleep, being merely *ideal* (as it may be called, in oppoſition to the ſerious and real perſonification) and put into the mouth of a perſon whoſe mind was neither too ſerious nor too languid for it, is extremely agreeable :

> How many thouſands of my pooreſt ſubjects
> Are at this hour aſleep! Oh gentle Sleep,
> Nature's ſoft nurſe, how have I frighted thee,
> That thou no more wilt weigh my eyelids down,
> And ſteep my ſenſes in forgetfulneſs!
> Why rather, Sleep, lieſt thou in ſmoaky huts,
> Upon uneaſy pallets ſtretching thee,
> And huſh'd with buzzing night-flies to thy ſlumber,
> Than in the perfumed chambers of the great,
> And lull'd with ſounds of ſweeteſt melody?
> Oh thou dull god! why lieſt thou with the vile
> In loathſome beds, and leaveſt the kingly couch,
> Beneath rich canopies of coſtly ſtate;
> A watch-caſe to a common larum-bell?
> Wilt thou upon the high and giddy maſt
> Seal up the ſhip-boy's eyes, and rock his brains,
> In cradle of the rude imperious ſurge,
> And in the viſitation of the winds,
> Who take the ruffian billows by the top,
> Curling their monſtrous heads, and hanging them
> With deaf'ning clamours in the ſlippery ſhrouds,
> That with the hurly death itſelf awakes.—
> Canſt thou, Oh partial Sleep, give thy repoſe
> To the wet ſea-boy, in an hour ſo rude;
> And, in the calmeſt and the ſtilleſt night,
> With all appliances and means to boot,

Deny

Deny it to a king? Then happy, lowly clown,
Uneasy lies the head that wears a crown.

Second Part of HENRY IV. Act III. Scene 1.

Such personification as this is the exercise, or rather the *play*, of a mind at ease, which first of all seeing things to be what they really are, is afterwards struck with their resemblance in point of form, situation, cause, effect, &c. to thinking beings, and amuses itself with compleating the resemblance, and thus transforms them, as it were, by a voluntary effort of imagination, into real persons. Whereas in the *serious personification* the mind is under a temporary deception, the personification is neither made nor helped out by the speaker, but it obtrudes itself upon him; and, while the illusion continues, the passions are as strongly affected, as if the object of them really had the power of thought. It is impossible we should be affected in this manner by objects that we ourselves personify, and consequently cannot but know that we personify. The effect of a real personification is a real passion; but an ideal, or *rhetorical personification*, presents only the *ideas* of thought, sense, and passion; which are sufficient to enliven a composition, and please the *fancy*, but can never reach the *heart*. Those emotions can hardly be called real passion, which a person works himself into by the force of his own imagination.

For this reason a writer who is greatly in earnest will not use this figure. If he introduces a person greatly agitated with passion, he may put the serious personification into his mouth; but whatever objects he himself personifies, he will do it with more delicacy, and with a view to *enliven*, and never to *move* and *affect*, by a real illusion. No person in the circumstances of a writer can be supposed to be under such an illusion himself. It would
.be

be highly abſurd, therefore, to write as if he were. Though we are moved in reading ſome fine and ſtriking inſtances of perſoni- fication in Plato and Cicero, it is not that the objects perſonified inſpire any paſſion: they only ſerve to introduce, in a lively manner, ſentiments which, on account of their native force and propriety, are adapted to affect us.

It requires a greater ſtrength of imagination, after having given life to inanimate objects, to conceive them to *act* or *ſpeak* in their new characters, and yet it hath been very often done with great ſucceſs. The imagination, either exhilarated and enlivened, or, as we may ſay, *attendered* with paſtoral ſcenes in particular, eaſily admits, not only that all the parts of inanimate nature ſhould have life and ſenſe, but likewiſe that they ſhould act and ſpeak in conſequence of it. Do not all paſtoral writers, from Theocritus down to the preſent times, exhibit ſuch ſcenes as the following of Mr. Pope:

> No more the mounting lark, while Daphne ſings,
> Shall liſt'ning in mid air ſuſpend her wings.
> No more the nightingales repeat their lays,
> Or huſh'd with wonder, hearken from the ſprays:
> No more the ſtreams their murmur ſhall forbear,
> A ſweeter muſic than their own to hear.
> But tell the reeds, and tell the vocal ſhore,
> Fair Daphne's dead, and muſic is no more.
>
> Her fate is whiſper'd by the gentle breeze,
> And told in ſighs to all the trembling trees.
> The trembling trees, in ev'ry plain and wood,
> Her fate remurmur to the ſilver flood.
> The ſilver flood, ſo lately calm, appears
> Swell'd with new paſſion, and o'erflows with tears.

The

The winds and trees, and floods, her death deplore,
Daphne our grief, our glory, now no more.

In the fame ftrain are the following lines of Virgil:

Illum etiam lauri, illum flevere myriæ,
Pinifer illum etiam, fola fub rupe jacentem,
Mænalus et gelidi fleverunt faxa Lycæi.

and have not all readers eafily adopted and relifhed fuch fentiments?

With what fuccefs doth Plato give life to the dead, in his celebrated funeral oration, and afcribe a long fpeech to them.
Equally happy was Cicero in introducing Rome as a venerable
matron expoftulating with Catiline, who was engaged in a con-
fpiracy againft his country. And who hath not been charmed
with the behaviour and fpeeches of *virtue* and *vice* perfonified in
the *Choice of Hercules?*

Thefe are all inftances of *ideal perfonification*, which admits of
being drawn out to a greater length than that which is ferious.
The only queftion, with regard to the propriety of thefe defcriptive perfonifications, is, whether the nature of the work in which
they are introduced will admit of fuch a play of the imagination.
For if any inanimate object affect a writer in fo lively a manner,
as to fuggeft to him the appearance of thought and fenfe, and
his fubject admit his mind to be at liberty to attend to that refemblance, and to indulge the fiction, it is with as much propriety that he afcribes *actions* and *language* to fuch objects as that
he admitted the firft idea of their having *life*. For the very fame
reafon that a perfon might fay, " the pleadings of virtue, with
" difficulty, prevented a youth from being allured with the

2   " charms

" charms of vice," he might draw out the fcene at full length, with every circumftance and decoration fuitable to it, as in the *Choice of Hercules.* In ferious perfonification, indeed, he would not proceed fo far, becaufe no illufion of this kind can laft fo long ; but in ideal perfonification there is no more illufion at the firft than in the laft part of the allegory. That works of this kind will admit of being drawn out to a very great length is manifeft from Spenfer's *Fairy Queen,* the *Dunciad,* and many other allegorical works.

It is neceffary, indeed, that every object perfonified fhould make a figure in the work in which it is introduced, in proportion to the extent of the perfonification. The *hand,* in the following lines of Virgil, is not of importance enough to bear fo minute a perfonification.

> Te decifa fuum, Lecide, dextera quærit
> Semanimefque micaht digiti, ferrumque retractant.
>
> *Æneid.* X. *395.*

The *earth* is kept too long in view, and made of too much importance, by the perfonification in the following lines of Shakefpeare :

> She fhall be dignified with this high honour,
> To bear my lady's train, left the bafe earth
> Should from her vefture chance to fteal a kifs,
> And, of fo great a favour growing proud,
> Difdain to root the fummer-fwelling fhower,
> And make rough winter everlaftingly.
>
> THE TWO GENTLEMEN OF VERONA, Act II. Scene 7.

The

The perfonification of our *native country* feems to be tedious and difgufting in the following fpeech of King Richard upon his landing in England, to fupprefs the rebellion of Bolingbroke:

> ———— I weep for joy,
> To ftand upon my kingdom once again.
> Dear earth, I do falute thee with my hand,
> Though rebels wound thee with their horfes hoofs.
> As a long-parted mother with her child
> Plays fondly with her tears, and fmiles in meeting;
> So weeping, fmiling, greet I thee, my earth,
> And do thee favour with my royal hands.
> Feed not thy fov'reign's foe, thou gentle earth,
> Nor with thy fweets comfort his rav'nous fenfe;
> But let thy fpiders, that fuck up thy venom,
> And heavy-gaited toads, lie in their way,
> Doing annoyance to the treach'rous feet,
> Which with ufurping fteps do trample thee.
> Yield ftinging-nettles to mine enemies;
> And when they from thy bofom pluck a flower,
> Guard it, I pray thee, with a lurking adder,
> Whofe double tongue may, with a mortal touch,
> Throw death upon thy fov'reign's enemies.
> Mock not my fenfelefs conjuration, lords.
> This earth fhall have a feeling, and thefe ftones
> Prove armed foldiers, ere her native king
> Shall faulter under foul rebellious arms.
>
> RICHARD II. Act III. Scene 2.

That this was not intended to be a ferious perfonification, is evident from the addrefs to the lords, which fucceeds it. Indeed, if it had, it would have been much too long; and yet, the mind

of

of the fpeaker feems to have been too ferioufly engaged to be at
liberty for fo long an *excurfion of fancy*.

We are often offended with a perfonification, when it is not
merely the perfonification that occafions our difguft, but the extravagance of the fentiment conveyed by it. We are not fo much
offended that the *air* is perfonified, or that actions are afcribed to
it in confequence of the perfonification, in the following paffage ;
as that the air in the market-place fhould be in love with Cleopatra, and be reftrained from quitting its place to go to her, by the
dread of a vacuum.

> ————————— The city caft
> Its people out upon her, and Antony
> Inthroned.i' the market-place did fit alone,
> Whiftling to them ; which, but for vacancy,
> Had gone to gaze on Cleopatra too,
> And made a gap in nature.

ANTONY AND CLEOPATRA, Act II. Scene 3.

So natural is this figure of fpeech, that it requires but little
elevation of fancy to admit it even very near the beginning of a
work. In fome compofitions it is quite eafy in the very firft
fentence. No perfon can be fuppofed to fit down to write or read
a poem upon the *Seafons*, with lefs elevation of fancy than is fufficient to make him relifh Thompfon's invocation of them at the
opening of each :

> Come, gentle Spring, ethereal mildnefs, come,
> And from the bofom of yon dropping cloud,
> While mufic wakes around, veil'd in a cloud
> Of fhad'wing rofes, on our plains defcend.

L l 2

From bright'ning fields of ether fair difclofed,
Child of the fun, refulgent Summer comes.

Crown'd with the fickle and the wheaten fheaf,
While Autumn, nodding o'er the yellow plains,
Comes jovial on, the Doric reed, once more,
Well-pleafed, I tune.

See Winter comes to rule the vary'd year,
Sullen, and fad, with all his rifing train,
Vapours, and clouds, and ftorms.

I fhall only add one remark more on this fubject of perfonification, which is, that no object perfonified ought to have attributes
afcribed to it unfuitable to its nature, confidered as not perfonified. Thus it feems to be abfurd in Mr. Pope to reprefent any
perfons worfhipping the goddefs *Dulnefs* ; fince dulnefs is a thing
which all perfons, not excepting the dulleft, profefs a contempt for.

I cannot conclude this article without obferving, that the ftructure of the Englifh language is peculiarly favourable to diftinct
perfonification. In languages in which every thing is male or
female, there can be no diftinction between what hath real fex and
what hath none : fo that, in fuch language, it will not appear
when a writer means to perfonify, and when he doth not. Whereas in Englifh, the words *he* or *fhe*, being appropriated to things
which have *fex*, immediately intimate when a writer paffes from
plain language to the perfonification of things without life.

LECTURE

LECTURE XXX.

Of IMITATION, *and the Satisfaction we receive from the* Completeness *of things.*

TO the account of the pleasures we receive from the introduction of *human sentiments* into composition, we may conveniently subjoin an account of those we receive from a perception of the effects of the *human understanding*; a species of pleasure nearly related to the former, but something different from it.

The idea we universally conceive of the excellency of reason, of the innumerable advantages of it, and the sense of honour and dignity which from hence attends the consciousness of it, furnish a source of pleasing ideas, which are excited by the perception of the marks of design in human works. Moreover, the greater the design, and the more difficult we imagine the execution of it to be, the greater pleasure we receive from seeing the performance.

This is the principal source of the pleasures we universally receive from *imitations* of all kinds; in all which there is *design* and *execution* manifest. The pleasure we receive from the view of a happy imitation, is clearly distinguishable from the pleasure which the object itself is qualified to give us, notwithstanding it be necessarily

cessarily mixed with it. Were they of the same nature, the pleasure we receive from the original would always exceed, however, it would never fall short of, that we receive from the *copy*, because no copy can do more than exactly resemble the original. But we find that an imitation generally gives a more sensible pleasure to the imagination than an original. The pleasure must, therefore, be of a different kind. It could take from the original no more, nor other qualities than it was itself possessed of. Who is not sensible that a good *picture* gives more exquisite entertainment, particularly to a connoisseur, than the scene from which it was drawn? A fine landscape, particularly when it opens all at once, strikes the mind with a lively sense of pleasure; a good drawing of the same landscape, as far it suggests the same pleasurable sensation, doth the same, but must do it fainter. The reason then why we can take equal pleasure in gazing upon it, is, that amends is more than made for that faintness, by the additional pleasure it suggests, from presenting a view of the *effects of human genius* in executing the imitation.

We may perceive more clearly the nature of this additional pleasure, if we consider how it increases with every circumstance attending the imitation that increases the difficulty of it. All imitations please more upon our being informed that they were executed with inconvenient materials and utensils, by persons who were very young, or who had little or no instruction, &c. Of two pieces of painting, equally good, one said to be done by the master, and the other by the scholar, that done by the scholar would be the most gazed at. What else but ideas derived from these principles could have induced Ketel to throw aside his pencil, and paint with his fingers; and afterwards, thinking that practice too easy, and not sufficiently wonderful, to confine himself to the use of his toes? Though

Though common fenfe is far from juftifying this extravagance, it could not have exifted without fome foundation in nature. A landfcape in needle-work engages the attention more than the fame landfcape, much better executed, in drawing or painting. It is well known that in mufic, the difficulty of execution gives a pleafure which often bears away the mind from attending to the excellence of the compofition. And the fame difcourfe, delivered *extempore*, will always be heard with more pleafure than if it were pre-compofed ; or, fuppofing it to be pre-compofed, it will give more pleafure delivered from the memory than from notes. In moft of thefe cafes we clearly perceive that it is our admiration of the effects of human genius (which are more wonderful in proportion to the difadvantages it labours under, and the impediments it hath to remove) that gives the pleafure which imitation conveys, additional to what it can derive from the object itfelf ; becaufe this pleafure manifeftly increafes with the *admiration*.

We may perceive this fpecies of pleafure in the pureft kind, and freeft from all foreign mixture, in the imitation of objects which are in themfelves not in the leaft pleafing, or even difagreeable, and therefore have no agreeable qualities to communicate, fuch as are met with in pictures of toads, and various kinds of infects ; of fcenes in very low life, as perfons of a mean appearance ; beggars, for inftance, clothed in rags, in a forry houfe, with wretched furniture, and in every refpect fo circumftanced and employed, that no perfon could look upon the fcene itfelf with any pleafure. A picture of fuch a fcene as this, well imagined, and drawn to the life, would be valued. In thefe cafes, the difguft with which the objects themfelves would naturally infpire us, is loft in the pleafure we receive from the *powers of imitation*.

2

The

The fame obfervation is applicable, in fome meafure, to pictures of rocks, precipices, monfters, tempefts, battles, and the reprefentation of infamous characters and villainies upon the ftage. Only there may be a mixture of the *fublime* in fome of thefe views; and perhaps the very high pleafure with which tragic fcenes are received, when they are reprefented upon the ftage, and the uncommon avidity with which dramatic writings of the tragic kind are read, preferably to the comic, may be owing, in a great meafure, to this, that the ftrong fenfations, excited by fcenes of terror and compaffion, are fo much diminifhed by a conviction of their being only imaginary, as to fall within the limits of pleafure: fince pleafure hath been defined to confift of fenfations moderately vigorous, and pain of fenfations exceeding that degree. Befides, ideas of difficulties and danger cannot but contribute, in fome meafure, to give us pleafure, by means of the reflection which, in thofe circumftances, we unavoidably and every moment make on our own fecurity.

That the pleafure we receive from tragical reprefentations is not wholly owing to the views they give us of the marks of genius and defign in the imitation of fuch fcenes, is pretty evident from the refemblance it bears to the pleafure which many people take in cock-fighting, bull-baiting, boxing-matches, horfe-races, &c. Thefe fpectacles roufe and agitate the mind, but not to a degree exceeding the limits of pleafure.

It may to fome appear a paradox, that an imitation may be too perfect to give pleafure; but it is plainly neceffary that every imitation bear evident marks of its being an imitation, and not an original, before it can excite, in a fenfible manner, thofe peculiar pleafureable ideas which are annexed to the perception of imitation. A ftatue coloured, and with the eyes painted, &c. in order

to

to make it more nearly refemble real life, is obferved by connoiffeurs to be not near fo pleafing as if it were of the natural colour of the ftone, or other materials, of which it was made. When
coloured, it excites an idea which coincides exactly with the idea
of a real human perfon, fuch as we fee every day. Without that
colour, which brings it fo near to life, it bears evident marks of
its being only an imitation, and excites the proper correfponding
feelings with vigour. Being told that it is a ftatue, or even feeling it to be nothing more, is not, in this cafe, it feems, fufficient.
A coloured ftatue, or a well-executed piece of wax-work, has fo
much the appearance of life, that we are ftruck as with a kind of
horror to find it otherwife, and are affected as we fhould be at
feeing living perfons fuddenly ftruck dead and motionlefs.

On the other hand, a *picture* being generally in a frame, and
upon a furface evidently plane, cannot be without marks enow
of its not being a reality. A picture, therefore, admits of being
coloured, and of every other advantage to make it refemble life
as much as poffible, without any fear of its not giving us all the
pleafure it might give us as an imitation.

It is, perhaps, poffible that a tragedy, by being acted to great
perfection, may give only the fame kind of pleafure that we
fhould receive from the fame fcene in real life, and the
art of the poet and actors be wholly loft upon us for the time.
What is it we admire in actors, but that command of their words
and geftures, which gives them the appearance of other perfons than
they really are; that is, in exhibiting an *imitated* and not a natural character: fo that if they fhould, in the courfe of the performance, really forget themfelves (continuing to fpeak and act
in a manner fuitable to the character they began with affuming)
the reafon of our admiration would certainly ceafe. But if the

scenes be such as are in themselves sufficiently agreeable or interesting, and such as did not need, and would be rather hurt by, any foreign ornament, the performance is the more valuable. But in a variety of dialogues, and other things which are exhibited upon the stage, it is manifest that several circumstances, which every moment demonstrate the scene to be no reality, have a good effect. Otherwise *prose* would be universally more agreeable than *verse*, because no person ever speaks seriously in verse.

It is said that when a player was asked by a bishop why *plays* were heard with more attention than *sermons*, he answered, " The reason is, that we speak fiction as if it were a reality, " while preachers speak of things real as if they were fiction." But perhaps we may be able, from these principles, to give a more just idea of the comparative difficulty of their respective provinces, and of their different success.

Besides that the theatre, and the subjects of plays, contain a thousand things more engaging to the bulk of spectators than the furniture of a church, or the subjects of the generality of sermons, it is really much more difficult to *preach* well, than to *act* well. To an accomplished actor a mixture of nature and art is requisite, which renders what are called imperfections in acting, which are really deviations from nature, necessary to his success. Should actors behave exactly as the persons whose character they assume would have done, all appearance of their *art*, and all their reputation would vanish. It is not their business, therefore, to exhibit a borrowed character exactly, which would perhaps exceed the abilities of any human being, who retained any idea of his own real character, and did not absolutely forget himself, and is what the professed admirers of players do not sufficiently attend to. They even mistake the cause of their own applause: for when they cry

out

out that such a piece of acting is *pure nature*, they only mean
nature happily *imitated*, and therefore *seen* to be imitated, that
is, *not pure nature.*

On the other hand, all the words and gestures of a preacher
must be *nature* unmixed with any appearance of *art*, which it is
impossible to conceal from an observer of tolerable discernment.
And yet, speaking in earnest is not alone sufficient. In an accomplished preacher we expect a *graceful earnestness.* He must deliver
himself as well as if he had prepared every word and gesture, and
yet no appearance of *preparation* must appear in either. Besides,
he has his *own character* to support, and his own sentiments and
language to deliver; while the actor assumes the character, sentiments, and language of *another*; a consideration which must
certainly throw a greater weight of solicitude and anxiety upon
the former than the latter. And though the former be in itself
more easy, it is required to be *perfect in its kind*; whereas in
the latter only a certain nearness to perfect imitation must be
aimed at. I now proceed to note other effects of the same general cause.

Why is the pleasure we receive from *verse*, in any case, superior
to the pleasure we should receive from the same things said in *prose*,
but because it is of this kind; namely, that which results from the
perception of the marks of human genius? It is more *difficult*
to compose in verse than in prose. Why, moreover, is *rhyme*
more agreeable, as it confessedly is, in some cases, than blank
verse? Undoubtedly, not merely from the chiming of the same
sound at the end of the lines, but chiefly because to construct
words in this manner is more difficult, and shows greater art and
skill: for nothing is more universally disgusting than rhyme,
when it is not the effect of art and design.

By

By this principle it may, perhaps, be no very difficult matter to determine the proper ufe of *profe, blank verfe,* and *rhyme.* In confidering a ferious fubject, which wholly engroffes the mind, we are not at liberty to attend to any other ideas than thofe which the naked fcene exhibits. It cannot be fuppofed, therefore, that any perfon defcribing fuch a fcene, and properly impreffed with it, fhould at the fame time attend to, and introduce into his defcription, any other ornaments than thofe which neceffarily belonged to it. In thofe cafes, confequently, plain profe, the only language of real ferious emotions and paffions, is the only mode of expreffion that is tolerable. The appearance of *verfe* of any kind, which fhews a *double attention,* could not be borne.

On the other hand, if the compofition be not intended to raife any very ferious emotion, but be of fuch a nature as that it may eafily leave the mind at liberty to attend to, and relifh, a variety of different kinds of pleafures, *verfe,* and even *rhyme,* giving one of thefe *foreign fpecies of pleafure,* may give an additional poignancy and relifh to it. In works of an intermediate nature, namely, fuch as moderately elevate and affect the mind, without wholly engroffing it, *blank verfe* may be moft fuitable.

It muft be impoffible to fix any precife limits in this cafe, efpecially in a thing that is relative to the ftate of the human mind; which is fo extremely various, and variable. However, this muft be allowed, that the more manifeft figns there are of *art* in any compofition, the more the mind is drawn off from an attention to the fubject of it, if it do at all tafte the foreign pleafures which refult from an attention to thofe marks of art and defign; and that there are more of thofe marks of artful compofition in blank verfe than in profe, and more of them in rhyme than in blank verfe.

In

In compositions in rhyme there is, likewise, a great variety, in the *degrees* of art and design, according to the number of objects attended to at the same time. That which is usually called *Heroic measure* (that is, the five feet Iambic, in which every other line rhymes to the preceding) approaches the nearest to blank verse; and the various measure of the *Ode*, consisting of stanzas, recedes farther from it. Accordingly, the practice of our poets seems to shew that the rhyming heroic is better suited to serious subjects, such as grave historical narration, than the form of the ode. The measure of Spenser, which was copied from Tasso, is intirely and justly disused in heroic poetry. The stanza is, indeed, generally applied to sublime and serious subjects, treated in the form of hymns and adapted to contemplation; but that is because the regular division of the ode into stanzas is most easily suited to the detached thoughts and sentiments of which hymns and such compositions generally consist; besides that the structure of the ode makes it peculiarly adapted to music. However, intricate stanzas do certainly by no means suit very serious subjects. The pleasure we receive from such complicated marks of genius and design are by no means of the same *tone*, as we may say, with very *serious emotions*, though it may suit extremely well with those which are of a light and moderate nature.

Upon some occasions more complicated marks of design than mere rhyme, and the variation of the length of the verses can furnish, are well relished; as in *acrostics*, and other species of witty versification. But because there are very few occasions which these very artful compositions suit, and they are, therefore, generally ill applied, they are usually ranked among the species of *false wit*.

It

It is from the fource of pleafure here treated of that *regular bodies* have a more pleafing appearance than thofe which are irregular. We fee marks of defign and contrivance in the one, and not in the other. If there be any thing in what fome perfons talk of the relative *perfection of figures*, it muft depend upon the greater or lefs defign that is requifite to form them. Thus, the circle and the fquare may be confidered as exceedingly perfect, becaufe they admit of no variety but of greater and lefs, and therefore require more exactnefs and fkill to draw them; whereas the parallellogram, the rhombus, &c. admit of greater variety, and therefore require lefs exactnefs and fkill to draw them. In numbers, a progreffion in a fimple ratio is pleafing; but a more complex ratio, if it be properly comprehended, pleafes more, as being the effect of a greater and more comprehenfive defign. In examining the productions of nature, likewife, the more defign we difcover in them, that is, the more we fee of an intended fubferviency of means to an end, the higher doth our pleafure in contemplating them arife.

It is hardly neceffary to obferve, with refpect to imitation of every kind, in painting, poetry, or compofition in general, that (provided it bear fufficient marks of its being an imitation) its merit is in proportion to its likenefs to the original; and that the correctnefs of our tafte in fuch works of genius muft be in proportion to our knowledge of the originals. If a child be drawn with the wrinkles of an old man, or an old man with the plumpnefs of a child, we fay it is abfurd; or if a perfon be reprefented as fpeaking in a manner that we have no remembrance or idea of a perfon of his character and ftation fpeaking, we are difgufted with the impropriety; and the more, in proportion to our knowledge of the perfon's character or ftation. If we be unacquainted with the originals, the exactnefs of the imitation

4

will

will give us no pleasure, becaufe it is unknown to us; neither will a defect in the imitation difguft, becaufe it is equally unknown.

A regard ought to be had to the known manners, cuftoms, and prevailing fentiments of the times in which any thing is reprefented to have happened, as well as to the perfonal propriety and uniformity of character in the fpeakers themfelves. And though fuch anachronifms as thefe be no objection to a perfon's abilities as a writer or a poet, yet they are to his character of a *general fcholar*; and no perfon ought to undertake to defcribe any fcene, unlefs he be acquainted with every thing effential to it. Shakefpeare is frequently guilty of miftakes of this kind. In the life and death of King John, *canons* are perpetually mentioned as ufed in the times of that monarch. The Baftard gives him the title of *majefty*, which the Kings of England had not then affumed; and the King is reprefented, in the following fpeech, as inveighing againft the Pope, in fuch a manner as there is no reafon to fuppofe any prince in chriftendom, in that age, was capable of talking. The fundamental principles of proteftantifm were not then fo well underftood:

> What earthly name to interrogatories
> Can tax the free breath of a facred King?
> Thou can'ft not, Cardinal, devife a name
> So flight, unworthy, and ridiculous,
> To charge me to an anfwer, as the Pope.
> Tell him this tale, and from the mouth of England
> Add thus much more, that no Italian prieft
> Shall tithe or toll in our dominions:
> But as we, under heaven, are fupreme head;
> So under it, that great fupremacy

Where

Where we do reign we will alone uphold,
Without th' affiftance of a mortal hand.
So tell the Pope.   All reverence fet apart
To him and his ufurp'd authority.

K. Philip.   Brother of England, you blafpheme in this.

K. John.   Though you, and all the Kings of Chriftendom,
Are led fo grofsly by this meddling prieft,
Dreading the curfe that money may buy out;
And by the merit of vile gold, drofs, duft,
Purchafe corrupted pardon of a man,
Who in that fale fells pardon from himfelf;
Though you, and all the reft, fo grofsly led,
This juggling witchcraft with revenue cherifh,
Yet I alone, alone, do me oppofe
Againft the Pope, and count his friends my foes.

Act III. Scene 3.

Examples of other kinds of proprieties and improprieties in imitations have been given upon various occafions in the courfe of thefe lectures, fo that it is needlefs to multiply them in this place.

Let any perfon but recollect his feelings when a mufician ftops before he has finifhed his tune; when a bad rhyme, or no rhyme at all, occurs in a poem compofed in generally good rhyme; or when a perfon, who is reading, makes an unexpected paufe, and leaves a fentence unfinifhed, and he will perceive the force of another inftance of the affociation of ideas, fimilar to the effect of imitation, the obfervation of which is of confiderable ufe in criticifm; namely, that the mind is impatient of the interruption

2   of

of a chain of ideas ſtrongly connected, and is pleaſed to ſee every thing carried to its proper concluſion, according to the ideas previouſly formed of it. For this reaſon, a member of a ſentence, unuſually long, or unuſually ſhort, is heard with a ſenſe of pain and diſappointment, and any diſſimilarity of ſtyle in the ſame compoſition offends. A ſhort verſe, in the midſt of a poem conſiſting chiefly of long ones, would diſpleaſe; but a ſhort verſe recurring alternately with ſhort ones, as the pentameter among hexameters; recurring at equal intervals, as the adonic verſe in the ſapphic, doth not diſpleaſe, becauſe it is *expected*; nay, we ſhould feel the want of it very diſagreeably, if it were omitted.

But the ſatisfaction ariſing from the coincidence and agreement of things, with the ideas previouſly exiſting in our minds, is heightened, if, in ſome things, it be not perfectly complete; the *diſſimilarity* in the one caſe forming a pleaſing contraſt with the ſimilarity in the other. For example; though a great interruption in the order of the words that compoſe a ſentence, by parentheſes, be diſagreeable, yet a ſmall deviation from the natural, uſual, and expected order, is agreeable; and though a line that is perfectly proſe would have a moſt diſagreeable effect in a poem, yet we find that a little variation in the feet of our heroic verſe hath a good effect, as a *trochee* for a *ſpondee*, in the following line:

Ārms ănd thĕ mān I ſing, who forc'd by fate,——

Two inſtruments ſounding in uniſon, pleaſe; but two ſounds that are chords to one another, pleaſe more. Sometimes an imperfect chord is preferred to a perfect one, and ſometimes a diſcord is preferred to both.

N n   The

The expectation and defire of feeing every thing full and complete, according to our ideas of perfection, extends much farther than to the ftyle of compofition. It often directs our hopes and fears in the moft important concerns of life, and even contrary to reafon and experience. Hence the fears that men formerly had of dying in their grand climacteric; the fear that Iphigenia's brother (according to the account that Ariftotle gives of an old play) had of being facrificed, when he found himfelf in the fame fituation in which he believed his fifter had been facrificed. Hence the apprehenfion of the people of London, that, as they had had an earthquake on the fame day of two fucceeding months, and the fecond more violent than the firft, they fhould have a third on the fame day of the month following, more fatal than either of the former. Hence many rules that common people have with regard to the weather; as that, if it be fair or rainy on fuch a particular day, it will be fair or rainy fo much longer. And hence the fatisfaction they receive from the accomplifhment of a prediction. Rather than the event fhould not anfwer to it, they would take confiderable pains to bring it about. Shake-fpeare hath noted this weaknefs in Henry the Fourth.

K. *Henry.*　Doth any name particular belong
　　　　　Unto that lodging where I firft did fwoon?
Warwick.　'Tis call'd Jerufalem, my noble Lord.
K. *Henry.*　Laud be to God! even there my life muft end.
　　　　　It hath been prophefy'd to me, many years,
　　　　　I fhould not die but in Jerufalem;
　　　　　Which vainly I fuppofed the Holy Land.
　　　　　But bear me to that chamber, there I'll lie:
　　　　　In that Jerufalem fhall Henry die.
　　　　　　　Second Part of HENRY IV. Act IV. Scene laft.

LECTURE XXXI.

Of CLIMAX, *and the Order of Words in a Sentence.*

IN a world conftituted as this is, a view of a gradual rife and improvement in things cannot fail to make an agreeable profpect. The continual obfervation of this furnifhes us with a ftock of pleafing ideas, which are conftantly accumulating, and which are eafily transferred, by affociatiou, upon every thing, either in compofition, or in any other field of view, which prefents a fimilar appearance. How agreeable to all perfons is the idea of the days growing longer, of fpring advancing, and of children growing up to men !

This is one, but not the only caufe of the remarkably ftriking effect which a well-conducted *climax* hath in compofition. When a feries of terms rife, by nearly-equal degrees, above one another in greatnefs and ftrength, they ftand in the faireft fituation for being *compared* and *contrafted* to one another ; by which means the terms mentioned laft in fuch a fucceffion affect the mind much more ftrongly than if they had occurred fingly. Likewife, together with the preceding terms, they contribute (as was obferved befote) to form the *fublime*.

Befides, that order of terms which conftitutes the happieft climax generally coincides with the *order of time and nature*, in which the things they exprefs really ftand related to, or are con-

nected

nected with one another. Confequently, it is agreeable to repeat that coincidence ; and it is a painful interruption of a long-
eftablifhed affociation of ideas, to break that order, This we
may perceive in the following climax of Cicero : *In urbe luxuries
creatur, ex luxuria exiftat avaritia neceffe eft, ex avaritia erumpat
audacia, inde omnia fcelera ac maleficia nafcuntur.* Pro Rofcio. In
this paffage the terms *luxury, avarice, impudence,* and *licentiouf-
nefs* rife regularly above one another, both with regard to their
heinoufnefs as vices, and their pernicious effects in the ftate ;
and they likewife fucceed one another in the order of time and
of caufe and effect, the preceding article being always the caufe
of the following.

The words *rocks, feas,* and *fkies* ftand in a happy climax in the
following paffage of Pope's Ode on St. Cecilia's day :

> So, when the firft bold veffel dared the feas,
> High on the ftern the Thracian raifed his ftrain
> While Argo faw her kindred trees
> Defcend from Pelion to the main.
> Tranfported demi-gods ftood round,
> And men grew heroes at the found,
> Enflamed with glory's charms.
> Each chief his feven-fold fhield difplay'd,
> And half-unfheathed the fhining blade
> And rocks, and feas, and fkies rebound,
> To arms, to arms, to arms.

The order of climax not only adds to the ftrength and fublimity of ftyle, it is likewife eafily adapted to heighten the poignancy of wit and humour. Of this Cicero, in his treatife de
Oratore tells us that Craffus took a happy advantage, in quef-
tioning

tioning a witnefs againft his client. " Perhaps," fays the orator, " the perfon from whom you heard this was angry when
" he fpoke it." The witnefs making no reply; he adds, " Per-
" haps you did not take him right." The witnefs ftill continuing filent; he adds again, " Perhaps you did not hear it
" at all."

As all things that can be exhibited in the fame view, fo as to
be named together in a fentence, muft be related to one another,
(becaufe in that fituation they muft have a like dependence upon
fomething going before, or coming after) and fince it is impoffible that things which are really different fhould have the fame
relations, there muft always be a reafon for naming fome
firft and others laft, and the difpofition of them cannot be quite
arbitrary. The order of *caufe and effect*, of *time or place*, and of
worth, *dignity*, and *importance*, are of principal influence in this
affair. So habitually do we attend to thofe relations, that a confiderable offence againft them, even in common converfation,
would be inftantly perceived, and give a fenfible difguft.

The difguft which this inverfion of order occafions is exactly
fimilar to what we feel when the ufual order of words in a fentence is altered, or any other grammatical miftake is made. It
baulks, as it were, *our expectation*; and the fentence thus conftructed doth not coincide with our ideas of perfection formed by
previous affociations of ideas, which was explained before. Befides, if this inverfion of order gave no fenfible pain, the difpofition of things which conftitutes a climax is fo agreeable, that it
is a pity it fhould be neglected, when it prefents itfelf without our
feeking for it.

The order of *time* is obferved in the following feries from
Swift:

" It

" It is a fhame for an Englifh lady not to relifh fuch difcourfes,
" not to improve by them, and endeavour, by reading and in-
" formation, to have her fhare in thofe entertainments."

A regard to relative weight and importance may be obferved in
the following fentence of the fame author:

" The books read at fchool and colleges are full of incitements
" to virtue and difcouragements from vice, and drawn from the
" wifeft reafons, the ftrongeft motives, and the moft influencing
" examples."

The order of *caufe and effect* is confpicuous in fuch phrafes as
thefe: *She was in the bloom of youth and beauty*; *Old age and in-
firmities came upon him*, &c. Sometimes the effect may precede
the caufe; but this order is not generally quite fo natural. *Joy
fitting in every face, content in every heart.* BOLINGBROKE.
Though, in defcription, as in this cafe, there may be a propriety
in mentioning the effect which is vifible firft, and the caufe
which is invifible afterwards.

In this fentence of the laft-mentioned author—*The genuine effect of efteem, confidence, and affection*, the term *confidence* is mifplaced; becaufe confidence is the refult of efteem and affection,
and therefore ought to be named after them. But the arrangement of the terms in the following fentence is much more faulty:

" No king, who is not, in the true meaning of the word, a
" patriot, can govern Britain with eafe, fecurity, honour, dig-
" nity, or indeed with fufficient power and ftrength."

The capital fault in this fentence is, that after a gradual rife in
the ideas, from *eafe* to *dignity*, the writer goes back to an article

profeſſedly below them all, when he concludes the aſcending climax with the words, " *or indeed with ſufficient power and ſtrength.*" Every term introduced as this is, ought to be the laſt of a deſcending ſeries. In the next place, *ſecurity* ought to have preceded *eaſe*, for the ſame reaſon that he hath made both ſecurity and eaſe to precede *honour* and *dignity.* Laſtly, I do not ſee a ſufficient diſtinction between *ſecurity*, and *ſufficient power and ſtrength.*

I have now enumerated the principal ſources of pleaſure which enter into works of genius and imagination; and, for the ſake of illuſtration, have given, under each head, a ſelect number of examples, from the moſt celebrated authors, of paſſages which derive their merit from each of them. I ſhall now give a view of the whole in a very ſhort compaſs.

Every thing that hath a ſtriking or pleaſing effect in compoſition, muſt either *draw out and exerciſe our faculties*, or elſe, by the principle of aſſociation, muſt *transfer from foreign objects ideas that tend to improve the ſenſe*; the principal of which are *views of human ſentiments*, of the *effects of the human genius*, and of a *riſe and improvement* in things.

If it be thought that ſome other ingredients contribute to render a diſcourſe engaging, I apprehend it will be found, upon reflection, that thoſe advantages belong to the *ſubject* of a diſcourſe, and are by no means in the choice of a compoſer: whereas the beauties that have been enumerated and explained in theſe lectures, are ſuch as depend upon the *compoſition*, and therefore ſuch as may be neglected and overlooked by a compoſer. If any perſon ſhould imagine that the *moral ſenſe*, the *ſenſe of honour*, of *benevolence*, and of *devotion*, ought to have been allowed ſome
influence

influence in works of genius and imagination; it is acknowledged that the fubjects of compofition may pleafe, by reafon of their exhibiting fcenes adapted to gratify thofe fenfes. But then we ought, for the fame reafon, not to have excluded the external fenfes, or any faculty whereby we receive pleafure; becaufe it may be faid, with refpect to them all, that ideas may be prefented in a difcourfe or compofition, which could have had no power to pleafe or to affect us but in confequence of our having fuch fenfes. It is in reality, for the reafon above mentioned, equally foreign to the bufinefs of *criticifm*, to take notice of any of them, any farther than they are neceffarily connected with the pleafures of the imagination.

LECTURE

L E C T U R E XXXII.

Of PERSPICUITY *in Style.*

IT may not be amifs to conclude this account of what it is that makes ftyle *pleafing*, with a few obfervations on what tends to make it *perfpicuous*; efpecially as, in fact, this property is the more effential of the two. For, certainly, the firft care of a judicious writer will be to make his meaning eafily underftood, and therefore to keep his ftyle free from ambiguity.

A fentence muft be ambiguous when it is impoffible to determine, from the ftructure of it, to which antecedent a relative refers, or to what principal claufe of a fentence a circumftance introduced into it belongs. In the following fentence from Middleton, it doth not appear whether *miracles* or *battles* be the antecedent to the relative *which*.

" They have alfo many churches and public monuments erected
" in teftimony of fuch miracles, viz. of faints and angels, fighting
" for them in their battles, which, though always as ridiculous"—

The conftruction would direct us to *battles*, but the fenfe to *miracles*.

The circumftance [with great care and diligence] in the following fentence is not placed where it is apparent, at firft fight, to what it belongs.

O o   " This

" This morning, when one of Lady Lizard's daughters was
" looking over some hoods and ribbands, brought by her tire-
" woman, with great care and diligence, I employed no less in
" examining the box which contained them." Guardian.

These ambiguities will be prevented, if, in a case like the former,
the relative be always placed immediately after its proper antecedent; and, in the latter, if the circumstance be immediately sub-
joined to that clause of a sentence to which it belongs, provided
it never be placed between two clauses to which it may equally
belong. It is not a sufficient vindication of passages which are
left ambiguous for want of attending to these particulars, that
the *sense* will determine to which the relative or the circumstance
refers : for the structure of a sentence ought to be such, as to
leave the hearer or reader no trouble to find out the meaning, by
comparing one thing with another.

It favours perspicuity, and procures every member of a sentence the degree of attention that is due to it, when the incidental circumstances of an affirmation are introduced pretty early in
a sentence, and the principal ideas are reserved to the last; for
were those circumstances placed after the principal idea, they
would either have no attention at all paid to them, or they would
take from that which is due to the principal idea; and, in either
case, a sentence constructed in that manner is flat and languid.
The circumstances attending Mr. Woolston's recantation, are well
introduced in the following sentence :

" At Saint Bride's church, in Fleet-street, Mr. Woolston (who
" wrote against the miracles of our Saviour) in the utmost terrors
" of conscience, made a public recantation."

But

But in the next, the claufe [in the fixth book of the Æneid] is aukwardly introduced :

" Virgil, who hath caft the whole fyftem of Platonic philofo-
" phy, fo far as it relates to the foul of man, into beautiful al-
" legories, in the fixth book of his Æneid, gives us the punifh-
" ment," &c.————

If it be thought proper to crowd a number of circumftances into one fentence, it is advifeable not to place them all together, but to intermix them with the principal members of the fentence.

There may be one inconvenience in referving the principal members of a fentence to the laft, that if any thing which precedes it be abfolutely unintelligible without it, and pretty remote from it, it will be difficult for the reader to connect in his mind thofe disjointed members, fo as to make the fenfe eafy. The neceffity for inverfion in blank verfe frequently obliges the writers of it to make the reader wait for any fenfe at all, through the whole of a pretty long fentence; as Milton hath done in the beginning of Paradife Loft :

> Of man's firft difobedience, and the fruit
> Of that forbidden tree, whofe mortal tafte
> Brought death into the world and all our woe,
> With lofs of Eden ; till one greater man
> Reftore us, and regain the blifsful feat,
> Sing heav'nly mufe.————

The name of the perfon we are fpeaking to is introduced *with the moft refpect* in the beginning of the fpeech, but it is generally introduced in a more *eafy and familiar manner* after the firft or

fecond

second claufe of a fentence, or even later. Of both thefe obfervations we have a happy example in Milton :

> Oh, father, what intends thy hand, fhe cried,
> Againft thy only fon ? What Fury, oh fon,
> Poffeffes thee, to bend that mortal dart
> Againft thy father's head.
>
> PARADISE LOST, Book II. Line 727.

The only objection to this paffage is, that the hafte the fpeaker
may reafonably be fuppofed to be in, would more naturally throw
her words into too much diforder, to preferve fo minute a diftinction between the manner of accofting a fon and a father.

It is an offence againft perfpicuity when the conftruction of
different claufes in a fentence is unneceffarily varied. This refembles changing the fcene, and placing objects in different points
of light, which tends to embarrafs a reader. The Greek and
Latin claffics were too negligent of this, and, indeed, many other
helps to perfpicuity.

Thus Livy :

" Id jugum, ficut Apennini dorfo Italia dividitur, ita mediam
" Greciam deremit."——

And Cicero :

" Honos alit artes, omnefque incenduntur ad ftudia gloriâ;
" jacentque ea femper quæ apud quofque improbantur."

Whether a *fimilarity* or *contrariety* be intended to be exhibited
in things, it is of advantage that they fhould have a *fimilar fitua-*
tion

tion in the fentence. For, fince the ideas both of fimilarity and contrariety are relative, and perceived by a comparifon, the more obvious and eafy is the comparifon, the more fenfible and ftriking are the ideas refulting from it. So that if we ftudy perfpicuity, we ought to make the greateft uniformity poffible in the ftructure of thofe members of a fentence that have any correfpondence in their meaning. Even negative and affirmative copulatives do not follow one another without fome confufion of ideas; as in Horace:

> Nec horret iratum mare, forumque vetat.

The term *productions* doth not fufficiently correfpond to *minifters* in the following fentence of Swift:

" I have obferved, of late, the ftyle of fome great minifters,
" very much to exceed that of any other productions."

Perhaps the latter part of the following fentence from the Spectator had better have been made to tally more nearly with the former:

" The wife man is happy when he gains his own approba-
" tion; the fool, when he recommends himfelf to the applaufe
" of thofe about him."

Very often, indeed, writers plainly ftudy to vary the form of expreffion in two correfponding members of a fentence. This, certainly, fhews a greater command of language, and in fhort fentences, where every thing elfe is uniform, may have no bad effect; as in the following of Mr Addifon:

I

" A

" A friend exaggerates a man's virtues, an enemy inflames
" his crimes."

The omiffion or redundancy of articles, or copulatives, though
it may be made without any material prejudice to the fenfe,
ought not, however, to be made at random ; becaufe this circumftance, when conducted with judgment, may contribute to
indicate fome particulars in the fituation of a writer's mind,
which it is of fome moment to attend to, as the knowledge of
them may make his meaning more obvious. For example ; it
is convenient to make as little feparation, by the article, or other
words, as poffible between terms, the ideas belonging to which
are reprefented as united ; but if they be fpoken of as disjoined,
the words had better be placed at a greater diftance. Speaking
of the two fuppofed conftituent parts of human nature as compofing one being we fhould always fay, *the foul and body* ; treating of their different properties, we fhould naturally fay, *the
foul and the body.*

The omiffion of the copulative, when feveral things are named
in fucceffion, expreffes hurry and impetuofity ; a redundancy of
them, on the other hand, expreffes deliberation, and a defire to
have each particular of the feries of terms carefully attended to.
A copulative would have intirely fpoiled Cæfar's laconic account
of his expedition to Pontus : *Veni, vidi, vici*; whereas a redundancy of them is of advantage in the following expreffion of
Cicero : *Me pre cæteris et colit, et obfervat, et diligit.*

Poffibly, the reafon why the omiffion of a copulative is lively
and animating may be, becaufe the repetition of the members of
a fentence in an unconnected manner refembles an interrupted
fucceffion of founds; which, confifting of feveral changes from
one

one ftate to another, roufes the attention more than an uniform
continued found.   Or it may be enough to fay, that it produces its
effect by furprizing, in confequence of its being unufual and unexpected.   The repetition of this copulative before every member of a feries of terms draws the attention to each more ftrongly, becaufe it makes every term appear to be the *laft,* for which
we always referve a greater fhare of our attention.

If we judge of ftyle by the effect it hath upon the mind of the
hearer, we fhall not always condemn the ufe of *fynonymous words,*
or fuch as are nearly fo (perhaps there are none perfectly fynonymous) or even the *repetition* of the fame word, any more than
we fhould univerfally condemn a periphrafis.   Both may contribute
to give a clearer and ftronger idea of a perfon's meaning than any
fingle words could do.   Moreover, we have the example of our
moft chafte and correct writers for this liberty.   Thus Swift :

" It would be endlefs to run over the feveral defects of ftyle
" among us.   I fhall therefore fay nothing of the *mean* and
" the *paltry* (which are ufually attended by the fuftian);
" much lefs of the *flovenly* or *indecent.*"

A regard to perfpicuity will direct us rather to multiply fentences, than crowd into the fame fentence things which have no
relation to one another.   As Burnet, in giving Lord Sunder-
land's character : " His own notions were always good ; but he
" was a man of great expence."

Every paragraph ought certainly to be independent, in grammatical conftruction at leaft, of any other ; and yet Mr Lawfon,
in his Lectures on Oratory, frequently begins a paragraph with
a relative, the antecedent of which is in the preceding paragraph ;

2   as

as at page 276 : *Which reafoning*, &c.—This might eafily have
been rectified by ufing *This* inftead of *Which*.

Sometimes the reader is embarraffed by a fentence which he
haftily condemns as ungrammatical, when not the principles of
grammar, but an attention to common fenfe only, can rectify it.
Thus when Swift fays————*and cleanlinefs, qualities fo oppofite to thofe animals*; the fault is not in the grammar, but the
fenfe : for *qualities* can be oppofed only to *qualities*. The following fentence, likewife, of Mr. Sheridan is faulty; not becaufe it is ungrammatical, but becaufe it is abfurd to fay that the
attempt was impoffible, though the *fuccefs* might.

" This is but a fmall fpecimen of the irregularities to be found
" in the ftate of our written language ; yet it may ferve to fhew
" how different, nay impoffible, the attempt muft be to acquire
" a knowledge of the true pronunciation of the Englifh ; unlefs
" learners be furnifhed with a proper clue to guide them through
" this labyrinth."

LECTURE

L E C T U R E   XXXIII.

Of the Resemblance between SOUND *and* SENSE.

HAVING considered words as they serve to convey the *sense*, I come now to consider the properties of them as mere *sounds*, or as they affect the external ear only.

Speech consists of sounds divided by a great variety of *intervals*. All ideas, therefore, either of real sounds, or of intervals, and consequently all ideas analogous to those of sounds and intervals, admit of a natural expression by words: that is, the words may not be mere *arbitrary* signs of such ideas, but bear a real *resemblance* to them; so that a person, without being previously acquainted with the meaning of the words, might be made sensible of it, by the pronunciation only: or, at least, if he could not perceive the *particular ideas* they denoted without an explanation, he might be *affected* by the sound of the words only, in a manner similar to what he would have been by the sentiment.

That mere sounds are capable of this kind of expression, is evident from the well-known power of music, which, according to the different species of it which are employed, is capable of introducing very different states of mind. And indeed, since these states of mind may afterwards, by association, introduce particular ideas, the ideas themselves may, with propriety enough, be

P p

be said to be excited by the power of mufic, that is, of mere found.

All the properties of founds, befides thofe which depend upon their effential differences (as confifting of particular combinations of vowels and confonants) are the greater *eafe* or *difficulty* of pronouncing them, and the *longer* or *fhorter time* which the diftinct pronunciation of them requires; which properties arife from the forementioned radical differences.

Articulate founds may refemble thofe which are inarticulate, becaufe the former are often copied from the latter; as the *bleating* of the fheep, the *lowing* of the ox, the *roaring* of the lion, the *clangor* of arms, &c. It is by this advantage that Pope defcribes the falling of trees, in the following paffage, which fo happily correfponds to the fenfe:

——— deep-echoing groan the thickets brown,
Then ruftling, crackling, crafhing, thunder down.

Milton's defcription of the found made by the opening of hell-gates is equally happy, on the fame account:

——————— On a fudden open fly,
With impetuous recoil and jarring found,.
Th' infernal doors, and on their hinges grate
Harfh thunder, that the loweft bottom fhook
Of Erebus.

A fentence conftructed fo as not to be pronounced without difficulty (which, by the way, it requires very little ingenuity to do, in our language) may very naturally reprefent any effort of labour and difficulty. Thus Milton hath well defcribed Satan ftruggling through chaos:

So

> So he with difficulty and labour hard,
> Mov'd on, with difficulty and labour he.

Mr. Pope hath not been quite fo happy in his profeffed imitation of Ajax's effort to throw a rock, and of the expreffion of that effort in words :

> When Ajax ftrives fome rock's vaft weight to throw,
> The line too labours, and the words move flow.

The latter of thefe lines, in particular, is by no means of more difficult pronunciation than the generality of Englifh verfes. It runs much fmoother, and more eafily, than his defcription of the gentle flow of a current :

> And the fmooth ftream in fmoother numbers flows.

But this mifcarriage is not owing primarily to the poet, but to the language, in which every poffible advantage was not taken of all the properties of found. This is alfo the cafe in another particular.

Nothing is more obvious than that fhort fyllables may aptly reprefent *fpeed*, and long fyllables *flownefs*, and that quicknefs and flownefs are analogous to a variety of other mental concep-tions, which, by this means, might likewife be expreffed by founds. But, unfortunately, the ftructure of moft languages is fuch as to take little or no advantage of this property of found, any more than of the former. In no language, perhaps, are the fyllables of the words which exprefs *fwiftnefs*, upon the whole, fhorter than thofe of words which exprefs *flownefs*. In Latin, we find the penultima of *velox* and *feftino* unnaturally long, while the penultima of *mora* and *piger* is fhort, as alfo thofe of *labor*

and

and *opus*, which is an unfortunate circumſtance for the following often-quoted line of Virgil:

> Hic lăbor, hoc ŏpus eſt.

On this account Pope's deſcription of Camilla's *ſwiftneſs* (which Engliſh word, by the way, is far from correſponding to the idea it conveys) is very unfortunate:

> Not ſo when ſwift Camilla ſcours the plain,
> Flies o'er th' unbending corn, and ſkims along the main.

His own ſucceſs might have taught him that an Alexandrine verſe is more proper to expreſs ſlowneſs and heavineſs than ſpeed:

> A needleſs Alexandrine ends the ſong,
> Which, like a wounded ſnake, drags its ſlow length along.

However, the univerſal admiration with which, till very lately, every body read that paragraph of the *Eſſay on Criticiſm*, from which theſe extracts are made, ſhews us how naturally we tranſfer the properties of *ideas* upon the *words* which expreſs them. Hence it is eaſy to *imagine* a reſemblance of the ſound to the ſenſe in almoſt every thing. But ſince this is wholly the work of the reader's imagination, a writer doth not need to give himſelf trouble about it. Thoſe who underſtand the language will *imagine* the correſpondence, and it will hardly ever be tried by the only fair teſt, the *ear of a foreigner* (or rather the *eye*, for if it were read, he would be impoſed upon) whether the correſpondence be any thing more than imaginary.

The *pauſes* or *intervals* of ſound a writer hath more command of, as they are, in a great meaſure, independent of the caprice of language. Indeed, greater advantage may be taken of this property of fpeech to make the found an echo to the fenfe, than of the mere found of the words themfelves. In particular, *intervals* are peculiarly adapted to exprefs a variety of affections of the mind. For it is manifeft that the breaks or refts we make in our voice, the length or fhortnefs of our fentences, and the like, vary with the ftate of the mind with which we deliver ourfelves upon any occafion. For inftance, when the mind is agitated, the voice is interrupted, and a man expreffes himfelf in fhort and broken fentences. A foliloquy, alfo, is expreffed in a more disjointed manner than a converfation equally calm. In fhort, every train of thought, and every circumftance attending it, hath its own peculiar *divifions*; and therefore if the paufes of a fentence be difpofed in fuch a manner as to correfpond to the intervals of thought, the found will be a juft echo to the fenfe, and this independent of the peculiar characters of the words themfelves.

By the artful difpofition of the paufes of a fentence, Mr. Pope hath defcribed the catching of a butterfly, in a manner which gives us a lively idea of the action:

> I faw and ftarted from its vernal bower
> The rifing game, and chaced from flower to flower.
> It fled, I follow'd; now in hope, now pain.
> It ftop'd, I ftop'd; it moved, I moved again.
> At laft it fix'd. 'Twas on what plant it pleafed,
> And where it fix'd the beauteous bird I feized.
>
> Dunciad, B. IV. v. 425.

A full

A full paufe in an unufual place very aptly reprefents the ftopping of a ftone, after an impetuous courfe down a hill, in the following paffage in Pope's tranflation of Homer:

> From fteep to fteep the rolling ruin bounds,
> At ev'ry fhock the crackling wood refounds.
> Still gath'ring force, it fmokes, and, urged amain,
> Whirls, leaps, and thunders down impetuous to the plain ;
> Then ftops. So Hector. Their whole force he proved,
> Refiftlefs when he raged, and when he ftopp'd, unmoved.

The whole of this paffage, particularly the defcription of the rolling of the ftone down the hill, is a happy example of defcriptive imitation.

The frequent paufes of meditation and foliloquy are happily imitated by Shakefpeare upon many occafions, and particularly in Hamlet's meditation on death:

> To be, or not to be—that is the queftion.
> Whether 'tis nobler in the mind to fuffer
> The ftings and arrows of outrageous fortune,
> Or to take arms againft a fea of troubles,
> And by oppofing, end them. To die, to fleep—
> No more—and by a fleep to fay we end
> The heart-ach, and a thoufand nat'ral fhocks
> That flefh is heir to. 'Tis a confummation
> Devoutly to be wifh'd—to die, to fleep—
> To fleep—perchance to dream. Ay, there's the rub—
> For in that fleep of death what dreams may come,
> When we have fhuffled off this mortal coil,
> Muft give us paufe—

4

A great

A great variety of juſt expreſſion of ſenſe by ſound, or at leaſt intervals of ſound, may be obſerved in various parts of Pope's Ode on St. Cecilia's Day; particularly at the beginning, where he deſcribes ſeveral inſtruments of muſic:

> Deſcend, ye Nine, deſcend and ſing,
>   The breathing inſtruments inſpire;
> Wake into voice each ſilent ſtring,
>   And ſweep the ſounding lyre.
> In a ſadly pleaſing ſtrain
> Let the warbling lute complain;
>   Let the loud trumpet ſound,
>   Till the roofs all around
>   The ſhrill echoes rebound.
> While in more lengthen'd notes and ſlow
> The deep, majeſtic, ſolemn organs blow.
>   Hark the numbers ſoft and clear
>   Gently ſteal upon the ear;
>   Now louder, and yet louder riſe,
>   And fill with ſpreading ſounds the ſkies.
> Exulting in triumph now ſwell the bold notes,
> In broken air trembling the wild muſic floats;
>   Till, by degrees, remote and ſmall,
>   The ſtrains decay,
>   And melt away,
>   In a dying, dying fall.

And afterwards, when he deſcribes the death of Orpheus:

> But ſoon, too ſoon, the lover turns his eyes.
> Again ſhe falls, again ſhe dies, ſhe dies.
> How wilt thou now the fatal ſiſters move?
> No crime was thine, if 'twas no crime to love.

Now

Now under hanging mountains,
Befide the fall of fountains,
Or where Hebrus wanders,
Rolling in meanders,
   All alone,
   Unheard, unknown,
   He makes his moan,
   And calls her ghoft,
   For ever, ever, ever loft.
Now with furies furrounded,
Defpairing, confounded,
   He trembles, he glows
   Amidft Rhodope's fnows:
See, wild as the winds, o'er the defart he flies —
Hark—Hæmus refounds with the Bacchanals cries—
   ————Ah fee—he dies.

From reading the former of thefe paffages, in particular, it
muft be apparent how much it is in the power of *pronunciation*
to affift and help out this expreffion of fenfe by found and intervals of found ; and becaufe, if we feel the fentiment, we unavoidably do give the language all the affiftance we can from pronunciation, the powers of *written language* have been fuppofed
to be as extenfive as thofe of *language* and *pronunciation* together. The obfervation of the different manner in which the
words *great* and *little* are pronounced, according to the *degree of
the quality* we intend to exprefs,' may fuffice to fhew us both
how naturally we endeavour to favour the fenfe by the found,
and alfo how far we are able to do it. The peculiar beauty,
particularly, of the former of the two paffages quoted from Pope
may be loft by an injudicious pronunciation. Alfo the words

fal'n,

fall'n, fall'n, fall'n, fall'n, in Dryden's *Feaſt of Alexander,* require
to be pronounced with a tone of voice growing continually more
and more languid, to preſerve the beauty of the paſſage in which
they are introduced.   Indeed no perſon, who reads the poem
with any feeling and taſte, can avoid doing it.   There are many
ideas and turns of thought which a *ſpeaker* may imitate very
ſuccefsfully, when a *writer* (unlefs languages had been conſtruct-
ed in a manner very different from what they are) is not able to
contribute much to the ſuccefs of the imitation.

LECTURE

LECTURE XXXIV.

Of HARMONY *in* VERSE.

ALL fpeech naturally divides itfelf into *long* and *fhort fylla- bles*. Whatever language we fpeak, or whether it be *quantity* or *accent* that we attend to in it, we pronounce fome fyllables with more rapidity than others ; and the art of verfifi- cation univerfally confifts in the difpofition of the long or fhort fyllables, according to fome rule. In fome kinds of verfe, indeed, there is more latitude than in others ; but an utter inattention to the length of the fyllables would quite deftroy the harmony of any verfification in the world.

The regular difpofition of the long and fhort fyllables neceffa- rily divides every verfe into certain diftinct portions, or *feet*, and the harmony of a verfe is moft diftinctly perceived when thefe portions or feet are kept as diftinct as poffible ; becaufe then the regular difpofition of the long and fhort fyllables, in which the effence of verfe confifts, is moft apparent. To keep thefe divi- fions of verfe quite diftinct (which the mind, according to an obfervation lately made, naturally inclines to do, in order to *perfect* the harmony) a momentary paufe muft be made after each of them, and this paufe will be peculiarly eafy and natural, if fuch divifion, or foot, clofe with a long fyllable.

I

In order to have any perception of the harmony of verse, and to feel the pleasure we receive from it, unmixed with that which we receive from other beauties of poetry, we must dispose *unmeaning syllables*, or such as have no other properties than *length* or *shortness*, in metrical order, and observe how we are affected by the pronunciation of them. By this method we shall also perceive the peculiar beauty of the versification in use in any country, independent of any advantages it may derive from the peculiar *properties of the language*, or the *art of the poet*. For the sake of brevity, I shall here apply this method to English heroic verse only, using the syllables that the ingenious Mr. Mason contrived for this purpose; viz. *tum* for the long syllable and *ti* for the short one. The following line then will be the general standard of English Iambic verses:

Tĭtūm | tĭtūm || tĭ tūm | tĭ tūm | tĭ tūm.

Let any person only pronounce these syllables at his leisure, and he must perceive a disposition to pause a little after every long syllable, and most of all after the second foot, leaving the latter part of the verse longer than the former; by which means it hath the additional beauty of a *climax*. Accordingly, it will be found by experience that those verses, *separately taken*, are the most musical, in which the words are so disposed, that those pauses shall be the most distinctly perceived; that is, where the division made by the words and the sense coincides with the metrical pause. To this, no doubt, is owing, in a great measure, the remarkable harmony of that stanza of Denham's, which Dryden proposes as a paradox to be explained by the wits of his age:

Tho' deep, yet clear; || tho' gentle, yet not dull:
Strong without rage; || without o'erflowing, full.

Anciently, I believe, in all nations, mankind were so captivated with the charms of verse, that, in reciting poetry, no regard
was paid to any thing but the metrical pause ; which made the
pronunciation of verse a kind of *singing* or *chanting :* and accordingly, we never read of *poems* being *read*, but always of their being
sung by them. Nor shall we wonder at this, if we consider that,
even in our own age, all persons who have not been instructed
in the true art of pronunciation (which is governed wholly by the
sense) naturally pronounce verse in the same manner, and quite
differently from their manner of pronouncing prose ; so that it
generally requires a good deal of pains to correct that vicious
habit. Even among persons of a liberal education, we find some
lean more to the pause of the *metre*, and others more to the
pause of the *sense* ; and there are no persons, not even those who
contend the most strenuously that verse ought to be pronounced
exactly like prose, but distinguish the metrical pause as much as
a regard to the sense will admit. Indeed, if we have a just taste
for *harmony*, we shall perceive that a little interruption of the
metrical pause by the division of the sense hath no disagreeable
effect, *musically considered,* as it contributes to throw an agreeable
variety into the structure of verse.

If we pay any regard to the sense, we must make no pause in
the middle of a word, or between two words which together present only one idea, and separately are of no signification ; as between prepositions, or adjectives, and their substantives, which
are as inseparable in pronunciation as if they were single words.
The greater is the coincidence of the metrical pause with the
pause of the sense, and the more distinguishable is verse from
prose : and verses grow less and less distinguishable as a regard to
the sense throws the pause farther and farther from its natural
place.

place. If the metrical paufe be excluded intirely, the verfe, not-withftanding the regular diftribution of the long and fhort fylla-bles, will not be diftinguifhable from profe, nor pafs for a verfe, except among others.

This a judicious ear will be able to obferve in a comparifon of the following verfes in *Pope's Effay on Man*; in which the paufes are very various. I have marked the proper paufe to be made in the pronunciation, which is always as near to the metrical paufe (namely, after the fecond long fyllable in the line) as a regard to the fenfe will admit:

> All nature is but art ‖ unknown to thee :
> All chance, ‖ direction, which thou can'ft not fee,
> All difcord, ‖ harmony not underftood ;
> All partial evil, ‖ univerfal good.
> And fpite of pride, ‖ in erring reafon's fpite,
> One truth is, clear ; ‖ whatever is is right.

In thefe verfes, the paufe which falls neareft to the beginning of the verfe, is after the fecond fyllable, which is rarely graceful ; and that which falls neareft to the end is after the fixth fyllable. Sometimes the paufe may fall, and not ungracefully, one fyllable later, as in the following :

> Some place the blifs in action, ‖ fome in eafe.

If the paufe fall earlier or later than thefe, it has a bad effect upon the harmony of the verfe, unlefs it anfwer the purpofe of making the found an echo to the fenfe, as in this :

> Celeftial voices to the midnight air
> Sole, ‖ or refponfive to each other's note.

The

The following verſes, by the cloſe coherence of the words in grammatical conſtruction, admit of no metrical pauſe, at leaſt none that is ſufficiently ſtriking:

> Shoots far into the boſom of dim night,
> Oft leaving what is natural and fit.

It is only little more than the *tranſpoſition of the words* that gives the next line an air different from that of proſe:

> The God who darts around the world his rays.
>
> POPE'S HOMER.

If the words be reſtored to their natural order, though the *meaſure* of verſe will be preſerved, the *effect* of it will be wholly loſt:

> The God who darts his rays around the world.

For this reaſon *polyſyllables* are, for the moſt part, unhappily re-fuſed admittance into the moſt muſical Engliſh verſes, viz. be-cauſe they can hardly be ſituated where they will not occupy the moſt convenient place for the principal pauſe; and it is evident they muſt neceſſarily occupy the place of an inferior pauſe, at leaſt. On this account, though theſe verſes may contribute to throw an agreeable variety into a poem, they ſeldom ſound mu-ſically when pronounced ſingly. The following are rather too profaic:

> A noble ſuperfluity it craves.
> In magnanimity of mind reſolved.

But, if polyſyllabic words can be ſo diſpoſed as not to interfere with the principal pauſe, they have a very good effect, on account of

of their accent being fo diftinguifhable.   Let the melody of the
following lines be attended to :

> ———————————— Him th' Almighty Power
> Hurl'd headlong, flaming from th' etherial fky,
> With hideous ruin and combuftion, down
> To bottomlefs perdition; there to dwell
> In adamantine chains and penal fire,
> Who durft defy th' Omnipotent to arms.

On the other hand, Englifh verfes, confifting wholly of *mono-*
fyllables, have feldom a ftriking effect, becaufe they are not, in
general, fufficiently diftinguifhable into long and fhort.   As it is
only the *accent* which determines the length of fyllables in our
language, the *quantity* of all words which have no accent muft
be arbitrary; and accordingly we do pronounce them long or
fhort at pleafure.   Unlefs, therefore, there be *accented words* intermixed with monofyllables, there is nothing to direct the pronunciation of them, and without fome determinate difference in
the length of the fyllables, the metre vanifhes.   The following
lines may ferve as examples of this obfervation :

> The God that made both air, and earth, and heaven
> Nor the deep tract of hell.   Say firft what caufe
> To caft him out from heaven with all his hoft

Notwithftanding the meafure of the greater part of our monofyllables is arbitrary, and therefore they generally do neither
good nor harm in a verfe; yet fome of them are fo *eafy*, and
fome fo *difficult* to pronounce, that a regard to *quantity*, properly
fo called, neceffarily fubftitutes itfelf in the place of accent.
Monofyllables, the quantity of which is remarkably different,

may,

may, when properly difpofed, make very mufical verfes ; or, difpofed improperly, they may greatly injure the melody. The following are very harmonious verfes, though (except the laft) they confift wholly of monofyllables :

> Arms and the man I fing, who forc'd by fate
> I truft in thee, and know in whom I truft
> For which we bear to live, nor fear to die
> Afk of the learn'd the way ; the learn'd are blind ;
> This bids to ferve, and that to fhun mankind.

This next verfe has no harmony, becaufe the monofyllable *the*, in the place of a long fyllable, is not capable of being pronounced long :

> This nymph, to the deftruction of mankind

If the paufe in the middle of a line cannot be excluded without a lofs of the harmony, much lefs can the ftill greater paufe at the end of a line be excluded without that inconvenience. No two verfes, therefore, ought to be fo clofely connected in grammatical conftruction, as that a juft pronunciation of them fhall leave no paufe between them. Neverthelefs, Milton hath often offended againft this rule, as in the following examples :

> What thanks fufficient, or what recompence
> Equal have I to render thee, divine
> Hiftorian. Book VIII. l. 5, 6.

> ———————— Unlefs an age too late, or cold
> Climate, or years damp my intended wing.
> Book IX. l. 44.

Invefted

> Invefted with bright rays, jocund to run
> Her longitude thro' heaven's high-road : the grey
> Dawn, and the pleiades before him danced.
>
> Book VII. 1. 373.

Milton, however, had the example of the Greek and Roman poets to miflead him, who often clofe verfes in the middle of a word; and yet the nature of an *hexameter verfe* (the clofe of which hath fo remarkably uniform and peculiar a cadence) makes a paufe at the end of it much more neceffary than in our *Iambic verfes*, in which the fame difpofition of fyllables which clofes a verfe, ufually begins the next. Englifh verfes, of the length of our heroics, may run into one another, fo that it fhall hardly be perceived where one ends and another begins, but it may always be perceived where an hexameter ends. Univerfally, a paufe in the fenfe ought to be made to coincide with the metrical paufe, and to be in proportion to the quantity or diftinctnefs of that paufe. A regard to this one rule will direct that the fenfe come nearer to a clofe at the principal paufe than at the inferior paufes of the fame verfe, at the end of an hexameter than of an Iambic verfe, at the end of a couplet or rhyme than of blank verfe, and at the end of a ftanza than of a fingle couplet; becaufe, in the latter of all thefe cafes, there is a more fenfible paufe in the metre than in the former : yet, in violation of this rule, we fometimes fee no paufe made at the end of a couplet, or even of a ftanza of Englifh verfe; and the liberty of drawing on the fenfe from one blank verfe to another hath been greatly abufed.

A very few examples will fhow the importance of attending to the metrical paufe in the difpofition of words in Latin as well as

R r

Englifh

Englifh verfe. The coincidence of the metrical paufe with that
of the words, makes the following of Virgil exceedingly harmonious :

> Tityre tu patulæ recubans fub tegmine fagi
> Ludere quæ vellem calamo permefit agrefti
> Eurydicen toto referebant flumine ripæ.

A want of this coincidence makes this next, of Ennius, very un-
harmonious :

> Romæ mænia terruit impiger Hannibal armis.

Who could have imagined that the two following verfes could
have the fame meafure, and that the difpofition of the paufe only
could make fo great a difference in the harmony :

> Ad talos ftola demiffa, et circumdata palla.   Horace.

> Placatumque nitet diffufo lumine cœlum.   Lucretius.

Sometimes, inftead of one principal paufe, there may be two
equal paufes, at nearly equal diftances from the middle of the
verfe, as in the following of Dr. Young :

> From darknefs | teeming darknefs | where I lay.

If the principal paufe immediately fucceed a long fyllable, it may
be obferved to be more *vigorous*; if a fhort fyllable be wanting
to finifh a word, the effect is more *languid*. If the chief paufe
at the end of a verfe be fucceeded by a fhort fyllable, it is wholly
unfit to exprefs grandeur and fublimity, and is beft adapted to
jocofe fubjects. It is impoffible to read a line thus conftructed,
and not perceive this effect; for inftance, the following of
Dryden :

Then

Then all for women, painting, rhyming, drinking,
Befides ten thoufand freaks, that died in thinking.

In many of the verfes quoted above, it muft have been apparent that a trochee at the beginning of a verfe hath even a good effect. It is *enlivening*, as in the following of Philips :

Happy the man, who, free from care and ftrife

For the fame reafon, a trochee is leaft difagreeable after the principal paufe; becaufe after that we, as it were, begin again. Thus the following verfes, though admitting a trochee, as it is after the principal paufe, are not wholly void of harmony :

Had they prevail'd ‖ dārknĕfs had clofed our days,
And death and filence had forbid his praife.

Hov'ring on wing ‖ ūndĕr the cope of hell.

The foot which fucceeds the principal paufe in the following line of Pope, is rather a trochee than a fpondee, and yet doth not, perhaps, contribute to the intended heavinefs of the line :

And, like a wounded fnake, ‖ drāgs hĭs flow length along.

Notwithftanding a perfect uniformity in the meafure of verfe is univerfally tirefome in a long poem, and variety is generally agreeable; yet, when there is any correfpondence in the fenfe of two lines, the moft perfect uniformity in the cadence is the moft agreeable, as in thefe of Mr. Pope :

Bright as the fun, ‖ her eyes the gazers ftrike;
And, like the fun, ‖ they gaze on all alike.

And

And alſo in theſe:

> Warms in the ſun, || refreſhes in the breeze,
> Glows in the ſtars, || and bloſſoms in the trees.
> Lives thro' all life, || extends thro' all extent,
> Spreads undivided, || operates unſpent.

The chief advantage of blank verſe, in point of harmony, is, that, not being divided into couplets, there is no neceſſity for, or expectation of a pauſe in the ſenſe at the end of any particular verſe; but the ſenſe may be continued, without any interruption, to almoſt any length that is thought proper. Other differences of blank verſe and rhyme were conſidered upon a former occaſion.

LECTURE XXXV.

Of HARMONY in PROSE.

THE harmony of *prose* doth not depend upon any regular
return of long or short syllables, for that would constitute
it *verse*, but is consistent with any disposition of long and short
syllables that is easy to pronounce, and at the same time favours
the sense. Very many long syllables coming together make a
style rough and heavy; and many short syllables have likewise a
disagreeable effect, because there is nothing to support the voice,
and for want of that it is apt to hurry on, and embarrass itself.
For this reason, people who are inclined to stammer (as I know
by experience) find great difficulty in pronouncing many short
syllables together. There are too many short syllables together
in the following sentence :

" This doctrine I apprehend to be erroneŏŭs, ănd ŏf ă pĕrni-
" cious tendency."

Those single words are the most agreeable to the ear, in which
the long and short syllables are the most remarkably distinguishable, because they contain the greatest variety of sound This
excellence we perceive in many polysyllables, as *rapidity*, *impetuosity*, *independent*, &c.

Pauses

Paufes muft be made in reading profe as well as verfe; and fince the voice muft reft, it is convenient that provifion be made for its refting at proper intervals. Since neither in verfe, or profe, ought thofe words to be feparated by the leaft interruption of found, which together prefent but *one idea*, it is proper that, at leaft, words fo clofely connected fhould not be fo many, as that it would be difficult to pronounce them in a breath. Moreover, fince the fyllables preceding the paufe are more diftinctly heard, and more attended to than any others, it is peculiarly neceffary that their natural and mechanical effect upon the mind fhould be confidered by a compofer. A paufe preceded by a long fyllable is always *vigorous*, and preceded by a fhort fyllable *feeble*. If the long fyllable be preceded by other long fyllables, it is *folemn*, if by fhort ones, *lively*. On the other hand, if a fhort fyllable preceding a paufe (which is in itfelf feeble) be itfelf preceded by a long one, it makes a clofe eafy and graceful. No perfon, who hath any notion of the analogy there is between intellectual ideas and thofe of fenfe (which has been fo often mentioned and explained in the courfe of thefe lectures) can be at a lofs to account for the propriety of thefe diftinctions. However, let facts fpeak for themfelves.

The paufes in our tranflation of the firft verfes of the book of Genefis, are chiefly preceded by long fyllables, and I appeal to the reader if they are not manly and vigorous:

" In the beginning | God created | the heavens | and the
" earth; || and the earth | was without form | and void; || and
" darknefs | was upon the face | of the deep ||."

The laft paufe of the following fentence of Bolingbroke is weak and bad:

" If

" If the heart of a prince be not corrupt, thefe truths will find
" an eafy ingreffion through the underftanding to it."

BOLINGBROKE.

This next fentence is graceful :

" Wherever I find a great deal of gratitude in a poor măn, | I
" take it for grăntĕd | there would be as much generōsĭty | if
" he were a rīch măn |."

And the clofe of this is folemn :

" I feldom fee a noble building, or any great piece of magni-
" ficence and pomp, but I think how little is all this to fatisfy
" the ambition, or to fill the idea of an īmmōrtāl fōul."

A fentence is beautifully conftructed when there is a climax in
the length of the words ; and a period, when there is a climax
in the length of the claufes that compofe it.   Something of this
beauty may be perceived in the following fentence :

" Many men have been capable of doing a wife thing, more a
" cunning thing, but very few a generous thing."

When things are either compared or contrafted, it is beautiful
to have every thing in the fentence fo fimilar, as that even the
names of them fhould begin with the fame letter.   Of this take
the following example :

" The peacock, in all his pride, doth not difplay half the co-
" lour that appears in the garments of a Britifh Lady, when fhe
" is dreffed either for a *ball* or a *birth-day*."

SPECTATOR, No. 265.

My

My life's companion and my bosom friend,
One *faith*, one *fame*, one *fate* shall both attend.

DRYDEN'S TRANSLATION OF THE ÆNEID.

In any other case, however, many words that are near one
another cannot begin with the same letter without having a difagreeable effect; and a similar sound in two neighbouring words,
which are no otherwise related to one another, is peculiarly of-
fensive; as the following of Mason:

" Many things that *deserve* to be *observed* on this subject"—

When a word is found out of its usual place and connection,
though the sense be quite obvious, our ears are offended as with
a disagreeable sound: but this is rather a part of an observation
made upon another occasion. I shall, however, in this place,
subjoin a few examples of it:

" I have, *indeed*, not found among any part of mankind"—

RAMBLER, No. 38.

" These, therefore, we must principally hunt out, but, above
" all, preserve a laudable prolixity, presenting the whole and
" every side *at once* of an image to view."

ART OF SINKING.

" A man was obliged to produce all the wealth of his mind
" to view, and he was rated to the sum he produced: no one
" could *therefore* pass for rich who was not so."

SHERIDAN'S LECTURES.

I do not think I can close these observations on the harmony of
style in prose and verse, better than with advising, that a *secondary*

I   attention

attention only to be paid to them.   Let your primary regards be always to the *fenfe* and to *perfpicuity*; and in every competition between harmony and thefe more valuable objects, if no methods can be found to reconcile them, let the harmony be facrificed without hefitation.   Propriety of fentiment and expreffion will better cover a defect of harmony, than the harmony will cover a defect of propriety.

F I N I S.

S s

A CATALOGUE of BOOKS written by

JOSEPH PRIESTLEY, LL.D. F.R.S.

AND PRINTED FOR

J. JOHNSON, Bookseller, at No. 72, St. Paul's Church-Yard, London.

1. THE HISTORY and PRESENT STATE of ELECTRICITY, with original Experiments, illustrated with Copper-Plates. 4th Edition, corrected and enlarged, 4to. 1l. 1s. Another Edition, 2 vols. 8vo. 12s.

2. A Familiar INTRODUCTION to the STUDY of ELECTRICITY. The Second Edition, 8vo. 2s. 6d.

3. The HISTORY and PRESENT STATE of DISCOVERIES relating to VISION, LIGHT, and COLOURS, 2 vols. 4to. illustrated with a great Number of Copper-Plates, 1l. 11s. 6d. in Boards.

4. A Familiar INTRODUCTION to the THEORY and PRACTICE of PERSPECTIVE, with Copper-Plates. Price 5s. in Boards.

5. DIRECTIONS for impregnating Water with FIXED AIR, in order to communicate to it the peculiar Spirit and Virtues of PYRMONT WATER, and other Mineral Waters of a similar Nature, 1s.

6. Experiments and Observations on different Kinds of Air, with Copper-Plates. 3 vol. Price 16s. in Boards.

7. PHILOSOPHICAL EMPIRICISM: Containing Remarks on a Charge of Plagiarism respecting Dr. H——s, interspersed with various Observations relating to different Kinds of Air, 1s. 6d.

8. A New CHART of HISTORY, containing a View of the principal Revolutions of Empire that have taken Place in the World; with a Book describing it, containing an Epitome of Universal History. The Third Edition, 10s. 6d.

9. A CHART of BIOGRAPHY, with a Book, containing an Explanation of it, and a Catalogue of all the Names inserted in it. The Fourth Edition, very much improved, 10s. 6d.

10. An Essay on a Course of liberal Education for Civil and Active Life, with Plans of Lectures on, 1. The Study of History and general Policy. 2. The History of England. 3. The Constitution and Laws of England.

11. An EXAMINATION of Dr. REID's Inquiry into the Human Mind on the Principles of Common Sense, Dr. BEATTIE's Essay on the Nature and Immutability of Truth, and Dr. OSWALD's Appeal to Common Sense in Behalf of Religion. The Second Edition, 5s. sewed.

12. HARTLEY's THEORY of the HUMAN MIND on the Principle of the Association of Ideas, with Essays relating to the Subject of it, 8vo. 5s. sewed.   13. The

13. The Rudiments of English Grammar, adapted to the Use of Schools, 1s. 6d.

14. The above Grammar, with Notes and Observations, for the Use of those who have made some Proficiency in the Language. The Fourth Edition, 3s.

15. An Essay on the First Principles of Government, and on the Nature of Political, Civil, and Religious Liberty. The Second Edition, much enlarged, 5s.

16. Institutes of Natural and Revealed Religion, Vol. I. containing the Elements of Natural Religion; to which is prefixed, An Essay on the best Method of communicating religious Knowledge to the Members of Christian Societies, 2s. 6d. — Vol. II. containing the Evidences of the Jewish and Christian Revelations, 3s. sewed.—Vol. III. containing the Doctrines of Revelation, 2s. 6d. sewed.—The Fourth and last Part of this Work will contain an Historical Account of the Corruptions of Christianity.

17. A Harmony of the Evangelists, in Greek: To which are prefixed, Critical Dissertations, in English, 4to. 14s. in Boards.

18. A Free Address to Protestant Dissenters on the Subject of the Lord's Supper. The Third Edition, with Additions, 2s.

19. The Additions to the above may be had alone, 1s.

20. An Address to Protestant Dissenters on the Subject of giving the Lord's Supper to Children, 1s

21. Considerations on Differences of Opinion among Christians; with a Letter to the Rev. Mr. Venn, in Answer to his Examination of the Address to Protestant Dissenters, 1s. 6d.

22. A Catechism for *Children* and *Young Persons*. The Second Edition, 3d.

23. A Scripture Catechism, consisting of a Series of Questions, with References to the Scriptures, instead of Answers, 3d.

24. A Serious Address to Masters of Families, with Forms of Family Prayer. The second Edition, 6d.

25. A View of the Principles and Conduct of the Protestant Dissenters, with respect to the Civil and Ecclesiastical Constitution of England. The Second Edition, 1s. 6d.

26. A Free Address to Protestant Dissenters, on the Subject of Church Discipline; with a Preliminary Discourse concerning the Spirit of Christianity, and the Corruption of it by false Notions of Religion, 2s. 6d.

27. A Sermon preached before the Congregation of Protestant Dissenters, at Mill Hill Chapel, in Leeds, May 16, 1773, on Occasion of his resigning his Pastoral Office among them, 1s.

28 A Free Address to Protestant Dissenters, as such. By a Dissenter.

Diffenter. A new Edition, enlarged and corrected, 1s. 6d.—An Allowance is made to thofe who buy this Pamphlet to give away.

29. Letters to the Author of *Remarks on feveral late Publications relative to the Diffenters, in a Letter to Dr. Prieftley*, 1s.

30. An APPEAL to the ferious and candid Profeffors of Chriftianity, on the following Subjects, viz. 1. The Ufe of Reafon in Matters of Religion. 2. The Power of Man to do the Will of God. 3. Original Sin. 4. Election and Reprobation. 5. The Divinity of Chrift; And, 6. Atonement for Sin by the Death of Chrift. The Fifth Edition, 1d.

31. A FAMILIAR ILLUSTRATION of certain Paffages of Scripture relating to the fame Subject, 4d. or 3s. 6d. per Dozen.

32. The TRIUMPH of TRUTH; being an Account of the Trial of Mr. Elwall for Herefy and Blafphemy, at Stafford Affizes, before Judge Denton. The Second Edition, 1d.

33. CONSIDERATIONS for the USE of YOUNG MEN, and the Parents of YOUNG MEN, 2d.

Alfo, publifhed under the Direction of Dr. PRIESTLEY,

THE THEOLOGICAL REPOSITORY;

Confifting of Original Effays, Hints, Queries, &c. calculated to promote religious Knowledge, in Three Volumes, 8vo. Price 18s. in Boards.

Among other Articles, too many to be enumerated in an Advertifement, thefe Three Volumes will be found to contain fuch original and truly-valuable Obfervations on the Doctrine of the *Atonement*, the *Pre-exiftence of Chrift*, and the *Infpiration of the Scriptures*, more efpecially refpecting the *Harmony of the Evangelifts*, and the Reafoning of the Apoftle Paul, as cannot fail to recommend them to thofe Perfons, who wifh to make a truly-free Enquiry into thefe important Subjects.

In the Firft Volume, which is now reprinted, feveral Articles are added, particularly Two Letters from Dr. THOMAS SHAW to Dr. BENSON, relating to the Paffage of the Ifraelites through the Red Sea.

INDEX

A

Acting, 266

Addison, Joseph: amplification in his *Spectator,* 28; method, 66–67; simile, 167; perspicuity, 285–86; harmony in prose, 311

Adjuncts: a universal topic, 12; defined, 12; used by divines, moralists, 12; arguments referable to, 12; and sublime, 157

Aeneas, 80, 91, 234

Affectation, and natural propriety, 226–28

Akenside, Mark, sublimity in his *Pleasures of the Imagination,* 154, 155

Allegory: and uniformity and variety, 166; chief excellence of, 168; defined, 194; resemblance in, 194; and metaphor, 194–95; rules for use of, 195–96; and riddles, 223

Amplification: derived from topics, 26; confirms and illustrates, 26; Newton's use of, 27; principle sources of, 28–29; faults of, 29–30, 53; Locke's diffuse, 59

Analogy: a universal topic, 15; divines, lawyers, use of, 15–16; importance in science, 16; in analysis, 42; and uniformity and variety, 165; basis of comparison, contrast, 212–13

Analysis (analytic method): and science, 42, 44; method of investigation, 42, 56; and communication, 43–44; and synthesis, 44; method of experimental philosophy, 44; adopted by divines and moralists, 44–45, 63–65; process referred to logic, 56; in celebrated writers, 57–63; end of, 66. *See also* Synthesis

Antecedents: a universal topic, 13; historians, divines, use of, 13

Antithesis: and contrast, 201; caution in use of, 226

Antonius, Marcus, his style, 142

Apostrophe, caution in use of, 113

Approximation, method of, 57

Arbuthnot, John, his ironical humour, 217

Argumenta ad hominem: and authority, 18; caution in use of, 53

Argumentative discourse: concern of recollection, 6; analytic, synthetic method of, 42; adapted to understanding, 52; process of, 52–54; Locke's, Hutcheson's, 59; Hume excels in, 60–61

Argumentative method: analytic and synthetic, 42–69; order of nature, 52; faults of, 53. *See also* Method

Arguments: rules of logic judge, 3; recollection of, 5, 7–8; as proof, 7; from form and manner of their introduction, 21–22; intermediate and amplification, 26–27; arrangement of, 42; weight, number of, 50–51; disguised, 51; forms of address independent of, 108. *See also* Recollection

Aristophanes, his use of ridicule, 214

Aristotle, his use of human nature, 4

Arrangement. *See* Method

Art: improves on nature, 1; taste for fine, 74; and nature, 176, 266; appearance of, 226; and imitation, 266–68

Art of oratory: supplements nature, 2; limitations of, 2–3; assistance from, 2, 4–5; in narrative discourse, 6; and topics, 8. *See also* Oratory

Assent: and authority, 17; and forms of address, 73, 116; and reality, 89; mentioned, 50

Association of ideas: constant reference to in *Lectures,* i; explains in-